NEGOTIATING SOVEREIGNTY AND HUMAN RIGHTS

Brings together a fascinating collection of articles that explore new concerns and issues in the arena of international human rights politics. The critical evaluation of changing dynamics between state and human rights and the attention paid to new human right actors such as non governmental organizations, epistemic communities and multinational corporations will be of interest not only to professional social scientists but to policy makers, activists and anyone concerned about human rights, social justice, freedom and peace.

Sandya Hewamanne, Wake Forest University, USA

Provides a window into cutting edge developments in the field of human rights across a spectrum of issues, actors, institutions and norms. Contributors lay the groundwork by examining new challenges to state sovereignty and immunity through such institutional developments as the International Criminal Court, truth commissions, and the responsibility to protect; and across issues spanning mobilization to meet millennium development goals, the urgency of climate change, international control of small arms and light weapons, and the rights of persons with disabilities. The case studies are both conceptually and theoretically grounded, and bring together practitioner and scholarly perspectives that enrich comprehension of the dynamics of international relations from local to global contexts.

Janie Leatherman, Fairfield University, USA

Negotiating Sovereignty and Human Rights

Actors and Issues in Contemporary Human Rights Politics

Edited by

NOHA SHAWKI and MICHAELENE COX
Illinois State University, USA

Routledge
Taylor & Francis Group
LONDON AND NEW YORK

First published 2009 by Ashgate Publishing

Published 2016 by Routledge
2 Park Square, Milton Park, Abingdon, Oxon OX14 4RN
711 Third Avenue, New York, NY 10017, USA

Routledge is an imprint of the Taylor & Francis Group, an informa business

British Library Cataloguing in Publication Data
Negotiating sovereignty and human rights : actors and
issues in contemporary human rights politics.
1. Human rights. 2. Sovereignty. 3. International law.
4. Non-governmental organizations.
I. Shawki, Noha. II. Cox, Michaelene.
341.4'8-dc22

Library of Congress Cataloging-in-Publication Data
Shawki, Noha.
Negotiating sovereignty and human rights : actors and issues in contemporary human rights politics / by Noha Shawki and Michaelene Cox.
p. cm.
Includes bibliographical references and index.
ISBN 97807546777192
1. Human rights. 2. Human rights activists. 3. Sovereignty. I. Cox, Michaelene. II. Title.

JC571.S459 2009
323--dc22

2009008175

ISBN 9780754677192 (hbk)

Contents

PART II CURRENT ISSUES IN INTERNATIONAL HUMAN RIGHTS

List of Figures

List of Tables

Notes on Contributors

Cristina G. Badescu is a Social Sciences and Humanities Research Council of Canada Postdoctoral Fellow at the Munk Centre for International Studies, University of Toronto, and a Visiting Research Fellow at the Ralph Bunche Institute for International Studies, The Graduate Center, The City University of New York. She received her PhD in political science from the University of Western Ontario in 2007. She was a SSHRC Doctoral Fellow and a Canadian Consortium on Human Security Fellow. Her research projects focus on humanitarian intervention, human security, and the responsibility to protect. She is completing a book manuscript titled *The Responsibility to Protect: Solving the Humanitarian Intervention Dilemma.*

Daniel B. Braaten is a PhD candidate in Political Science at the University of Nebraska-Lincoln. His research interests are in international law, human rights, and American hegemonic legitimacy. He has work forthcoming in *Review of International Studies* with David P. Rapkin that puts forth a new conception of hegemonic legitimacy and in the *Encyclopedia of Human Rights* published by Oxford University Press on the WTO and Human Rights. He has presented scholarly work, most notably, at the International Studies Association annual conference, the Midwest International Studies Association annual conference and the Midwest Political Science Association annual conference.

Eric Brahm is currently a consultant with the International Human Rights Law Institute at DePaul University. Also, he has worked with the recently completed Liberian Truth and Reconciliation Commission Diaspora Project. His research focuses on human rights ranging from labor rights issues to post-conflict reconstruction. He has written a number of pieces on the evaluation of post-conflict justice mechanisms. In addition, he has completed a book manuscript, based on his doctoral dissertation that examines the contribution of truth commissions to democratization processes and to strengthening the protection of human rights in post-conflict societies. Another book manuscript in progress chronicles the global experience with truth commissions and considers the evidence for a range of hypothesized effects.

Sonia Cardenas is Associate Professor of Political Science and Director of the Human Rights Program at Trinity College in Connecticut. She has published more than a dozen articles and book chapters on human rights and national human rights institutions. She is also the author of *Conflict and Compliance: State Responses* *to International Human Rights Pressure* (University of Pennsylvania Press 2007); *Terror and Hope: The Politics of Human Rights in Latin America* (University of Pennsylvania Press 2009); and *Chains of Justice: The Global Rise of State Institutions for Human Rights* (University of Pennsylvania, forthcoming).

Anne L. Clunan is an assistant professor of National Security Affairs at the Naval Postgraduate School in Monterey, CA. She earned her PhD in political science at the University of California, Berkeley. Her research and teaching interests focus on how states define and respond to new and emerging security threats, and on the implications of globalization for state sovereignty, international law, and governance. Her most recent book is *The Social Construction of Russia's Resurgence: Aspirations, Identity, and Security Interests* (Johns Hopkins University Press 2009). She is co-editor, with Harold Trinkunas, of a forthcoming volume entitled *Ungoverned Spaces? Alternatives to State Authority in an Era of Softened Sovereignty*. She is co-editor with Peter R. Lavoy and Susan B. Martin of *Terrorism, War or Disease? Unraveling the Use of Biological Weapons* (Stanford University Press 2008). Other recent publications include "The Fight Against Terrorist Financing," in *Political Science Quarterly* (Winter 2006/2007), and "Globalization and the Impact of Norms on Defense Restructuring," in *Global Politics of Defense Reform* (Palgrave MacMillan 2008).

Michaelene Cox is Assistant Professor in the Department of Politics and Government at Illinois State University. She holds a PhD in political science from the University of Alabama. She teaches courses in Comparative Politics and International Relations, and is also the Director of the Peace and Conflict Resolution Studies program at ISU for which she teaches the Peace Studies course. Her general research interests include political participation, social capital, and conflict. In addition to journal articles, she has recently published two edited volumes entitled *State of Corruption, State of Chaos* (Rowman & Littlefield 2008) and *Social Capital and Peace-Building* (Routledge 2009).

Suzette R. Grillot is the Max and Heidi Berry Chair, Associate Director of International Programs, and Associate Professor of International and Area Studies at the University of Oklahoma. She teaches courses on International Relations Theory, International Security, International Organization and Regimes, and European Security. She has published articles in numerous academic journals, such as *The British Journal of Political Science*, *International Politics*, *Political Psychology*, *Contemporary Security Policy*, and *The Nonproliferation Review*. She co-edited and contributed to the books *Arms on the Market: Reducing the Risk of Proliferation in the Former Soviet Union* (1998) and *Arms and the Environment: Preventing the Perils of Disarmament* (2001). She and Rachel Stohl have co-authored a forthcoming book (2009) titled *The International Arms Trade*. Dr. Grillot is also completing three additional book manuscripts — *Weapons Without Borders: The Global Spread and Control of Small Arms*; *Protecting Our Ports: The*

National and International Politics of Containerized Freight Security; and *Securing the Community: Reconciliation, Trust and Integration in the Western Balkans.*

Patricia B. Minikon is an immigration attorney and human rights practitioner in the Washington, D.C. metropolitan area and Adjunct Assistant Professor of Immigration Law at the University of Maryland University College. She is a degree candidate for a Masters in International Affairs from American University, where she focused on International Politics, Human Rights, and Conflict Resolution, with a regional emphasis on Africa; her thesis is on transitional justice and human rights institutions in Africa. She formerly served as Principal Attorney Editor of *Interpreter Releases*, a leading Thomson-West publication that provides analysis of immigration case law, policy, legislation, and regulations. She led legal education seminars, workshops, strategy sessions, and provided technical assistance to Minnesota Legal Services Coalition's staff attorneys in 35 offices. She served as the Co-Chair of the Education Committee of the Urban Coalition of Minnesota's Immigrant and Refugee Policy Coalition from 2000 to 2001. Her Juris Doctor degree was awarded by the University of Maryland and her bachelor's degree was awarded Magna Cum Laude, in the Administration of Justice, from Howard University.

Kenneth R. Rutherford is an Associate Professor of Political Science at Missouri State University and is co-founder of the Landmine Survivors Network. He is a renowned leader in the Nobel Peace Prize-winning coalition that spearheaded the 1997 Mine Ban Treaty and the 2008 Convention on Cluster Munitions. Rutherford was also a NGO delegation member to the negotiations on the Convention on the Rights of Persons with Disabilities, which was adopted in 2006. He is the author of *Humanitarianism Under Fire: The US and UN Intervention in Somalia* (Kumarian Press 2008), co-editor of two books, has been published in academic and policy journals, including *World Politics*, and testified before Congress. Rutherford is recipient of the Leadership in International Rehabilitation Award presented by Northwestern University's Institute for International Rehabilitation. His personal story of recovery from a landmine accident that resulted in the loss of both his legs has been profiled by the BBC, OPRAH, and Reader's Digest.

Benjamin N. Schiff received his PhD in political science from the University of California, Berkeley. Teaching at Oberlin College since 1979, he has authored *International Nuclear Technology Transfer: Dilemmas of Dissemination and Control* (Rowman and Allanheld 1983), about the International Atomic Energy Agency; *Refugees unto the Third Generation: UN Aid to Palestinians* (Syracuse 1995), about the United Nations Relief and Works Agency; and *Building the International Criminal Court* (Cambridge 2008). He co-authored, with June Goodwin, *Heart of Whiteness: Afrikaners Face Black Rule in the New South Africa* (Scribner 1995). Schiff was a visiting professor at Leiden University's Grotius Centre for International Legal Studies in The Hague, 2005 to 2006, and has published journal articles, chapters, newspaper op-ed pieces, and book reviews on international organization, international relations, foreign policy, and military topics.

Noha Shawki is Assistant Professor of Politics and Government at Illinois State University. She received her MA degree from the University of Trier in Trier, Germany and her PhD from Indiana University Bloomington in 2007. She was a visiting instructor at Carleton College from 2004 to 2007. Her teaching and research interests are in transnationalism, global governance, and human rights.

Susan Shepler is an Assistant Professor of International Peace and Conflict Resolution in the School of International Service at American University in Washington, D.C. Her ethnographic research is on youth and conflict generally, with a focus on the reintegration of former child soldiers in Sierra Leone. Other interests include post-conflict reconstruction, education and development, NGOs and globalization, and the search for local solutions to conflict. She is the recipient of fellowships from the Harry Frank Guggenheim Foundation, The Institute on Global Conflict and Cooperation, and the American Association of University Women. In addition to academic work, she has participated in evaluations of Talking Drum Studio in Sierra Leone for Search for Common Ground and of Defense of Children International programming in Sierra Leone. She is the author of several book chapters and journal articles in the fields of youth studies, human rights, and African politics.

Peter J. Stoett is Associate Professor and Chair of the Department of Political Science at Concordia University in Montréal. He earned a PhD from Queen's University in 1994. His main areas of expertise include international relations and law, human rights and environmental issues, and Canadian foreign policy. Recent books (authored, co-authored, and co-edited) include *Bilateral Ecopolitics: Canadian-American Environmental Relations* (Ashgate 2006); *International Ecopolitical Theory: Critical Reflections* (UBC Press 2006); and *Human and Global Security: An Exploration of Terms* (University of Toronto Press 2000). He also teaches at the United Nations' University for Peace in San Jose, Costa Rica. He is currently working on a forthcoming book, *Global Biosecurity: The International Politics of Denial, Fear, and Injustice*, to be published by Broadview Press 2010; and was awarded a SSHRC research grant on invasive species and global governance in April 2008.

Introduction

Noha Shawki and Michaelene Cox

Two extraordinary expressions of the universality of human rights highlight the relevance and expanding legitimacy of international norms promoting and protecting human dignity. They symbolize an enduring moral and political imperative to continue our engagement with human rights issues. One of these most notable articulations of the continuing salience of human rights is the translation of the Universal Declaration of Human Rights (UDHR) into more 300 languages and dialects, which makes it one of the most accessible and universal documents. The launching of the Declaration into space at the end of 2008 is another visible reminder of the significance of human rights. Placed aboard the International Space Station and orbiting around the Earth, the UDHR in this setting literally and figuratively transcends place and time. Both of these efforts reflect a growing international collaboration to promote justice, dignity, freedom and peace.

Cooperation in the area of human rights has been expanding since the adoption of the UDHR in 1948 and a plethora of other human rights agreements and programs. It is no surprise that the end of the Cold War facilitated opportunities for states and other actors to join forces in addressing a variety of global concerns, including human rights. In the 1990s, a renewed international commitment gave rise to what some have called the "human rights era" by the end of the decade. Now in the twenty-first century, contemporary human rights politics suggest that we pause to take stock of the development of relevant actors and issues. Sixty years after the adoption of the UDHR by the international community, and almost twenty years after the end of the Cold War, this is an opportune moment to reflect on what has been achieved in the area of human rights and think about remaining challenges and new opportunities. Our effort here is to contribute to a specific dimension of the larger debate by exploring the relationship between state sovereignty and human rights today. The title of this volume, *Negotiating Sovereignty and Human Rights*, aptly captures the dynamics of state sovereignty and rights.

The 12 chapters in this volume focus on actors and/or issues that are still on the fringe of the mainstream of international human rights politics. All chapter topics were selected for inclusion in this volume because they represent, in one way or another, a significant departure from the usual and established practice of human rights politics. More specifically, the chapters in this volume cover issues that: (a) have only recently emerged as an important part of the international human rights agenda and generated much advocacy, diplomacy and negotiations, and (b) entail a direct challenge to entrenched notions of state sovereignty and represent a departure form established ways of policymaking. This is either because they have necessitated that states further relinquish some of their traditional prerogatives in the area of human rights and international policymaking, or because the political process focusing on these issues has been spearheaded by non-state actors, or simply because they bypass national governments altogether. For example, Chapter 8 examining The Liberian Truth and Reconciliation Commission Diaspora Project and Chapter 11 on The Convention on the Rights of Persons with Disabilities find that it was the product of a process heavily influenced by non-governmental organizations. Another example of a political process that does not directly involve national governments is the UN Global Compact, which is addressed in Chapter 6. In addition, a number of issues in the volume are not well established on the international human rights agenda, and their status as human rights issues and the policies that are needed to address them are currently still very contested. These issues include development issues discussed in Chapter 9, environmental concerns in Chapter 10 and small arms and light weapons (SALW) in Chapter 12.

The range of topics addressed in the chapters herein illustrates the broad spectrum of discourse among the human rights community. Clearly, national governments continue to be key actors in that discourse, but as Chapters 1 and 5 illustrate, traditional state sovereignty is undergoing some change and there has been a remarkable expansion of other significant state and non-state actors. Some of these actors include national human rights institutions, as discussed in Chapters 2 and 3. Others include intergovernmental organizations and truth commissions, respectively addressed in Chapters 4 and 7. Readers will find references throughout the volume to additional important human rights actors, such as nongovernmental organizations, epistemic communities, and multinational corporations.

The chapters are divided into two parts with the first part focusing on structures, institutions and processes, and the second part of the volume focusing on emerging and current issues in human rights politics. In general, the questions addressed in this volume include:

- In what ways have contemporary international affairs reshaped established notions of state sovereignty, as related to human rights issues? What are the human rights issues that have posed a direct challenge to those norms of state sovereignty?
- Who are the actors that are able to shape current human rights discourse and practice? Which actors have benefited from increasing interdependence within the international community?

Contributors approach the nexus of state authority and human rights from multiple and critical perspectives. Some chapters document specific cases or advocacy campaigns, while all draw upon various conceptual and theoretical frameworks to evaluate the significance of recent human rights mechanisms. A number of novel instruments that span the bodies of soft and hard law and are addressed herein include the agreements mentioned above as well as the Paris Principles, the Rome

Statute of the International Criminal Court, the 2005 World Summit outcome document, and the Millennium Declaration. Thus, the reader will find here a well-balanced collection of previously unpublished studies that underscores changing dynamics between the state and human rights, and which serves as a useful and timely compendium for students of international human rights.

Taken together, the chapters in this volume demonstrate the growing visibility and diversity of actors, issues, and mechanisms for defining and protecting human. They complement the present research agenda and suggest avenues for future inquiry and policy initiatives. In particular, further attention to topics addressed in this volume and others outside the mainstream is still needed. Negotiating tensions between rights and responsibilities of the international community, national governments, and private citizens will continue to define the world in which we live.

Capturing the remarkable breadth of the debate surrounding sovereignty and human rights requires considerable cooperation from many individuals. We hope that this volume will make a contribution to that effort. It reflects the assistance and support of the publisher's editorial team, anonymous reviewers, our graduate assistants, and especially the collaboration of a diverse group of chapter contributors.

PART I
Actors, Institutions, and Institutional Innovations

Chapter 1
Redefining Sovereignty: Humanitarianism's Challenge to Sovereign Immunity

Anne L. Clunan[1]

State sovereignty is at root a set of rules about institutional boundaries that divide political and territorial space and determine who can do what to whom and for what reason (Bull 1977; Kratochwil 1989; Holsti 2004).[2] Human rights are seen as a critical challenge to state sovereignty, as they challenge its central premise of the state as the ultimate legal and political authority in world politics. How are the set of rules defining sovereignty—its boundary—changing, and what has produced those changes (Deutsch 1953; Haas 1964, 1990; Wendt 1999, 1994, Krasner 1999; Biersteker and Weber 1996; Ruggie 1993)? This chapter takes up these questions, and assesses how humanitarianism—in its legal forms—has undermined one of the classical tenets of state sovereignty—the immunity of state officials from prosecution for official acts—and yielded a new set of institutions and relationships among states and individuals.

State sovereignty has two components: internal sovereignty and external sovereignty (Bull 1977; Jackson 1990).[3] Internally, the classical state sovereign has exclusive authority over a particular territory, in other words freedom from outside interference. With the 1648 Treaty of Westphalia as a convenient historical marker, states over the next three hundred years increasingly recognized each other's rights to determine for themselves the structure and content of their internal political, economic, and social life. These rights were codified in the Charter of the United Nations. States, within a particular set of territorial and extraterritorial boundaries, have the authority to police their citizens and regulate their social, political, and economic relations. In the classical formulation of sovereignty, states have the right to establish the extent of hierarchical subordination of the individual to state authority.

Externally, the state sovereign has both the exclusive right to wage war, and international legal personality, allowing it to enter into binding contracts and generally conduct international relations (Roberts and Guelff 2000; Gray 2004;

1 The views expressed in this document do not represent the official position of the Department of Defense or the US government, but are sole responsibility of the author.

2 This focus on sovereignty on a set of rules is emphasized by the English School and constructivists.

3 Robert Jackson denotes these as negative and positive sovereignty.

Walzer 1977).[4] The institution of sovereignty creates clear rights and privileges as well as obligations and responsibilities of the state. Other actors do not have international legal personality, and cannot act as states internationally, including the right to sue a state. The right of legal personality is a core institution in international law, as it is in domestic law. It establishes which actors have the capacity to act within the institutional boundaries of legal orders. Sovereignty enshrines the state as the legal and the political actor at the international level. Without sovereignty, a state cannot legally enter into the game of international relations and its political clout is significantly hampered (Holsti 2004, 115).[5] Traditionally, state sovereignty has imposed obligations that are externally oriented: responsibilities to act or refrain from acting towards other states as well as to make reparations for wrongful acts (Carter et al. 2003).[6] The most important obligation is to refrain from interfering in the internal affairs of other states, as this would violate a state's right to internal sovereignty.

The erosion of the institution of internal sovereignty has received much attention in the academic literature. The notion of exclusive authority over a territory was questioned first by the literature on the impact of interdependence, then the newer focus on globalization's erosion of state control (Keohane and Nye 1989; Rosenau 1990; Strange 1996; Mathews 1997; Slaughter 2004). These works focus on the *de facto* erosion of internal sovereignty. Here the focus is on the reduced capacity of the state to control what occurs within its borders under the strains of increasing economic and information flows. As Stephen Krasner notes, such *de facto* challenges to internal sovereignty are not particularly new. He therefore argues against over-exaggerating the erosion of state sovereignty. Following the realist tradition, he views sovereignty less as a constitutive institution creating a society of sovereign states than as a cognitive script enacted whenever powerful actors deem it useful (Krasner 1993). Krasner argues that international institutions, including sovereignty, are fundamentally less institutionalized and path dependent than domestic institutions. As Krasner says,

> Compromising the sovereign state model is always available as a policy option because there is no authority structure to prevent it: nothing can preclude rulers from transgressing against the domestic autonomy of other states or recognizing entities that are not juridically autonomous (Krasner 2001).

4 The right of sovereigns to wage war was first institutionalized in just war doctrine that governed relations among European states since the eighteenth century. It has been codified and further refined in the law of armed conflict, otherwise known as international humanitarian law. The literature on just war doctrine and the laws of war is extensive.

5 The example of Taiwan, which has all the elements of *de facto* state sovereignty but lacks the legal recognition of it, demonstrates the political advantages of *de jure* sovereignty.

6 At the request of the United Nations General Assembly in 1947, the International Legal Commission determined the legal rights and responsibilities of states.

Krasner argues that because there is no hierarchy of authoritative rules at the international level, rulers will always be faced with situations in which different rules apply, and power and interest are most likely to determine how they act. Rulers will voluntarily or involuntarily abandon the institution of sovereignty as incentives and power dictate (Krasner 2001). As Krasner correctly notes, power remains at the center of international relations. Yet the international system is more institutionally developed than Krasner allows, and these institutions do affect the rights and powers of state sovereigns in important ways.

Recently sovereignty has been challenged *de jure* in ways that are undermining the basic and traditional powers of sovereigns. Material power alone cannot explain why states are changing the boundaries of the core institution that provides order and protects their rights internationally. Moreover, these changes have not only domestic but international consequences for states. One area in which the boundary of state sovereignty has been most changed is human rights and the emergence of international criminal law out of the laws of war and human rights. The creation and expansion of the human rights regime during the latter half of the twentieth century has been one of the most remarkable changes in international relations, setting the stage for the rise of post-Cold War innovations such as those examined in this volume. As Robert Jackson notes, the very "perception of international human rights violations presupposes general standards and expectations of humanitarian conduct," in effect placing sovereign states within a broader web of international societal institutions (Jackson 1990, 141).

The human rights regime has changed the institution of state sovereignty in two ways. First, because certain human rights are understood to be universal, it has reduced the legitimate scope of all states' internal sovereignty, in effect shrinking the exclusive jurisdiction of the state and increasing their accountability to other states. The past few years have seen efforts to institutionalize the norm of "contingent sovereignty" that links sovereign authority directly to the treatment of citizens (United Nations 2004). Second, it has given individual human beings legal personality to confront states. While at the time of their creation international conventions may have been entered into cynically and deemed to have little real significance, today these conventions have improved the capacity of individuals to act at the international level. They have also reduced the ability of states to act with legal impunity at home (Krasner 2001; Thomas 2001). A few examples help make this shift in sovereignty's boundaries evident.

State Sovereignty Confronts Extraterritorial Jurisdiction

Increasingly, sovereigns are no longer able to claim absolute immunity from other states' interference within their own boundaries or even beyond their borders. This applies both to the agents of the sovereign state as a whole, and to the head of state. The classical institution of state sovereignty conferred absolute immunity from laws and courts within other states on officials acting in the capacity of the state, regardless of the nature of the act.[7] This classical notion of state sovereignty held that states only had authority to apply, enforce, and adjudicate laws over their own citizens and private foreigners, but not against foreign state representatives, even after they had left office. At the same time, this institution limited states' accountability: sovereign states were not accountable to other sovereign states for acts committed within their sovereign jurisdiction or by their sovereign agents.[8] For centuries, sitting and former heads of state enjoyed absolute immunity from prosecution by foreign courts unless they consented to appear before such a court.

The rule of absolute sovereign immunity was first challenged in its application to private commercial transactions conducted by state agents (Sweeney 1963; Fox 2004).[9] The United States in 1952 replaced the absolute doctrine with the restrictive doctrine of sovereign immunity, in which "sovereign immunity should not be claimed or granted in actions with respect to real property…or with respect to the disposition of the property of a deceased person even though a foreign sovereign is the beneficiary."[10] This restrictive doctrine of immunity was recently codified in the 2005 UN Convention on Jurisdictional Immunities of States and Their Property. The restriction to exclude private property transactions (*jure gestionis*) from governmental actions (*jure imperii*) is easily explained through rationalist accounts of reciprocal policy coordination though it was never easy to practice (Robertson 2002, 405).

What is less easily explained in a straightforward rationalist manner is why states now increasingly exclude official human rights abuses from immunity. A shift in sovereignty's boundaries has placed gross human rights abuses under extraterritorial jurisdiction, removing states' exclusive jurisdiction over the persons on their territory. This shift has become the center of a battle royal between governments and judiciaries.

---

7 Sovereign immunity goes hand in hand with the Act of State Doctrine, which holds that domestic courts will not sit in judgment on the actions of a sovereign state within its own territory. As the US Supreme Court ruled in *Underhill v. Hernandez* (1897), "Every sovereign State is bound to respect the independence of every other sovereign State, and the courts of one country will not sit in judgment on the acts of the government of another done within its own territory" (Carter et al 2003: 619).

8 Traditionally, sovereigns were only accountable to other sovereigns for injuries arising from conditions menacing international peace, military accidents, and more recently, pollution emanating from within one state and harming another. In the event of such injuries, states are obligated to pay reparations to the harmed state.

9 Absolute sovereign immunity has not included immunity in cases dealing with private real property of state officials. See Sweeney 1963 and Fox 2004.

10 Jack B. Tate, Acting Legal Advisor to the Secretary of State, Letter to the Attorney General, 19 May 1952. The "Tate Letter" is widely accepted as the point at which the United States accepted the restrictive doctrine of sovereign immunity. This understanding of restrictive sovereign immunity was codified in the Foreign Sovereign Immunities Act of 1976. See Carter et al. 2003, Robertson 2002, 405.

The Pinochet Precedent

1998 was a seminal year for international human rights. The arrest and 17 month detention of General Augusto Pinochet in London on a Spanish warrant set a precedent that has further reduced the boundaries of sovereignty immunity (Agence France Presse 2001).[11] As a consequence, individual legal access to state officials dramatically increased and the privileges of state sovereigns have been further eroded. The mere act of serving a former head of state with an arrest warrant was an historic event, as states rarely place their human rights obligations above the "political benefits of avoiding international disagreements." (Rothenberg 2002, 928) The Pinochet case fundamentally undermined the role of the sovereign state in two ways: immunity for official violations of human rights was revoked, and national courts exercised extraterritorial jurisdiction to punish human rights crimes in foreign countries, despite the diplomatic consequences.

The Pinochet precedent was not set overnight, and did not start or end in Great Britain. In 1996 Spanish and later non-Spanish citizens and their families filed suit in Spain in a special court, the Audencia Nacional, designed to investigate crimes such as drug trafficking that occur outside of Spanish territory. They charged former leaders of Argentina and leaders of the Chilean junta with terrorism and genocide. The Spanish high court overruled government lawyers' arguments that these cases were not subject to Spanish jurisdiction.

Traditionally, states may claim jurisdiction over an alleged crime on the basis of the territory on which the act occurred (the territorial principle), the effects on a sovereign (the effects principle), the personality of the alleged perpetrator (the personality principle) or victim (the passive personality principle). By far the most common and accepted is the territorial principle, which reinforces a sovereign's control over acts and persons within its territory. Jurisdiction to hear the cases involving Spanish victims of Chilean acts falls under the passive personality principle that states have the right to protect their citizens while abroad. States rarely assert this right to hear cases of foreign criminal acts, such as terrorism or political violence, involving their citizens. However, this principle does not cover non-citizens; for such a claim, the state must claim that the alleged crime is universally illegal. Until 2003 Spanish law specifically affirmed the principle of universal jurisdiction for certain crimes including genocide and terrorism. Because of the inclusion of non-Spaniards in the Argentinean and Chilean cases, the Spanish investigating judge argued that the alleged crimes were subject to universal jurisdiction (Rothenberg 2002, 933).

Universal jurisdiction is a part of customary international law that recognizes that some acts are so reprehensible that *any* state, not just the state in which the acts occurred or which suffered injuries as a result, may take jurisdiction over the perpetrator "because the offenders are 'common enemies of mankind and all nations have an equal interest in their apprehension and prosecution.' " (Browne-Wilkinson

11 Agence France Press, "A Chronology of the Pinochet Affair" 9 July 2001.

1999) Universal jurisdiction was used in the eighteenth and nineteenth centuries to prosecute pirates and slave traders. It fell out of use until the Nuremberg war crimes trials at the end of World War II. There, the allies relied explicitly on universal jurisdiction to prosecute Nazi officials for acts that were not illegal under Nazi Germany's laws, but were deemed to be "crimes against humanity" (Bass 2000).

Using the argument that the alleged crimes committed in Chile were subject to universal jurisdiction, the Spanish investigating judge issued arrest warrants and an extradition request in late October 1998 while General Pinochet was on an unannounced visit to Great Britain for medical treatment. After his arrest, the Pinochet case went straight to Britain's highest court, the Law Lords. The first panel of Law Lords ruled 3–2 in favor of extraditing the former Chilean head of state to Spain to stand trial on charges of crimes against humanity, unless the Home Office interfered. Remarkably, Home Secretary Jack Straw refused to step in after the first trial, "finding," as Geoffrey Robertson puts it, "no reason not to let the law take its course." (Robertson 2002, 397–8) Straw explicitly rejected the notion that Pinochet enjoyed immunity for the alleged crimes, and held that Britain's obligations under international law overcame the usual deference to state sovereignty (BBC News World Service 1998).[12] After a personal connection between one of the Law Lords and Amnesty International was made public, a second trial was held to establish the legality of extraditing Pinochet. This seven judge panel ruled 6–1 in favor of extradition, again subject to the Home Office's determination that such extradition would not be unduly onerous (Browne-Wilkinson 1999). Straw ruled on 15 April 1999 that Pinochet should be extradited to Spain. After the second Law Lords ruling, medical examiners declared in October 1999 that Pinochet was mentally unfit to stand trial on the grounds that he had suffered brain damage following two strokes. After asking for a medical examination of the general, Home Secretary Straw allowed Pinochet to leave Great Britain for Chile in March 2000 (BBC News World Service 2000; AFP 2001). Subsequently, and much to the surprise of Chileans and international observers, the Chilean Supreme Court rescinded Pinochet's life-time immunity (granted to him in 1990 as a condition of his transfer of power to a civilian government), and stripped him of immunity in three human rights cases (BBC News World Service 2004a, 2005).

Beyond Pinochet

What stands out for our purposes is that "In its ruling of 24 March 1999, the British Law Lords definitively rejected General Pinochet's claim of immunity as a

12 It is usual for a foreign court to give deference to a home court if that court is undertaking proceedings on the same issue and has a stronger claim of jurisdiction. Chilean politicians argued that Pinochet should be tried in Chile; Straw rejected the argument that the possibility of this trial superseded Britain's requirement to obey its commitments under the European Convention on Extradition.

former head-of-state" (Wilson 1999, 977). Subsequent acts suggest the precedent has been set for a changed boundary of sovereign immunity. The Mexican Supreme Court in June 2003 ruled that a former Argentine military officer be extradited to Spain for alleged atrocities he committed in Argentina in the 1970s and 1980s (Peters 2003). Argentina itself has shifted its position and has detained 46 former military officials and repealed laws and edicts granting them and other officials' lifetime immunity in preparation for extradition to European countries. Its Supreme Court ruled in August 2004 that there is no statute of limitations for crimes against humanity (Rohter 2003; Jonas 2004; BBC News World Service 2004b). In June 2004, the US Supreme Court upheld the Alien Tort Statute of 1789 (ATS), which allows US courts to assert jurisdiction for well-defined crimes committed outside the United States and against foreigners that are against the law of nations or self-executing treaties. The Court expressly rejected the claim that the ATS was meaningless, and affirmed the right of foreigners to use federal courts to seek damages for a limited set of acts. The Court also reaffirmed the judiciary's role in enforcing well-defined customary international law, such as the prohibition on state-sanctioned torture and genocide.[13] In March 2005 a US Appellate Court upheld the first judgment in the United States against a Chilean military officer for acts committed in violation of the ATS and the Torture Victim Protection Act (American Society of International Law 2005a). European courts continue to issue arrest warrants and extradition requests, in some cases even against current government officials. In 2000, Belgium issued a warrant for the arrest of the then Foreign Minister of the Democratic Republic of Congo (DRC) for alleged crimes in violation of the 1949 Geneva Conventions.

What made these changes possible in part was states' own admission of the existence of human rights laws through their adoption of the Convention against Torture (CAT) and the Genocide Convention. International treaties such as these are firmly institutionalized when they become a part of domestic law through the passage of implementing legislation. It was the fact that the UN Convention against Torture was part of domestic British law that led the Law Lords to hold that Pinochet had indeed committed extraditable offenses. However they went well beyond this

13 542 US *Sosa v. Alvarez-Machain* (2004). The Court in this ruling gave federal courts the ability to decide which acts violate customary international law, but made very clear that only very specifically defined acts that were clearly accepted as prohibited were permissible grounds for taking jurisdiction. They specifically referenced state-sanctioned torture and state- or privately-sanctioned genocide as passing this threshold. They reaffirmed the role of US courts in enforcing customary international law set out in the *Paquete Habana* (1900) and *Filartiga v. Pena-Irala* (1980) cases. *Filartiga* turned solely on whether torture was prohibited under customary international law, while the *Paquete Habana* set the precedent that US courts would apply the customary law of nations. Official torture is widely understood to be against the law of nations, as codified in the Convention on Torture (ratified by the US in 1994 and executed in the Convention Against Torture Implementation Act). To bolster the prohibition on torture, the US enacted the Torture Victims Protection Act in 1991 after the *Filartiga* case.

to argue that these offenses were crimes against humanity that dissolved the claims of sovereign immunity. The Torture Convention explicitly defines and criminalizes torture as certain acts conducted by *representatives of a state*. It is for this reason that the Law Lords rejected the claim of sovereign immunity for state-sponsored acts of torture as such acts are specifically illegal under the CAT, and are laid out as crimes requiring universal jurisdiction (Browne-Wilkinson 1999; Robertson 2002, 398).[14] The reverse side of this coin is that sovereigns are extending their national jurisdiction beyond their borders on the basis of international agreements requiring universal enforcement. They are agreeing to prosecute former and sitting state officials. The result is that individuals have increased ability to seek grievances against their own state officials, even in foreign courts.

Courts vs. Politics: Sovereign Immunity and International Law in National Courts

This shift in the boundary of sovereign immunity has not gone unnoticed by governments. The line between sovereign and individual human rights is currently hotly contested. The International Court of Justice ruled in 2002 in favor of the DRC that certain government officials, "such as accredited diplomats, current heads of state (or heads of government such as prime ministers) and current foreign ministers, are entitled to a temporary procedural immunity from the criminal jurisdiction of foreign states" for the duration of their official term, but that the immunity lapses once they are out of office (International Court of Justice 2002; Bhuta and Schurr 2006). Governments have taken the ICJ ruling as an opportunity to restrict the applicability of universal jurisdiction for human rights violations to former officials and to reestablish political, rather than legal, criteria for grants of immunity. When pursuing cases, they have focused on more traditional appeals to the principles of nationality (of the alleged perpetrator) and passive personality (the nationality of victims) instead of relying on universal jurisdiction.

Under severe pressure from the United States after Secretary of Defense Rumsfeld was charged there with war crimes, Belgium modified its law to apply only to Belgian nationals or residents (thus relying on the passive personality rather than the universal principle for extraterritorial jurisdiction). However, it has continued to prosecute alleged perpetrators of humanitarian crimes committed outside of Belgian territory, convicting two Rwandans of genocide in July 2005 (American Society of International Law 2005). Several European states have

14 Lord Saville wrote in *Ex Parte Pinochet*, "Each state party has agreed that the other state parties can exercise jurisdiction over alleged official torturers found within their territories, by extraditing them or referring them to their own appropriate authorities for prosecution; and thus to my mind can hardly simultaneously claim an immunity from extradition or prosecution that is necessarily based on the official nature of the alleged torture." (Browne-Wilkinson 1999)

declined to exercise jurisdiction over current foreign officials. German courts went beyond the 2002 ICJ ruling to hold that a *former* Chinese head of State was entitled to immunity from German criminal jurisdiction. European countries have also taken steps to limit the right of individuals to bring suit against foreign officials and have enacted legislation shifting this authority to state prosecutors (Bhuta and Schurr 2006, 8–13, 25–7). French courts held in a 2007 case alleging torture against former Secretary of Defense Donald Rumsfeld that he was immune from prosecution for acts committed while he was in office, following the dismissal of similar cases in Germany (Center for Constitutional Rights 2009). The African Union in 2008 condemned the abuse of universal jurisdiction to target African leaders and resolved that warrants for the arrest of African leaders under this principle would not be executed by AU member states (Assembly of the African Union 2008).

Yet at the same time, the number of cases prosecuted in Western Europe under universal jurisdiction has steadily risen since 2000. Spain's Constitutional Court upheld the application of universal jurisdiction to cases falling with Spain's international legal commitments in 2005 in its ruling on the *Guatemalan Generals* case (Bhuta and Schurr 2006, 25). In 2006 Spain's Audencia Nacional accepted jurisdiction over a case concerning the Chinese government's alleged policy of genocide in Tibet (Bakker 2006, 595–601). In 2008, Spain and France issued warrants for the arrest of Rwandan officials, leading to the arrest in Germany of Rwandan Minister of Protocol Rose Kabuye and her extradition to France to await trial (AFP 2008; McGreal 2009). Spain and France both consider foreign amnesties to be irrelevant to their ability to exercise universal jurisdiction over human rights cases (Bhuta and Schurr 2006, 25, 86). Several European countries have developed dedicated police and investigatory units to handle international crimes including human rights abuses. The European Union has set up a "network of contact points in respect of persons responsible for genocide, crimes against humanity and war crimes" to facilitate EU-wide cooperation in investigation and prosecution of international crimes and emphasized the need for EU members to prosecute such cases (Bhuta and Schurr 2006, 3, 10–13, 21). In 2004 Interpol began organizing Expert Meetings on these crimes in response to the increasing number of universal jurisdiction prosecutions (Bhuta and Schurr 2006, 21–3). Latin American countries have participated in a "justice cascade," stripping former officials of immunity and trying them for human rights violations (Lutz and Sikkink 2000, 633, 654–7, 2001). In 2007, Chile's Supreme Court approved the extradition of former Peruvian head of state Alberto Fujimori to Peru for trial on human rights abuses and corruption charges (Romero 2007). African countries may favor local application of universal jurisdiction while opposing European and international application, as suggested by the 2000 indictment in Senegal of the former President of Chad for torture and crimes against humanity and the filing of suits against him in Chad by alleged victims (Amnesty International 2001).

Many countries have retained domestic laws allowing the exercise of universal jurisdiction for human rights violations (Amnesty International 2007).[15]

The Decline of Sovereign Immunity regarding International Human Rights

What the struggle over the acceptance of universal jurisdiction masks is that a substantial shift in the institution of sovereign immunity has still occurred. The shift has three parts. First, courts are increasingly asserting jurisdiction over events that took place on the sovereign territory of another state through more vigorous use of the passive personality principle. Classically, states did not base their claims to extraterritorial jurisdiction on the passive personality principle (the nationality of the victims); at best, passive personality was a secondary rationale for asserting extraterritorial jurisdiction, as established in the 1927 *Lotus* case. Yet the legislation enacted in the past few years suggests that states are now much more willing to ignore claims to sovereign immunity for human rights violations committed against their citizens. Second, they more regularly assert jurisdiction over former government officials, when formerly such officials were considered immune both during and after their government service. Third, courts are also claiming the authority to rule on actions of these officials that previously would have been classified as part and parcel of their official duties (and therefore covered by immunity). These actions, now seen as violations of international human rights law, are no longer considered to be covered by sovereign immunity, much as commercial transactions have ceased to be considered public or officials acts. While not the full scale victory for universal jurisdiction that human rights activists hoped for this three-part shift still carries important political implications, as states increasingly accept that their sovereign rights are circumscribed by human rights. Moreover, domestic courts are still exercising universal jurisdiction over human rights cases. What made these shifts possible was the development of other institutions, in particularly the creation of a new set of crimes—crimes against humanity—in the body of international humanitarian law and its entrenchment with the creation of international criminal law.

Crimes against Humanity and the Erosion of Sovereign Immunity

The challenge to absolute sovereign immunity started not with a frontal assault on sovereign immunity but with an innovation in the boundaries of the institution known as the law of armed conflict or international humanitarian law which led to the establishment of a new institution: international criminal law. The law of

15 In September 2001, over 125 countries had domestic criminal law allowing for universal jurisdiction over some form of human rights abuses. Over 80 state parties to the Convention Against Torture may exercise universal jurisdiction for torture.

armed conflict arose to limit the discretion of military officers and their political commanders in the conduct of an activity that is legally recognized as being the right only of states: war.[16] This institution sought to constrain the authority of war makers by stipulating the humanitarian boundaries beyond which they could not go—in effect bounding the jurisdiction of war within the institutional limits of humanity.[17]

This boundary change was formalized in recent times in the Nuremberg Charter adopted by the Allies on 8 August 1945. Through the Nuremberg Charter, foreign states, the Allies, defined a right of jurisdiction over crimes against humanity in addition to war crimes that occurred in Germany and elsewhere. While crimes against peace and against agents of the belligerents (the laws of armed conflict) reflect the traditional notion of war as an affair conducted between states, crimes against humanity were something else.[18] This innovation gave foreign states the right to try German officials for crimes committed against German citizens and in Germany, who were not covered by the law of armed conflict. Moreover, it established jurisdiction over these crimes even if the acts were not crimes under local law (Orentlicher 1998, 9). In effect, Nuremberg removed the boundary of state sovereignty over a belligerent's citizens in times of interstate war. It enforced a set of international social values (humanitarian principles) on agents of the state and constrained sovereign authority to regulate and organize society through inhumane means.[19]

---

16 The 1899 and 1907 Hague and 1949 Geneva Conventions codifying the laws of war expressly recognize authorized state agents as the only legal combatants in conflict. Other combatants are illegal as they do not have legal authority to act.

17 This is expressly laid out in the Martens clause, included in the preambles to the 1899 and 1907 Hague Conventions Respecting the Laws and Customs of War:

> Until a more complete code of the laws of war has been issued, the High Contracting Parties deem it expedient to declare that, in cases not included in the Regulations adopted by them, the inhabitants and the belligerent remain under the protection and the rule of the principles of the law of nations, as they result from the usages established among civilized peoples, from *the laws of humanity*, and the dictates of the public conscience. [Emphasis added]

Hague Convention (No. IV) Respecting the Laws and Customs of War on Land, with Annex Regulations, 18 October 1907. See also Diane Orentlicher, "The Law of Universal Conscience: Genocide and Crimes Against Humanity," paper presented at the Committee on Conscience conference *Genocide and Crimes Against Humanity: Early Warning and Prevention* on 9 December 1998, at the United States Holocaust Memorial Museum, 8.

18 The law of armed conflict stipulates the responsibility of foreign armies with respect to enemy civilians, but does not lay out the responsibilities of a belligerent state towards its own population.

19 This was not the only time that the society of states had sought to bind state sovereignty. States also sought to ban slave-trading and mercenary armies.

The humanitarian bounding of a state's authority over its citizens in times of interstate conflict expanded to times of interstate peace as well.[20] While the Nuremberg Charter had limited international jurisdiction to those crimes against humanity that were committed in connection with war crimes or crimes against peace (Orentlicher 1998, 11), that linkage was soon broken. The Allies created a new uniform code for the prosecution of Nazi war criminals in their zones of occupation that de-linked crimes against humanity from wartime activities (Orentlicher 1998, 13–14). This effectively removed a temporal limitation on when a crime against humanity could occur (only within wartime), as well as a geographic limitation (only in regions where there was interstate conflict). A new body of international law was born: international criminal law.

This expansion of the extraterritorial jurisdiction over crimes against humanity was codified in the UN Security Council's adoption of the Statute establishing the International Criminal Tribunal for the Former Yugoslavia (ICTY). The ICTY Statute gave the Tribunal authority to prosecute crimes conducted in either interstate or internal armed conflicts (ICTY Statute 1993).[21] The temporal expansion was institutionalized in the Statute of the International Criminal Tribunal for Rwanda (ICTR) and the International Criminal Court, which do not require that the acts be conducted in times of armed conflict, only that they be "part of a widespread or systematic attack on any civilian population" (Rome Statute of the ICC 1993).[22] All three stipulate that no state can conduct either genocide or crimes against humanity. Regardless of whether a state of armed conflict is in existence, these crimes are justiciable, and starting with Nuremberg, there is no statute of limitations on when individuals can be prosecuted for crimes against humanity. Another incursion on the traditional boundaries of sovereignty and sovereign immunity that Nuremberg began was that of individual responsibility for state-sanctioned crimes. The Nuremberg Tribunal, ICTY, ICTR and ICC all enshrine the principle that not only are those in official command responsible for crimes, but so are the individuals who actually commit or aid and abet these crimes. This further erodes the sovereign state's ability to shelter its own officials and those it empowers from societal norms. It also alters the authority relationships within state institutions.[23]

---

20 The human rights regime expanded throughout the second half of the twentieth century. Important international treaties include the 1945 UN Charter, Article 55, 1948 Universal Declaration of Human Rights, 1948 Genocide Convention, 1966 International Covenant on Civil and Political Rights, 1966 International Covenant on Economic, Social, and Cultural Rights, 1966 Convention on the Elimination of all Forms of Racial Discrimination, 1979 Convention on the Elimination of all forms of Discrimination Against Women, and 1984 Convention Against Torture.

21 ICTY Statute, Article 5, adopted 25 May 1993.

22 Rome Statute of the ICC, Article 7, adopted 17 July 1998. See also ICTR Statute, Article 3, adopted 8 November 1994.

23 The US Uniform Code of Military Justice stipulates that military personnel are required to disobey an illegal order. The scandal over the torture of prisoners in Iraq highlighted this issue, as soldiers went public stating either that they had been instructed

The most controversial of these institutions is the International Criminal Court. The Nuremberg Tribunal, the ICTY and the ICTR can all be labeled as cases of the victors creating new rules to apply to the vanquished. The ICC was a new creature—a universal regime that applied to all state parties from July 2002 onwards. The ICC Statute entered into force on 1 July 2002. As of July 2008, it had 108 State Parties, including Canada, Australia, New Zealand, 30 African, 16 Eastern European, 14 Asian, 23 Latin American, and 22 Western European states. The Court began hearing cases in 2004 and its first trial was begun in January 2009. It gives individuals the right to petition the Prosecutor to begin investigating a case, much as in the Spanish case regarding Pinochet and Argentinean officials.

The ICC also directly challenges the boundaries of sovereign immunity. Following on clauses built into the ICTY and ICTR and the precedent set at Nuremberg, the official position of the individual does not make them immune from prosecution. Contrary to the 2002 ruling of the International Court of Justice—a forum in which only states, not individuals can bring cases—that sitting officials maintain their sovereign immunity for crimes against humanity, the ICC makes no distinction between former (such as Pinochet) and current officials. As is well-known, ICTY Prosecutor Carla del Ponte indicted a sitting head of state, Slobodan Milosevic. The ICC explicitly rejects sovereign immunity for current or former state officials. ICC Statute Article 27.2 states, "Immunities or special procedural rules which may attach to the official capacity of a person, whether under national or international law, shall not bar the Court from exercising its jurisdiction over such a person."

The ICC Prosecutor's case against Sudanese officials regarding the atrocities in Darfur further reinforces the shift away from immunity of current and former officials for human rights violations, a move for the first time called for by the UN Security Council in 2005 (ICC 2007).[24] The case represents a clear statement that, when it concerns the treatment of populations, the internal affairs of states and the actions of state officials are no longer separate from international politics in law or in deed.

While the Clinton Administration initially championed the establishment of the ICC and the campaign to end impunity for human rights violations, it feared the political use of such charges to limit US military engagement abroad. Under the Clinton Administration, the US fought hard to ensure that the ICC Statute contained provisions that prevented politically-motivated prosecutions and limited

---

to commit these abuses and had not known they were illegal, or that they had known that such acts were illegal and therefore refused to participate and reported it to their superiors. See *Manual for Courts-Martial United States* (2000 Edition) (Washington, D.C.: US Government Printing Office), IV-19-IV-20.

24 ICC, "Facts regarding the situation in Darfur, Sudan" Document No ICC-PIDS-PR-20070502-214A_En; Available at: http://www2.icc-cpi.int/NR/rdonlyres/59BD94DF-74B4-47BA-B9BF-809A541E81E2/144043/ICCPIDSFR20070502214A_En1.pdf (accessed 19 December 2008).

ICC jurisdiction to only those cases where a state refused or failed to prosecute the alleged crimes at home. It failed however in gaining blanket immunity for US military personnel in the Statute (Tepperman 2000). The US Congress stepped into the act in 2000 when Senator Jesse Helms introduced the American Service-Members Protection Act (ASPA), which President George W. Bush signed into law on 2 August 2002. The APSA prohibits US cooperation with the ICC and seeks to regulate US cooperation with the United Nations and foreign countries to guarantee US protection from ICC actions. It also bars any US military assistance to states that have ratified the ICC treaty unless the President waives this requirement. The ASPA was quickly dubbed the "Hague Invasion Act" because it authorizes the US President to "use all means necessary and appropriate to bring about the release of any person…detained or imprisoned by, on behalf of, or at the request of the International Criminal Court" (American Society of International Law 2002, 975–7).

The Bush Administration went much farther in its efforts to restore the traditional institution of sovereign immunity; it sought to reverse the bounding of state sovereignty within human rights and humanitarian law and choke off the development of international criminal law. It revoked the US signature on the ICC Statute. It also exerted a tremendous amount of time, pressure and threats to force countries, especially parties to the Statute, to sign bilateral immunity agreements (BIAs) covering US officials and military personnel, claiming the right to do so under Article 98 of the ICC Statute. The EU Council subsequently pronounced that such BIAs are illegal, and counseled member states not to sign them as they would violate their legal obligations under international law (Akande 2004, 407–33). The US also sought to reverse the institutionalization of universal jurisdiction within domestic legal systems.[25] The US acted in part for practical reasons, given its extensive basing of military personnel abroad.

Much US behavior under the Bush Administration, however, appeared to be driven by an ideological rejection of state sovereignty and executive power as bounded by broader societal norms. In this version of US exceptionalism, newer institutions of international society undermine the core values of popular sovereignty enshrined in the US Constitution which require a societal commitment to the traditional institution of sovereign immunity. In this view, US international

25 The US Attorney General filed friend of the court briefs in two court cases involving the Alien Tort Statute (ATS), *Sosa v. Alvarez Machain* and *John Doe v. UNOCAL*, a case filed by Burmese citizens against US energy company UNOCAL. In both briefs, the Justice Department argued that US courts should deny foreigners the right to sue in US courts under the ATS. The US also successfully threatened Belgium to change a 1993 anti-atrocity law. Belgium had passed the legislation first in order to comply with its obligations under the Convention against Torture and then amended the legislation in 1999 to comply with its obligations under the ICC Statute. The US threatened to stop funding the construction of a new NATO headquarters in Belgium and to stop sending US officials to Belgium unless the law was amended. The Belgian parliament amended the law so as to give only Belgian citizens, and not foreigners, the right to bring suit in Belgium for atrocities committed worldwide. See Richey 2004; Black and MacAskill 2003; Forero 2003.

commitments are bounded by the overarching institution of US popular sovereignty, embodied in the Executive Branch (Kahn 2003; Spiro 2000, 9–15). The United States' actions reflected an effort to make international society less institutionalized and more like Krasner's realist world of power hierarchies.

Conclusion: The Implications of Eroding Sovereignty

The political significance of this shift in jurisdictions has not been lost on state actors. In particular, the United States government sought to shore up classical sovereign immunity by attacking the growing acceptance of universal jurisdiction for crimes against humanity. The vehemence with which the Bush Administration sought to strangle the ICC at birth and to circumvent the Convention Against Torture and the Geneva Conventions in its war on terror indicates the intense political struggles that boundaries engender, as well as the lengths states will go to determine which actors—states or individual human beings—have the authority to act both domestically and internationally. These struggles arise precisely because of the important ways in which changes to one institution, the law of armed conflict, have rippled through human rights law to establish international criminal law and along the way erode another institution, sovereign immunity.

What are the consequences of this erosion of state sovereignty? Aside from the important effect of promoting greater accountability for human rights and reducing the impunity of dictators, this shift has altered the legitimate realms of authoritative action of states and individuals. On the one hand, states appear to be increasingly subjecting themselves to a reduced sphere of exclusive sovereign authority and to greater international accountability. On the other hand, states have expanded their claims to domestically adjudicate cases that have traditionally been off limits, protected by the boundary of state sovereignty. As a result, individuals have much greater ability to access national and international courts to seek redress for acts committed by state officials. The institutional boundaries of state sovereignty are now more permeable. While sovereignty may never have been as institutionalized as domestic institutions, this change in its sacrosanct nature through the alteration and creation of international law has real political consequences, not all of which have been welcomed, but which appear likely to persist.

References

AFP. 2008. *Rwanda's Kabuye in French custody on Wednesday: Paris* [Online 14 November]. Available at: www.google.com/hostednews/afp/article/ALeqM5haUdjw46WY87 o2iVjPynUtDWGWg [accessed 30 January 2009].

Agence France Presse. 2001. *A Chronology of the Pinochet Affair*, 9 July 2001. Available at: http://www.globalpolicy.org/intljustice/wanted/2001/pino2.htm [accessed 05 February 2009].

Akande, D. 2004. International Law Immunities and The International Criminal Court. *The American Journal of International Law* 98(3), 407–33.

American Society of International Law. 2002. American Service-Members Protection Act. *The American Journal of International Law* 96(4), 975–7.

American Society of International Law. 2005a. *International Law in Brief* [Online April 12]. Available at: http://www.asil.org/ilib/2005/04/ilib050412.htm#j3 [accessed 28 August 2005].

American Society of International Law. 2005b *International Law in Brief* [Online 19 July]. Available at: http://www.asil.org/ilib/2005/07/ilib050719.htm#b1 [accessed 27 August 2005].

Amnesty International. 2001. *Universal Jurisdiction: The Duty of States to Enact and Implement Legislation* (AI Index: IOR 53/002-018/2001). Available at: http://web.amnesty.org/ pages/legal_memorandum [accessed 22 February 2007].

Amnesty International. 2007. *Universal Jurisdiction: Questions and Answers*. Available at: http://web.amnesty.org/library/index/engIOR530202001 [accessed 22 February 2007].

Assembly of the African Union. 2008. *Decision on the Report of the Commission on the Abuse of the Principle of Universal Jurisdiction Doc.* Assembly/AU/14 (XI), 11th Ordinary Session, Sharm El-Sheikh, Egypt, 30 June–1 July 2008.

Bakker, C. A. E. 2006. Universal Jurisdiction of Spanish Courts over Genocide in Tibet: Can it Work? *Journal of International Criminal Justice* 4(3): 595–601.

Bass, G. J. 2000. *Stay the Hand of Vengeance.* Princeton: Princeton University Press.

BBC News World Service. 1998. *Straw Sets Out his Reasons* [Online 9 December, 17:57 GMT]. Available at: http://news.bbc.co.uk/1/hi/uk_politics/231775.stm [accessed 23 August 2004].

BBC News World Service. 2000. *The Pinochet Case: Timeline* [Online 12 January, 10:53 GMT]. http://news.bbc.co.uk/2/hi/americas/600617.stm [accessed 30 January 2009].

BBC News World Service. 2004a. Court Lifts Pinochet's Immunity [Online 28 May, 19:05 GMT]. http://news.bbc.co.uk/1/hi/world/americas/3758005.stm [accessed 22 August 2004]

BBC News World Service. 2004b. *Vital Rights Ruling in Argentina* [Online 24 August, 23:45 GMT]. Available at: http://news.bbc.co.uk/1/hi/world/americas/359631 6.stm [accessed 25 August 2004].

BBC News World Service. 2005. *Court Strips Pinochet of Immunity* [Online 6 July 2005, 16:37 GMT 17:37]. Available at: http://news.bbc.co.uk/1/hi/world/americas/4657509.stm [accessed: 30 January 2009].

Bhuta, N. and Schurr, J. 2006. Universal Jurisdiction in Europe: The State of the Art. *Human Rights Watch Report* [Online 27 June]18(5) (D). Available at: http://www.hrw.org/en/reports/2006/06/27/universal-jurisdiction-europe [accessed 30 January 2009].

Biersteker, T. J. and Weber, C. (eds). 1996. *State Sovereignty as Social Construct.* New York: Cambridge University Press.

Black, I. and MacAskill, E. 2003. US Threatens to Boycott Belgium Over War Crimes Law. *The Guardian* 13 June.

Browne-Wilkinson, L. 1999. *Regina v. Bartle and the Commissioner of Police for the Metropolis and Others Ex Parte Pinochet Regina v. Evans and Another and the Commissioner of Police for the Metropolis and Others Ex Parte Pinochet (On Appeal from a Divisional Court of the Queen's Bench Division)* [Online 24 March] House of Lords. Available at: http://www.parliament.the-stationery-office.co.uk/pa/ld199899/ldjudgmt/jd990324/pino1.htm[accessed 30 January 2009].

Bull, H. 1977. *The Anarchical Society.* New York: Columbia University Press.

Carter, B., Trimble, P. R. and Bradley, C. A. (eds). 2003. *International Law.* New York: Aspen Publishers.

Center for Constitutional Rights. 2009. *French War Crimes Complaint Against Donald Rumsfeld, et al.* [Online]. Available at: http://ccrjustice.org/ourcases/current-cases/french-war-crimes-complaint-against-donald-rumsfeld [accessed 30 January 2009].

Deutsch, K. W. 1953. *Nationalism and Social Communication.* Cambridge: MIT Press.

Forero, J. 2003. Rights Groups Overseas Fight US Concerns in US Courts. *New York Times* 26 June.

Fox, H. 2004. *The Law of State Immunity.* Oxford: Oxford University Press.

Gray, C. 2004. *International Law and the Use of Force.* Oxford: Oxford University Press.

Haas, E. B. 1964. *Beyond the Nation State.* Stanford: Stanford University Press.

Haas, E. B. 1990. Reason and Change in International Life. *Journal of International Affairs* 44(1), 209–40.

Holsti, K. J. 2004. *Taming the Sovereigns: Institutional Change in International Politics.* Cambridge: Cambridge University Press.

International Court of Justice. 2002. *Case Concerning the Arrest Warrant of April 2000 (Democratic Republic of the Congo v. Belgium).* I.C.J. Rep., H 295.

Jackson, R. H. 1990. *Quasi-states: Sovereignty, International Relations, and the Third World.* Cambridge, England; New York: Cambridge University Press.

Jonas, S. 2004. The Ripple Effect of the Pinochet Case. *Human Rights Brief* 11(3), 3–38.

Kahn, P.W. 2003. Why the United States Is So Opposed. *The Crimes of War Project Magazine* [Online December]. Available at: http://www.crimesofwar.org/print/icc/icc-kahn-print.html [accessed 30 January 2009].

Keohane, R. O. and Nye, J. S. 1989. *Power and Interdependence.* New York: Harper Collins Publishers.

Koh, H.H. 2003. Wrong on Rights. *Yale Global* 18 July.

Krasner, S. D. 1993. Westphalia and All That, in *Ideas and Foreign Policy* edited by J. Goldstein and R. O. Keohane. Ithaca: Cornell University Press, pp. 235–64.

Krasner, S. 1999. *Sovereignty: Organized Hypocrisy.* Princeton: Princeton University Press.

Krasner, S. D. 2001. Rethinking the Sovereign State Model, in *Empires, Systems and States: Great Transformations in International Politics,* edited by M. Cox, T. Dunne, and K. Booth. Cambridge and New York: Cambridge University Press, pp. 17–42.

Kratochwil, F. V. 1989. *Rules, Norms, and Decisions.* Cambridge: Cambridge University Press.

Lutz, E. L. and Sikkink, K. 2000. International Human Rights Law and Practice in Latin America. *International Organization* 54(3), 633–59.

Lutz, E. L. and Sikkink, K. 2001. The Justice Cascade: The Evolution and Impact of Foreign Human Rights Trials in Latin America. *Chicago Journal of International Law* 2(1), 1–34.

Mathews, J. T. 1997. Power Shift. *Foreign Affairs*, 76(1), 50–67.

McGreal, C. 2009. Top Rwandan Aide Chooses French Terror Trial [Online 10 November]. Available at: http://www.guardian.co.uk/world/2008/nov/10/rwanda-congo-kabuye [accessed 30 January 2009].

Orentlicher, D. 1998. The Law of Universal Conscience: Genocide and Crimes Against Humanity. *Committee on Conscience Conference on Genocide and Crimes Against Humanity: Early Warning and Prevention.* United States Holocaust Memorial Museum, Washington, D.C..

Peters, G. 2003. Mexico Gives Boost to Universal Jurisdiction. *Christian Science Monitor* 13 June.

Richey, W. 2004. When Can Foreigners Sue in US Courts? *Christian Science Monitor* 30 March.

Roberts, A. and Guelff, R., 2000. *Documents on the Laws of War.* Oxford: Oxford University Press.

Robertson, G. 2002. *Crimes Against Humanity.* New York: The New Press.

Rohter, L. 2003. Argentines Face Human Rights Trials in Europe. *New York Times* 28 July.

Rome Statute of the International Criminal Court. 1998. Available at: http://www.icc-cpi.int/NR/rdonlyres/EA9AEFF7-5752-4F84-BE94-0A655EB30E16/0/Rome_Statute_English.pdf [accessed 8 February 2009].

Romero, S. 2007. Court Approves Extradition of Fujimori. *The New York Times* [Online 21 September]. Available at: http://www.nytimes.com/2007/09/21/world/americas/22chile.html?scp=10&sq=supreme%20court%20chile%20&st=cse [accessed 30 January 2009].

Rosenau, J. 1990. *Turbulence in World Politics: A Theory of Change and Continuity.* Princeton: Princeton University Press.

Rosenau, J. N. 2003. *Distant Proximities: Dynamics Beyond Globalization.* Princeton: Princeton University Press.

Rothenberg, D. 2002. 'Let Justice Judge': An Interview with Judge Baltasar Garzon and Analysis of His Ideas. *Human Rights Quarterly* 24(4), 924–73.

Ruggie, J. G. 1993. Territoriality and Beyond: Problematizing Modernity in International Relations. *International Organization* 47(1), 139–74.

Slaughter, A.-M. 2004. *A New World Order.* Princeton: Princeton University Press.

Spiro, P. 2000. The New Sovereigntists. *Foreign Affairs* 79(6), 9–15.

Statute of the International Tribunal for the Former Yugoslavia. 1993. Available at: http://www.icls.de/dokumente/icty_statut.pdf [accessed 8 February 2009].

Statute of the International Tribunal for Rwanda. 1994. Available at: http://69.94.11.53/ENGLISH/basicdocs/statute/2007.pdf [accessed 8 February 2009].

Strange, S. 1996. *Retreat of the State: The Diffusion of Power in the World Economy.* Cambridge: Cambridge University Press.

Supreme Court of the United States. 2004. *Sosa v. Alvarez-Machain et al.* 542 US 692.

Sweeney, J. M. 1963. *The International Law of Sovereign Immunity.* US Department of State Research Study.

Tepperman, J. 2001. Contempt of Court. *Washington Monthly* (November).

Thomas, D. C. 2001. *The Helsinki Effect: International Norms, Human Rights, and the Demise of Communism.* Princeton: Princeton University Press.

United Nations. 2004. *A More Secure World: Our Shared Responsibility: Report of the Secretary-General's High-Level Panel on Threats, Challenges and Change.* New York, United Nations.

United Nations. 2005. *In Larger Freedom: Towards Development, Security and Human Rights For All: Report of the Secretary General.* New York, United Nations.

United States Government. *Manual for Courts-Martial United States* (2000 Edition) (Washington, D.C.: US Government Printing Office).

Walzer, M. 1977. *Just and Unjust Wars.* New York: Basic Books.

Wendt, A. 1994. Collective Identity Formation and the International State. *American Political Science Review* 88(2), 384–96.

Wendt, A. 1999. *Social Theory of International Politics.* Cambridge: Cambridge University Press.

Wilson, R. J. 1999. Prosecuting Pinochet: International Crimes in Spanish Domestic Law. *Human Rights Quarterly* 21(4), 927–79.

Chapter 2

Sovereignty Transformed? The Role of National Human Rights Institutions

Sonia Cardenas

If the Cold War saw the internationalization of human rights norms, the post-Cold War period gave way to their internalization (Cardenas 2001). Nothing illustrates this more aptly than the global proliferation of national human rights institutions (NHRIs), permanent state agencies designed to protect and promote human rights. By the early 1990s, there was widespread consensus that domestic implementation was essential for sustainable human rights reform. Part of a broader global embrace of democracy, NHRIs came to be viewed as an institutional staple for democratizing, rights-protective regimes in a new world order (Reif 2000). International actors, for their part, actively promoted the growth of these institutions, often leading to unexpected results.

While these state institutions largely escaped the attention of observers drawn to parallel historical developments (new human rights treaties, humanitarian intervention, accountability mechanisms, and transnational activist networks) the rapid post-Cold War diffusion of NHRIs is no less intriguing, especially from the perspective of state sovereignty. Human rights norms have always posed an apparent challenge to traditional notions of Westphalian sovereignty. Hedley Bull described the dilemma for states in the late 1970s: "…in the present era the representatives of states, when they discuss the rights or the duties of individual human beings, do so in a muted voice: for if men have rights, which other states or international authorities may champion, there are limits to their own authority; and if men have duties, to causes or movements beyond the state of which they are citizens, the state cannot count on their loyalty" (Bull 2002, 80). Notions of human rights therefore challenged two longstanding taboos of the international system: state intervention in the internal affairs of other states (external sovereignty) and the loss of domestic legitimacy to external commitments (internal sovereignty).

As the human rights agenda gained unprecedented momentum after the Cold War, a debate quickly ensued over the changing nature of state sovereignty. Are notions of sovereignty in world politics, deeply engrained for three hundred years, being transformed and displaced by the forces of globalization? What exactly is the relationship between human rights and state sovereignty? (See, for example, Cohen 2008.) In this regard, NHRIs represent a noteworthy development: compared to most issues informing the human rights-sovereignty debate, focused on external developments or the role of non-state actors, NHRIs concern changes in internal state structures. Occupying a unique role (Smith 2006), NHRIs offer a promising vantage point from which to assess ongoing questions of sovereignty.

The chapter begins with an overview of the post-Cold War evolution of NHRIs, including key concepts and trends. The focus then shifts to the debate over human rights and state sovereignty, structured around three interpretations of the significance of NHRIs and the consequences for sovereignty. A concluding section argues that NHRIs, in all of their apparent inconsistencies, are best viewed as evidence of the socially constructed nature of sovereignty and institutional change.

The Evolution of NHRIs

The contemporary notion of a NHRI is closely implicated in post-Cold War norms and history, even though its roots also run deeper. Over 100 NHRIs exist today to protect and promote human rights domestically. Prominent NHRIs created in the early 1990s include Mexico's National Human Rights Commission, India's National Human Rights Commission, and the South African Human Rights Commission. NHRIs in Canada, Australia, and Denmark feature among older institutional leaders. (For general overviews, see OHCHR 1993; Reif 2000; Cardenas 2001; Ramcharan 2005; Murray 2007; Mertus 2009; Cardenas in press.)

The dual functions of protection and promotion cover a wide spectrum of activities. Protection can involve processing human rights complaints, monitoring rights conditions, consulting with related domestic bodies (including non-governmental ones), as well as cooperating with relevant international actors. NHRIs with quasi-judicial functions may have more extensive powers, including a greater capacity for conducting investigations and even the authority to compel witnesses to testify. NHRI decisions, however, are rarely binding, so that governments are free to disregard NHRI reports and recommendations. Promotional work generally entails human rights education, whether by initiating media campaigns to diffuse human rights information, offering professional training, or shaping school curricula (Cardenas 2005). These promotive efforts are seen as an integral step in socializing domestic actors.

In practice, NHRIs take various forms, including national human rights commissions, national ombudsman, a hybrid of the commission and ombudsman models, as well as specialized institutions focusing on vulnerable groups (United Nations 1995). More than one NHRI can co-exist in a country, in which case the need to collaborate and avoid institutional redundancy is especially important. Whether or not an institution is formally considered a NHRI depends largely on whether it is accredited internationally. The International Coordinating Committee, an 18-member group comprised of leading NHRIs, oversees the accreditation process, gauging compliance with baseline international requirements. Just over 60 NHRIs are currently accredited, while a few dozen other human rights institutions either have observer status, have not completed accreditation, or are in non-compliance with international standards (NHRI Forum). These human rights institutions vary enormously in terms of their resources, political independence, and overall effectiveness.

International Standards in Historical Context

Two key documents were especially instrumental in revitalizing and developing the idea of NHRIs in the immediate post-Cold War period: the 1991 Paris Principles and the 1993 Vienna Declaration and Programme of Action. The Paris Principles, the outgrowth of an international workshop convened under UN auspices, remain to this day the authoritative set of international standards or minimum requirements defining a NHRI. These guidelines call for institutions that are pluralistic and representative, adequately funded, and carrying stable mandates irrespective of the government in office. Above all, NHRIs are to be independent of the Executive if they are to be functionally effective.

The seminal Vienna Declaration and Programme of Action further reaffirmed the significance of NHRIs: "the important and constructive role played by national institutions for the promotion and protection of human rights, in particular in their advisory capacity to the competent authorities, their role in remedying human rights violations, in the dissemination of human rights information, and education in human rights" (Part I, para. 36). The Vienna Declaration, accepted by 171 states, was the concluding document of the World Conference on Human Rights in 1993, a turning point for human rights governance. The two-week conference was attended by approximately 7,000 participants, including over 800 non-governmental organizations (OHCHR 1993). The emphasis was on the interdependence of various rights (i.e., civil, political, economic, and social); linkages among rights, democracy, and development; the rights of marginalized groups like women, children, and indigenous peoples; and the creation of mutually reinforcing mechanisms at the international, regional, and national levels. Conceptually, NHRIs complemented closely evolving notions of global rights governance articulated in Vienna.

The Vienna Declaration's attention to NHRIs was itself the outgrowth of a series of regional meetings following the Paris Principles. These meetings included regional preparatory meetings for the Vienna Conference (Africa in November 1992, Latin America in January 1993, and Asia in March and April 1993), a Commonwealth Workshop on NHRIs in 1992, and a human rights workshop for the Asia-Pacific region in 1993 (United Nations 1993a). Even before formal regional networks of NHRIs convened later in the 1990s, regional meetings devoted to human rights issues permitted state and non-governmental representatives to collaborate and develop ideas about the structure and role of NHRIs.

All of these efforts, from the workshop producing the Paris Principles to a string of regional meetings and then the World Conference in Vienna, culminated in a General Assembly resolution in December 1993 devoted exclusively to NHRIs. The resolution reasserted the messages set forth in Paris and Vienna, further legitimating the creation of these institutions. It called for follow-up meetings and greater technical assistance, committing the United Nations to an ongoing "catalytic" role in supporting NHRIs (United Nations 1993a). The stage was set for the proliferation of these institutions worldwide.

Despite the significance of these developments, it would be inaccurate to portray the post-Cold War explosion in NHRIs as constituting an absolute break from the past. National human rights committees originally were envisaged shortly after the creation of the United Nations, initially as local counterparts to the UN Commission on Human Rights. In the 1960s the United Nations moved to promote NHRIs more actively, emphasizing their potential to protect and promote human rights nationally. Even countries like the United States that opposed greater internationalization of human rights concerns favored local human rights agencies (Cardenas 2003b). By the late 1970s, standard-setting and institution-building became more deliberate policy, as international guidelines were issued and new NHRIs appeared around the world. In the late 1980s, the United Nations began issuing annual resolutions, calling for concerted efforts to create and strengthen NHRIs (United Nations 1995; Pohjolainen 2006). If the end of the Cold War was a watershed for the proliferation of NHRIs, the diffusion of these institutions still depended on decades of international standard-setting and the experience of over a dozen NHRIs.

States were always free, moreover, to choose the particular kind of NHRI that most closely matched their interests. While the promotion of these institutions necessitates accepting the universality of at least basic human rights, international actors repeatedly have recognized the importance of national differences. Hence, the Vienna World Conference noted that, as long as a state abides by the Paris Principles, it is free "to choose the framework…best suited to its particular needs at the national level" (United Nations 1993b). In selecting the type of NHRI to create, state leaders often have fallen back on institutional models that resonated domestically. For example, some states (including in the Caribbean and Europe) have favored a national ombudsman, a centuries-old institution with Scandinavian roots focused on the maladministration of justice over the more recent "commission" model centered on human rights per se (Hossain, Besselink, and Selassie 2001). Institutional design has reflected historically conditioned national preferences within the boundaries set by international guidelines.

New Normative Directions

Without the end of the Cold War, NHRIs are unlikely to have proliferated as extensively. Although these institutions had been gaining ground for decades, they quickly multiplied after the Cold War. Of currently-accredited NHRIs, spread across every region of the world, over two-thirds of these were created after 1989. But the shift was not merely quantitative. While the Paris Principles built on existing guidelines, NHRIs after the Cold War reflected a broader set of commitments: greater emphasis on inclusiveness; attention to economic and social rights; and a turn to networking, internationally and regionally. The Paris Principles recognized some of these new priorities, calling on NHRIs to "develop relations with the non-governmental organizations devoted to promoting and protecting human rights, to economic and social development, to combating racism, to protecting particularly vulnerable groups (especially children, migrant workers, refugees, physically and mentally disabled persons) or to specialized areas" (Paris Principles). Democracy, development, and networking thus became integral to the notion of a NHRI.

International guidelines had long recommended that NHRI membership be representative of society, but beginning in the 1990s these principles became more socially inclusive: they paid closer attention to non-governmental organizations and to otherwise-marginalized vulnerable groups. First, there was stronger emphasis on NHRIs cooperating with domestic NGOs and treating them as partners in human rights implementation. This has not always worked out in practice, and NGOs remain among the most vocal critics of state human rights agencies. Still, the move to work alongside NGOs and even include them in NHRI decision making is significant, reflecting post-Cold War dynamics where non-state actors have played a more prominent role within international organizations.

NHRIs also became more inclusive in calling attention to vulnerable groups, including women, children, internally displaced persons, and the disabled. In some cases, this meant creating specialized NHRIs devoted to these previously overlooked groups; in other cases, existing institutions targeted the treatment of these groups for reform. While the rights of some vulnerable groups had been recognized previously, these rights were eclipsed during the Cold War by more blatantly "political" rights violations, i.e., deliberate acts committed by the state against its purported opponents. In contrast, once the Cold War ended, the status of vulnerable groups immediately rose on the rights agenda—illustrated vividly by the Convention on the Rights of the Child, which opened for signature a little over a week after the Berlin Wall's fall.

Social inclusiveness reflected a larger normative trend toward democratization. As more countries underwent political transitions and violent conflicts ended, international actors increasingly promoted democratic institution-building; and in the human rights arena, NHRIs became a key democratic political institution. Most major peace agreements, for example, proposed their creation, leading to NHRIs in El Salvador, Bosnia, Northern Ireland, Sierra Leone, and East Timor. Even Iraq's 2004 interim constitution called for a NHRI; likewise, the Bonn Agreement proposed a NHRI in Afghanistan, an institution established in 2002 to facilitate transitional justice. Parallel to international actors providing extensive technical assistance to bolster democratization processes, the United Nations and others offered technical assistance to democratizing and post-conflict states creating or strengthening a NHRI.

The post-Cold War period also saw much greater attention to economic and social rights in NHRI mandates (Gomez 1995; Kumar 2006). Both international actors and state institutions began emphasizing rights associated with health, housing, education, and employment. While the West had embraced civil and political rights almost exclusively during the Cold War, the end of superpower conflict made it possible for economic and social rights to lose their stigma as socialist or communist prerogatives. Systemic rights violations that had previously been all but neglected became visible and legitimate objects of reform. This growing attention to economic and social rights occurred in tandem with a more general inclination to recognize both the interdependence of all rights and close linkages between human rights and development.

The post-Cold War period further shaped NHRIs by facilitating extensive networking. While NHRIs had long been mandated to collaborate with international institutions, it is noteworthy that after the Cold War NHRIs began regular information exchanges with each other. This occurred on multiple levels of governance: internationally, regionally, and even sub-regionally (Cardenas 2003a). As detailed in the next chapter, well over a dozen networks of NHRIs exist around the world whose members meet regularly, issue statements, and place issues on relevant agendas. Parallel to the rise of other trans-governmental networks (e.g., of judges, regulators, and central bankers), NHRI networks represent the extension of this post-Cold War organizational form to the human rights arena (Slaughter 2004). And given the traditionally dominant role of non-state actors as active promoters of human rights, the rise of NHRI networks is an especially significant development. This networking shift reflects a trend towards multilateralism, as well as post-Cold War dynamics wherein globalization occurs alongside regionalization.

Overall, the evolution of NHRIs and the international standards defining them reflect new post-Cold War norms, as well as more gradual institutional developments dating to the creation of the United Nations. While the central purpose of NHRIs has always been to implement international human rights norms domestically, protecting and promoting them, post-Cold War standards have seen a much stronger emphasis on designing NHRIs that are inclusive, attentive to economic and social rights, and networked with one another. These institutions have now become much more global in scope; and their rising prominence has even led international organizations to grant them formal group standing, a sign of their institutional maturity. In a relatively short span of time, NHRIs have gone from relative obscurity during the Cold War to key players in the contemporary human rights arena.

Three Interpretations

Observers have interpreted the appearance of NHRIs in widely divergent ways, just as they have debated the extent to which human rights claims challenge traditional state sovereignty. On the one hand, human rights standards limit what the state is permitted to do within its borders, empowering others to intervene in a state's internal affairs when egregious human rights violations are at stake. On the other hand, many human rights commitments appear to be "empty promises" (Hafner-Burton and Tsutsui 2005), with states more often than not appearing to have the last word—the touchstone of sovereign authority, according to Jean Bodin in the sixteenth century. Interpretations of the role of NHRIs are similarly polarized, with these bodies simultaneously cast as essential new actors curtailing state authority versus hypocritical and ineffective institutions created to deflect criticism (Human Rights Watch 2001).

Despite these disagreements, NHRIs offer an important test of the extent to which human rights norms challenge state sovereignty. Unlike other developments linked to sovereignty, such as humanitarian intervention or transnational activist networks (e.g., Sikkink 1993), NHRIs are squarely concerned with the state itself *and* changing domestic structures. The state, alternatively treated as human rights villain or protector, remains central to the concept of human rights, which are essentially standards about the way the state should treat society. Given the state's centrality to human rights, it is useful to examine how if at all NHRIs have challenged sovereignty after the Cold War. Three possible interpretations, along with their relative merits, are sketched below.

Sovereignty Transformed

Perhaps the most popular view of NHRIs, certainly among international organizations, is that they are fundamental for human rights reform. In the words of an influential UN handbook,

> An institution which is in some way separated from the responsibilities of executive governance and judicial administration is in a position to take a leading role in the field of human rights. By maintaining its real and perceived distance from the Government of the day, such a body can make a unique contribution to a country's efforts to protect its citizens and to develop a culture respectful of human rights and fundamental freedoms (United Nations 1995).

Despite the problems of individual NHRIs, these institutions can be significant and their diffusion should be encouraged. NHRIs, moreover, inevitably challenge state sovereignty. Protecting human rights requires investigating the state and its agents, recommending changes in state behavior, and holding the state accountable. Promoting human rights, in turn, entails socializing people to make claims against the state. The degree to which NHRIs actually challenge state sovereignty will depend on the institution's effectiveness, with more effective NHRIs posing a greater challenge. Under the best of circumstances, NHRIs can be evidence of a "self-restraining" state (Schedler, Diamond and Plattner 1999).

Proponents of this view could point to recent trends as evidence that NHRIs limit the state's autonomy. For example, non-state actors and vulnerable populations can challenge the state directly by making costly demands, including calling on the state to guarantee economic and social rights. Network activism and formal standing within international organizations are other powerful symbols that NHRIs are actors in their own right: independent bodies mediating between state and society while transforming sovereignty.

A perspective that views NHRIs as evidence of the post-Cold War transformation of sovereignty can nonetheless be problematic. First, challenging a state's rights violations does not necessarily threaten its sovereignty. Many states, especially relatively democratic ones, create NHRIs because they are already committed in principle to human rights norms, not because they are coerced into doing so. Even if these states still violate human rights, it pays to differentiate between challenging a state's illegitimate actions versus challenging the state's legitimate authority to rule. NHRIs in democratic or democratizing contexts often do the former but not the latter.

Second, the assumption that NHRIs transform sovereignty may overlook state motives. Newer priorities associated with inclusiveness, economic and social rights, and trans-governmental networking can overshadow a state's ongoing capacity to have the last word. States may turn to these issues simply to defuse potential critics while side-stepping sensitive and politically charged rights issues; doing so can afford them continued control over the human rights agenda. Cooperating with NGOs, or potential critics, also can be a strategy of co-optation. Likewise, emphasizing the rights of vulnerable populations or economic and social rights can be a relatively effective appeasement strategy if the alternative is to focus on rights violations involving national security. This is evident, for example, when NHRIs exclude de jure or de facto from their jurisdiction certain issues, politically volatile zones, or the actions of particular state actors like the armed forces. It is also evident when, post-September 11, some NHRIs have been complicit in tacitly accepting domestic states of exception. Even when states appear to embrace human rights, assessing the changing nature of state sovereignty requires confronting possible ulterior motives, evident in the ongoing exclusion of certain rights or people from state protection.

Entrenched Sovereignty

An opposing view of NHRIs and state sovereignty downplays institutional changes and focuses on the persistence of human rights violations. This view is associated most closely with NGO and popular criticism of these institutions. Its adherents are not easily impressed by NHRI growth, highlighting instead the relative weakness of many of these institutions, including disproportionate attention to human rights promotion and education. This approach emphasizes how even abusive states create NHRIs and how these institutions often appear powerless before egregious violations. Amnesty International has referred to the inadequacy of NHRIs in confronting abuses, noting that "[t]his is an all too frequent failure of NHRIs around the world, and a major cause of frustration and cynicism towards NHRIs from victims and the general population within countries, as well as NGOs, especially when the actions of major violators of human rights have not been addressed in a satisfactory way" (Amnesty International 2001). The assumption is that, since protecting human rights is not always in a state's interest, NHRIs often are mere window-dressing (SAHRDC 1998). This skeptical account—closely associated with a realist perspective in international relations—can be deeply suspicious of the state's capacity to regulate itself, its interest in complying voluntarily with international norms and laws, and its willingness to trump other state goals for human rights concerns.

There is no shortage of evidence to support this critical view, as documented by virtually every case study of a NHRI. Numerous states have created NHRIs to appease human rights critics, especially international ones. In many cases, states that established NHRIs absent international pressure were also those that seemed to least need such institutions (e.g., Mertus 2009, for European cases). Once formed, even the most active NHRIs have not necessarily been able to constrain state action when it counts most, since human rights violations frequently persist, often quite viciously so. Though some states with NHRIs may engage in fewer rights violations than those without these institutions, there is no conclusive evidence that NHRIs themselves are responsible for improved practices. The fact that these institutions often have vague mandates, poor funding, and remain inaccessible to those most needing protection makes such influence unlikely. And even seemingly innocuous promotive work, such as human rights education, can have destabilizing effects: encouraging people to make human rights demands that states are unable or unwilling to meet could engender conflict (Cardenas 2005).

If the first perspective risks exaggerating progress, the entrenched sovereignty view may be too dismissive of institutional change. According to the argument, states create NHRIs either to garner benefits (by appeasing critics) or because it is not costly to do so (in the case of democratic or democratizing states). Yet this approach overlooks the potential costs of building these institutions. The construction of a human rights bureaucracy within the state apparatus is not as cheap as it may seem. It requires resources, staffing, budgets, and even physical space. States are also savvy enough historically to know that bureaucracies can carry unintended costs, just as they are privy through their networks to know that creating NHRIs has backfired for other states. Even if sovereignty remains largely entrenched in world politics, it is not altogether clear why traditional power-driven states would risk creating politically costly institutions

Negotiating Sovereignty

Some scholars have cautioned that sovereignty, like human rights, is not an all-or-nothing phenomenon; it needs to be disaggregated (e.g., Krasner 1999; Donnelly 2004). Sovereignty can have various dimensions, and it can refer both to a state's internal and external behavior. Accordingly, a NHRI could challenge one aspect of a state's sovereignty but not another (Cardenas 2002). NHRIs too have different institutional dimensions that should be evaluated distinctly. For example, a NHRI might be relatively effective in fulfilling its promotive but not its protective functions. And while some may be inclined to view human rights promotion as largely insignificant, hypothetically, such socializing efforts could prove fundamental in the long-term prevention of abuses.

The evidence that NHRIs challenge state sovereignty in partial and complex ways is strong. Though many states create NHRIs to appease international actors, institutional dynamics can take hold and have unintended consequences. When human rights are placed on the national agenda, even limited and symbolic reforms can serve as political opportunities for social actors to mobilize (Cardenas and Flibbert 2005); over time, social expectations about the state's obligations can be recast. In terms of institutional effectiveness, NHRIs may be consequential but not in ways that translate readily into improved human rights conditions. They may define national agendas, shape domestic rules and standards, socialize local actors, and promote accountability (Cardenas 2001, 2002). These may not seem substantial constraints on state authority, but they can change the nature of domestic interactions, opening the way for longer term reform.

If the state itself is disaggregated into various actors (such as the executive versus legislature, police versus military, various government ministries), a NHRI's complex effects become even more apparent. While an institution could seem generally effective, it may be differentially successful in influencing particular state actors (e.g., courts may cooperate but not the government). Or the NHRI may succeed in advancing some rights practices but not others, depending on underlying state dynamics. In federal systems, such as those of the Indian and Mexican commissions, a national institution might be more effective than its local human rights counterparts, or *vice versa*. In general, the evidence strongly supports an image of NHRIs that are variously influential against a complex modern state.

Some observers may object to this depiction, disputing its indeterminacy. Even if sovereignty is a complex phenomenon and NHRIs have multiple and discrete effects, sovereignty arguably should be evaluated in terms of state practice. As Stephen Krasner (1999) describes it, the international system is one of "organized hypocrisy," in which human rights have challenged the norm of state sovereignty but not its practice. Likewise, states often have created NHRIs, or chosen to change internal structures, precisely to retain broader sovereign control. Domestic institutional change and norm implementation are thus attempts to negotiate potential (not actual) threats to sovereignty.

An alternative view, closer to constructivism than realism in international relations, is more agnostic about states' attempt to negotiate potential challenges to sovereignty. This perspective would view NHRI interactions with state and non-state actors—each making claims and counterclaims—as the process by which the scope of legitimate authority acquires meaning and changes over time. Recognizing these multiple contingencies, Richard Falk notes that "sovereignty and human rights are linked in complex, contradictory ways" (Falk 2000; also Falk 1981). The complexity of these linkages means that NHRI effects could be signs of either institutional stasis or progress depending on the circumstances.

Conclusion: Sovereignty as Social Construct

The multiplicity of NHRI experiences since the end of the Cold War suggests that sovereignty itself is an evolving institution, whose meaning is variegated and contested as a result of interactions among actors. Viewing sovereignty as a social construct is nothing new, though it is not the conventional interpretation. In recent years, some scholars have argued that human rights do not challenge state sovereignty as much as re-construct its meaning (e.g., Barkin 1998; Levi and Sznaider 2006; Weinert 2007). Thus Christian Reus-Smit asserts that sovereignty and human rights are "two normative elements of a single, inherently contradictory modern discourse about legitimate statehood and rightful state action (2001, 519). If states could treat those within their borders however they wished in the past, contemporary human rights norms make it illegitimate for states to do so. And internally, human rights norms make a state's legitimate authority contingent on its respect for human rights. The crucial point is not that the state is no longer sovereign; it is that the notion of what constitutes sovereign authority in world politics has changed. Jack Donnelly articulates this nuanced position

> Sovereignty is not a hard shell, an impermeable barrier at the borders of a territory. It does not guarantee the efficacy of the unfettered will of the state. Sovereignty is a complex social practice.... Like all social practices, sovereignty both persists and is transformed over time.... Human rights, far from undermining or eroding sovereignty, are embedded within sovereignty. Dominant understandings of sovereignty (and human rights) have indeed been significantly reshaped. But sovereignty remains robust and, at least with respect to human rights, largely unchallenged (Donnelly 2004, 11).

At first glance, it would seem that NHRIs would not challenge state sovereignty as significantly as other human rights developments. In contrast to humanitarian intervention or international legal institutions, NHRIs do not lie outside the state or its purview; and in virtually all cases NHRIs lack enforcement powers against the state. Compared to UN and regional human rights institutions whose decisions also tend to be non-binding, a NHRI is part of the state, perhaps making it less likely that violators will self-regulate. For states that systematically abuse human rights, a state bureaucracy devoted to human rights may seem cosmetic pretense. For states that generally respect human rights, the creation of such an institution may seem unnecessary or even superfluous.

Yet insofar as sovereignty—like human rights—is socially constructed, NHRIs may be more innovative than they appear. While international enforcement seems a more obvious incursion of sovereignty, changing domestic structures in response to external pressures (whether via coercion or mimicry) is actually significant. For one, building a state bureaucracy can be costly, directly and indirectly. And if the goal is ultimately one of human rights protection and promotion, laying an organizational infrastructure could prove essential over time. Norm implementation, after all, is distinct from compliance; it entails concrete and technical steps to assure the routinization of compliance. Even when states are not under intense pressure to create a NHRI, it is pivotally important that the international context still provides standards and models for creating and sustaining these institutions, as well as opportunities for networking.

International human rights enforcement appears a dramatic assault on state sovereignty because it occurs in extreme cases; but it is precisely the mundane nature of NHRIs, enmeshed in the modern state's bureaucracy, that makes these institutions most consequential for sovereignty. The fact that states are negotiating the meaning of sovereignty while attempting to retain political control, and NHRIs yield mixed results, does not negate their potential significance in internalizing norms and reconstituting sovereignty. The post-Cold War diffusion of NHRIs signals a historic normative shift—implementing international human rights norms, or institutionalizing them in domestic structures, is a measure of state legitimacy. Neither human rights nor NHRIs displaces state sovereignty, or serves as an alternative focal point of authority. Rather, human rights and NHRIs constitute historically evolving and contested standards, infusing the state's sovereign legitimacy and authority with new meaning in a post-Cold War world.

References

Amnesty International. 2001. *National Human Rights Institutions: Amnesty International's Recommendations for Effective Protection and Promotion of Human Rights*. 1 October.

Barkin, S. 1998. The Evolution of the Constitution of Sovereignty and the Emergence of Human Rights Norms. *Millennium* 27(2), 229–252.

Bull, H. 2002. *The Anarchical Society: A Study of Order in World Politics*. 3rd edition. New York: Columbia University Press.

Cardenas, S. 2001. *Adaptive States: The Proliferation of National Human Rights Institutions*. Carr Center for Human Rights Policy, Kennedy School of Government, Harvard University. Working Paper Series T-01-04.

Cardenas, S. 2002. National Human Rights Commissions in Asia, in *Sovereignty under Challenge: How Governments Respond*, edited by J. D. Montgomery and N. Glazer. New Brunswick: Transaction Press, 55–82.

Cardenas, S. 2003a. Transgovernmental Activism: Canada's Role in Promoting National Human Rights Commissions. *Human Rights Quarterly* 25(3), 775–90.

Cardenas, S 2003b. Emerging Global Actors: The United Nations and National Human Rights Institutions. *Global Governance* 9(1), 23–42.

Cardenas, S. 2005. Constructing Rights? Human Rights Education and the State. *International Political Science Review* 26(4), 363–79.

Cardenas, S. (in press). *Chains of Justice: The Global Rise of State Institutions for Human Rights*. Philadelphia: University of Pennsylvania Press.

Cardenas, S. and Flibbert, A. 2005. National Human Rights Institutions in the Middle East. *Middle East Journal* 59(3), 411–36.

Cohen, J. L. 2008. Rethinking Human Rights, Democracy, and Sovereignty in the Age of Globalization. *Political Theory* 36(4), 578–606.

Donnelly, J. 2004. State Sovereignty and Human Rights. *Human Rights & Human Welfare*, Working Paper no. 21 (23 June).

Falk, R. 1981. *State Sovereignty and Human Rights*. New York: Holmes & Meier.

Falk, R. 2000. Sovereignty and Human Rights: The Search for Reconciliation. *Issues of Democracy* 5(1), 29–35.

Gomez, M. 1995. Social Economic Rights and Human Rights Commissions. *Human Rights Quarterly* 17(1), 155–69.

Hafner-Burton, E. and Tsutsui, K. 2005. Human Rights in a Globalizing World: The Paradox of Empty Promises. *American Journal of Sociology* 110(5), 1373–1411.

Hossain, K., Besselink, L. F. M. and Selassie, H. S. G. 2001. *Human Rights Commissions and Ombudsman Offices: National Experiences throughout the World*. The Hague, Netherlands: Martinus Nijhoff.

Human Rights Watch. 2001. *Protectors or Pretenders? Government Human Rights Commissions in Africa*. New York: Human Rights Watch.

Krasner, S. D. 1999. *Sovereignty: Organized Hypocrisy*. Princeton: Princeton University Press.

Kumar, C. R. 2006. National Human Rights Institutions (NHRIs) and Economic, Social and Cultural Rights: Toward the Institutionalization and Developmentalization of Human Rights. *Human Rights Quarterly* 28(3), 755–79.

Levi, D. and Sznaider, N. 2006. Sovereignty Transformed: A Sociology of Human Rights. *British Journal of Sociology* 57(4), 657–76.

Mertus, J. 2009. *Human Rights Matters: Local Politics and National Human Rights Institutions*. Stanford: Stanford University Press.

Montgomery, J. D. and Glazer, N. 2002. *Sovereignty under Challenge: How Governments Respond*. New Brunswick: Transaction Press.

Murray, R. 2007. *The Role of National Human Rights Institutions at the International and Regional Levels: The Experience of Africa*. Oxford: Hart Publishing.

National Human Rights Institutions (NHRIs) Forum. Available at: http://www.nhri.net [accessed 25 January 2009].

Office of the High Commissioner for Human Rights (OHCHR). *National Human Rights Institutions for the Promotion and Protection of Human Rights*. Fact Sheet No. 19. Available at: http://www.unhchr.ch/html/menu6/2/fs19.htm [accessed: 25 January 2009].

Office of the High Commissioner for Human Rights (OHCHR) 1993. *World Conference on Human Rights*. Available at http://www.unhchr.ch/html/menu5/wchr.htm [accessed: 25 January 2009].

Paris Principles. 1991. *Principles Relating to the Status and Functioning of National Institutions for Protection and Promotion of Human Rights*. Available at: http://www.unhchr.ch/html/menu6/2/fs19.htm#annex [accessed: 25 January 2009].

Pohjolainen, A. 2006. *The Evolution of National Human Rights Institutions: The Role of the United Nations*. Copenhagen: The Danish Institute for Human Rights.

Ramcharan, B. G. (ed.) 2005. *The Protection Role of National Human Rights Institutions*. Boston: Brill Academic.

Reif, L. 2000. Building Democratic Institutions: The Role of National Human Rights Institutions in Good Governance and Human Rights Protection. *Harvard Human Rights Journal* 13(Spring), 1–69.

Reus-Smit, C. 2001. Human Rights and the Social Construction of Sovereignty. *Review of International Studies* 27(4), 519–38.

Schedler, A., Diamond, L. J., and Plattner, M. F. (eds). 1999. *The Self-Restraining State: Power and Accountability in New Democracies*. Boulder: Lynne Rienner.

Sikkink, K. 1993. Human Rights, Principled Issue-Networks, and Sovereignty in Latin America. *International Organization* 47(3), 411–41.

Slaughter, A.-M. 2004. *A New World Order*. Princeton: Princeton University Press.

Smith, A. 2006. The Unique Position of National Human Rights Institutions. *Human Rights Quarterly* 28(4), 904–46.

South Asia Human Rights Documentation Center (SAHRDC) 1998. *National Human Rights Institutions in the Asia Pacific Region: Report of the Alternate NGO Consultation on the Second Asia-Pacific Regional Workshop on National Human Rights Institutions*. New Delhi: SAHRDC.

Sriram, C. L. 2006. Human Rights Claims vs. the State: Is Sovereignty Really Eroding? *Interdisciplinary Journal of Human Rights Law* 1(1), 107–120.

United Nations, Centre for Human Rights 1995. *National Human Rights Institutions: A Handbook on the Establishing and Strengthening of National Institutions for the Promotion and Protection of Human Rights*. New York and Geneva: United Nations.

United Nations, General Assembly. 1993a. National Institutions for the Promotion and Protection of Human Rights. 20 December. A/Res/48/134.

United Nations, General Assembly. (1993b). Vienna Declaration and Programme of Action. 12 July. A/CONF.157/23.

Weinert, M. S. 2007. Bridging the Human Rights-Sovereignty Divide: Theoretical Foundations of a Democratic Sovereignty. *Human Rights Review* 8(2), 5–32.

Chapter 3
A New Actor in Human Rights Politics? Transgovernmental Networks of National Human Rights Institutions

Noha Shawki

Introduction

With the third wave of democratization (Huntington 1991) and the end of the Cold War, increasing attention has been given by social scientists to the study of transitions to democracy and to the spread of human rights and the rule of law. The literature on democratization and human rights has explored the role of a number of different actors in processes of democratic transition: The state, individual leaders and elites, and civil society. National human rights institutions (NHRIs), however, have received comparatively little attention, and their potential contribution to democratization and the respect for international human rights standards has not yet been fully explored, even though NHRIs have in recent years been established in more and more countries of the world and, under the auspices of the UN, have formed transgovernmental networks. When they are studied, NHRIs are often not placed in the broader context of other phenomena and trends in international relations. Moreover, studies of NHRIs are often descriptive and do not draw on the broader theoretical literature in international relations to study and understand NHRIs and the networks they form.

This chapter argues that networks of NHRIs are potentially an important actor in human rights politics and transition processes and need to be given more scholarly attention. It maintains that recent research in international relations has provided theoretical lenses that are very useful for studying the potential significance and implications of the recent growth of networks of NHRIs. Using the framework developed by Anne-Marie Slaughter (2004) in her recent book *A New World Order*, this chapter applies the theoretical insights of recent research on global governance to NHRIs networks to a) argue that there needs to be a stronger research focus on *networks* of NHRIs, b) argue that these networks need to be studied in terms of global political trends and processes, c) explore how and why NHRIs can be influential actors in the expansion of human rights and democratic practices worldwide and in navigating sovereignty and human rights, and d) explore the relative strengths of this new actor compared to other actors who are active in the areas of human rights advocacy and promotion.

Chapter 2 in this volume addresses substantive issues surrounding National Human Rights Institutions. The present chapter also addresses the role of NHRIs in promoting human rights, but from a different perspective. I argue here that we need to begin studying *networks* of NHRIs. While the research focus on individual NHRIs has been very fruitful and has expanded our knowledge of NHRIs and their role in promoting human rights, I draw on different strands of international relations research to argue that we also need to study the *regional networks* that NHRIs have formed to better understand and assess their potential in promoting human rights. Previous research in international relations has shown that networks can diffuse new norms, and I maintain that regional networks of NHRIs can potentially be a non-mainstream channel of norm diffusion in the area of human rights. In other words, this chapter makes a case for researching networks of NHRIs instead of focusing solely on the role of individual NHRIs. In doing so, I draw on a number of theoretical approaches and apply them to NHRIs. The chapter should therefore be approached and read as a proposal to extend previous theoretical formulations and frameworks to a new topic. In this sense, this is very much a conceptual chapter that focuses on reviewing and tying together different related literatures and is less concerned with the empirical evidence for the efficacy of NHRIs in promoting human rights (or the lack thereof). I do, however, present some thoughts on future empirical research.

The chapter proceeds in two steps. First, I provide an overview of NHRIs, global governance and Anne-Marie Slaughter's approach to transgovernmentalism, arguing that these literatures can inform our study of NHRIs. Second, I discuss the question of why NHRIs can promote human rights, good governance and the rule of law internationally in ways that are not available to other actors in the area of human rights. I conclude the chapter with some brief comments on future empirical research.

National Human Rights Institutions (NHRIs)

According to Sonia Cardenas, national human rights institutions are "*government* agencies whose purported aim is to implement international norms domestically" (Cardenas 2003, 23). The number of NHRIs has rapidly increased worldwide since the end of the Cold War. A set of international guidelines, the Paris Principles, was developed during an international workshop in 1991 to set standards for the establishment of NHRIs and for their operation (Eldridge 2002, 212). The Paris Principles, which were adopted by the UN Human Rights Commission in 1992 and endorsed by the General Assembly in 1993 (Burdekin 2007; Pohjolainen 2006; Kabir 2001, 1–53), cover a number of different areas, including the independence of NHRIs from national governments and the necessity for adequate funding and a broad and meaningful mandate that allows NHRIs to be effective (Pohjolainen 2006, 6–16; Kabir 2001, 12). The Paris Principles also call for pluralism in NHRI membership and recommend that NHRIs establish ties with other actors in the human rights field, including NGOs and government agencies. Under the auspices of the United Nations and with the support of other international organizations and NGOs, NHRIs have created regional and international networks to promote exchange and cooperation. Regional and international events, including conferences and workshops, are held on a regular basis, and some events have thematic foci. Past areas of focus have included issues such as migration, prevention of torture, racism and discrimination as well as other issues.[1]

NHRIs are formally organized in various ways and with somewhat different mandates in different countries of the world. Linda Reif distinguishes between three types of NHRIs: the ombudsman, human rights commissions, and the hybrid human rights ombudsman (Reif 2000, 3–13). In a similar typology, Pohjolainen distinguishes between four types of NHRIs: human rights commissions and the ombudsman, which correspond to the two types Reif identifies, the advisory committee, and the human rights institute (Pohjolainen 2006, 16–20). The different types of NHRIs have different political and historical origins. They also differ in terms of their composition and the nature and scope of their mandates. In addition, NHRIs can differ along a number of other dimensions, including "the legal locus of founding instruments, … social and political conditions affecting their establishment, … their mediation role, and … the provision for selection of commission members" (Mohamad 2002, 238).[2]

Despite these formal and institutional and contextual differences, however, NHRIs share many common functions. The diverse functions that they perform can be categorized as regulative functions or as constitutive functions (Cardenas 2003, 25–7; Australian Human Rights Centre 2000, 259–21). Regulative functions refer to the tasks that are geared towards promoting national implementation of international human rights law and bringing national practice in line with international standards. Thus, regulative functions include promoting the ratification of international human rights treaties, legal assistance to victims of human rights violations, conducting investigations and inspections, and documenting the human rights record. In short, the focus of regulative functions is on protection from human rights violations. Constitutive functions, by contrast, are geared towards promoting a political culture that is favorable to upholding human rights. Constitutive functions encompass efforts to raise public awareness of human rights issues, to cooperate with and strengthen NGOs, and to conduct research at the national level. They also include efforts to network and cooperate with other NHRIs at the international level.

1 For more information on the regional and international networks and conferences as well as news and documents from specific conferences see the website of the National Human Rights Institutions Forum at www.nhri.net. The National Human Rights Institutions Forum is a website providing information about NHRIs and the networks that they form. This website is a service of the Danish Institute for Human Rights and the Office of the UN High Commissioner for Human Rights.

2 See also Mohamad, pages 238–41 for an overview of these differences.

In a nutshell, constitutive functions focus on the promotion of international human rights standards (Kabir 2001, 12). I argue that these important functions make NHRIs potentially influential actors in international human rights politics, especially considering that in recent years, the international community has supported and promoted the creation of (networks of) NHRIs. The UN, especially, has been at the forefront of efforts to strengthen NHRIs. Four main tools have been employed by the UN towards that end: Standard setting through defining and standardizing the tasks of NHRIs; capacity building through technical assistance and training programs; networking facilitation; and the granting of an official international status to NHRIs, with the right to attend certain UN human rights meetings (Cardenas 2003, 27–34).

The current research on NHRIs has increased our knowledge by providing excellent overviews about the origins, mandates, and organizational structures of NHRIs. Recent research has also explored specific issues that are relevant to the effectiveness of NHRIs, such as the nature of their independence and accountability (Smith 2006, 904–46) and their role in promoting economic, social and cultural rights (Kumar 2006, 755–79). Most of the current research, however, focuses on NHRIs in isolation from one another. Moreover, current research is mostly descriptive in nature and remains divorced from the larger theoretical debates about global governance. What we now need, therefore, are more studies that focus on *networks* of NHRIs and that are informed by the current theoretical literature on globalization and governance in an increasingly interdependent world. The remainder of this chapter further develops this argument and reviews the theoretical formulations that are relevant to the study of NHRIs.

Global Governance

The study of the role of non-state or sub-state actors in world politics was given impetus by the growing realization that current global problems require innovative approaches to global governance, approaches in which non-state and sub-state actors can and do make a significant contribution.

In a very basic conceptualization of global governance Jeffrey Hart and Aseem Prakash define governance as the organization of collective action and explain that it "entails the establishing of institutions; institutions being the rules of the game that permit, prescribe, or prohibit certain actions" (Prakash and Hart 1999, 1–24). Hart and Prakash proceed to argue that while formal organizations are often necessary to formulate rules, as well as to enforce them and monitor compliance with them, institutions can also function without formal organization, and can provide governance services outside the context of a nation state. This implies that governance is not to be equated with government, since non-governmental social institutions can perform governance functions and provide governance services (Prakash and Hart 1999, 1–24). Non-governmental institutions need not even be structural entities in the sense of being distinct actors or players in global affairs. As James Rosenau convincingly argues,

> (b)oth governance and government consist of rule systems, of steering mechanisms through which authority is exercised in order to enable systems to preserve their coherence and move towards desired goals. While the rule systems of governments can be thought of as structures, those of governance are social functions or processes that can be performed or implemented in a variety of ways at different times and places (or even at the same time) by a wide variety of organizations (2002, 72).

Global governance is thus a concept that is not state-centered. Non-state and sub-state actors involved in global governance include NGOs, research institutions and epistemic communities, businesses/the private sector, government regulators, and civil society groups as well as networks of such groups. Thus, the proliferation of the issues that need to be addressed at the international level has been accompanied by an increase in the number of international actors, many of whom are seeking to influence and shape the global agenda and global public policy. For this reason, James Rosenau has described international affairs as governed by a bifurcated system that is composed of the "…interstate system of states and their national governments that has long dominated the course of events" and "a multicentric system of diverse types of other collectivities that has lately emerged as a rival source of authority with actors that sometimes cooperate with, often compete with, and endlessly interact with the state-centric system" (2002, 72–3).

Finally, it is important to note that far from becoming obsolete, states will maintain a prominent role in world politics as strategic sites of authority that link and provide a point of reference for other actors in global governance. Indeed, most scholars acknowledge that states are still the central source of governance today (Koenig-Archibugi 2002, 46). In fact, bureaucratic or administrative units within states, including NHRIs, and the transgovernmental networks they form can be influential actors in global governance as Anne-Marie Slaughter has demonstrated.

Transgovernmentalism and the Disaggregated State

Anne-Marie Slaughter's point of departure is the proliferation of pressing issues and global policy problems that no single government can address on its own. Consequently, efforts of national governments to tackle these issues need to have global reach in order to be effective. Whereas other researchers argue that globalization, the increasing number and scope of global policy problems, and the rise of global non-state actors have led to a relative decline of the nation-state and may eventually lead to its demise, Slaughter maintains that while the modern nation state is undergoing changes, it is far from being in a process of steady decline. Rather, it is being transformed through the rise of transgovernmental networks that bring together public officials from different countries to address issues and problems that have international dimensions. In other words, Slaughter argues that "the state is not disappearing, it is disaggregating into its separate, functionally distinct parts. These parts—courts, regulatory agencies, executives, and even legislatures—are networking with their counterparts abroad, creating a dense web of relations that constitutes a new, transgovernmental order" (Slaughter 1997, 184).

Underlying this approach to studying cooperation between nation-states are several assumptions and premises, two of which are central to Slaughter's argument and important in the context of this chapter. First, Slaughter asserts that the unitary nation-state is a very important actor, but by no means the only actor in international relations (Slaughter 2004, 12–13). She argues that students of international relations have always assumed a unitary actor, an assumption that is very valid and helpful in some instances, especially when analyzing security issues, but that no longer holds in some other issue areas because it distorts the new realities of international relations. Slaughter therefore calls for drawing on the approaches developed by students of comparative politics, who unlike analysts of international relations, do not approach the nation-state as a unitary actor, but rather study the different institutions and their roles and functions within the nation-state. Second, Slaughter maintains that while the different component parts of the disaggregated nation-state reflect and promote the distinct national interests of the state, they also have professional values, experiences and identities that they share with their international counterparts and work to promote within and beyond their networks (Slaughter 2004, 18).

NHRI Networks: A Significant Actor in Global Governance and International Human Rights Politics?

Three important issues emerge from this brief review of the literature on NHRIs, global governance, and transgovernmentalism. First, NHRIs are expanding in number and are being promoted and supported by the United Nations. They are forming regional and international networks to address a number of different human rights issues and enhance cooperation and exchange. In that sense, they are slowly becoming more prominent actors in international human rights politics. Second, the concept of global governance provides a number of very valuable theoretical lenses that can be used to study NHRIs. The study of IR has historically been very state-centered, and, international relations scholars have long assumed explicitly or implicitly that the nation-state is a unitary actor that has a single unified set of interests, priorities and foreign policy goals as well as the capacity to act as a unified and coherent entity. The literature on global governance provides international relations analysts with the intellectual tools that are needed to better understand and explain those aspects of IR, for which the unitary actor assumption does not hold. This literature also provides an analytical framework that can help us understand novel trends and issues in international relations in an era of increasing interdependence that has resulted in the increase in the number of internationally significant actors. Third, within the literature on global governance, Anne-Marie Slaughter's approach focusing on transgovernmental networks as major actors in global governance and a new world order, is particularly helpful for students of international human rights politics who are interested in networks of NHRIs because it provides a conceptual and theoretical context with which the potential role and significance of NHRIs can be assessed. Taken together, these three points demonstrate one of the main arguments I make in this chapter, namely, that we need to study not only specific NHRIs, but also regional and global networks of NHRIs using the conceptual and theoretical lenses developed in the literature on global governance. The remainder of this chapter is an attempt to demonstrate some of the ways that research on global governance and trangovernmentalism can inform our study of NHRIs and help us understand and assess the potential of NHRIs and the networks they form in promoting human rights norms.

What is the potential role of NHRI networks in international politics, specifically in international efforts to promote democracy, human rights and the rule of law? Are NHRI networks potentially significant and influential actors in international relations? If yes, why? And if not, why not? These are the questions that are at the center of the following paragraphs, in which I review the compelling account that Anne-Marie Slaughter provides of the actual impact and potential future contributions of transgovernmental networks to global governance, focusing on those contributions that are more relevant to the issue of human rights. I also draw on the work of other authors to develop the argument that networks of NHRIs are especially promising transgovernmental networks that have the potential to diffuse human rights norms and standards internationally.

Anne-Marie Slaughter's Approach

Slaughter distinguishes between three categories of impact or influence that transgovernmental networks can exert: helping to bring about convergence on international rules and standards, enhancing compliance with international regulations, and enhancing and deepening international cooperation (Slaughter 2004, 24). These types of impact or influence are possible through different mechanisms of diffusion that are available to transgovernmental networks. I use the concept of diffusion in the sociological sense of the term, which Strang and Soule define as follows:

> (d)iffusion refers to the spread of something within a social system. The key term here is 'spread', and it should be taken...to denote flow or movement from a source to an adopter, paradigmatically via communication and influence... (T)he term 'practice'...denote(s)the diffusing item, which might be a behavior, strategy, belief, technology or structure. Diffusion is the most general and

> abstract term we have for this sort of process, embracing contagion, mimicry, social learning, organized dissemination, and other family members (Strang and Soule 1998, 266).

Among the most important mechanisms of diffusion that Slaughter outlines are regulatory export, technical assistance and training, the interpretation and dissemination of information to promote best practices, capacity building, and socialization. Regulatory export refers to the diffusion of the rules, regulations and laws existing in one country to one or more other countries via transgovernmental networks. The United States, for example, has been successful in exporting its environmental, antitrust and securities laws (Slaughter 2004, 172–7). A second related mechanism of diffusion is technical assistance and training. This is an instrument that is used to encourage regulatory export, and it has been used by the US to promote its laws and its enforcement mechanisms in other countries, including Mexico, the Netherlands, and other countries (Slaughter 2004, 172–7). The third mechanism of diffusion, the interpretation and dissemination of information, is not directly connected to regulatory export and technical assistance or training, but is in my view a very important channel of diffusion. The convergence of laws and practices in certain areas can be achieved through the authority and capacity that transgovernmental networks command to interpret and disseminate information. The credibility that transgovernmental networks enjoy in terms of the information they interpret and spread gives them substantial power: soft power, the same kind of non-coercive power that non-state actors, such as NGOs, can command "by creating a community of like-minded professionals who can frame a particular issue, create knowledge around it, and set the agenda for how to pursue it" (Slaughter 2004, 172–7).

Socialization, and capacity building are related processes. Socialization into the network's values and norms can be seen as a powerful diffusion mechanism. Drawing on sociological literature, Slaughter explains that "(a) socialized individual may want something intensely, but will not seek it if doing so would contravene prevailing social norms..." (Slaughter 2004, 198). Values and norms can be very influential in shaping both individual behavior and social practices, and Slaughter argues that the same socialization processes and dynamics that sociologists have observed in small groups take place within transgovernmental networks, which share with small groups several key features, including the existence of a common set of professional values and norms (Slaughter 2004, 199). For these reasons, socializing network members into international (human rights) standards and instilling common values in new network members can be an important and significant mechanism of diffusion, because socialized network members are national actors with decision-making and/or implementation competencies in national settings. In other words, socialization within networks can provide a mechanism that translates international norms and standards into domestic practices. This in turn can build and develop national governance capacities, especially in transitional societies, such as Iraq, when judges, regulators, and other professionals in these societies are active participants in transgovernmental networks (Slaughter 2004, 25–6).

Other Approaches

Slaughter's argument in many ways echoes arguments put forward by researchers adopting other theoretical perspectives on global governance or studying other issues areas in international politics. These approaches include the theoretical frameworks on norm diffusion, the epistemic communities approach and neofunctionalism. The first approach is grounded in the sociological literature. The second approach is used by constructivist IR scholars to explain a number of phenomena in international affairs, including the emergence of international environmental regimes (Haas 1999, 103–33). The third is an approach developed to study regional integration, particularly European integration.

In the context of this chapter, the social movement literature focusing on the diffusion of movement ideas and tactics is very relevant and lends support to Slaughter's arguments. According to this literature, diffusion involves a source, sometimes referred to as transmitter, an adopter, the item or practice that is diffused and a channel or medium of diffusion (McAdam and Rucht 1993, 59). This literature also distinguishes between diffusion within a society and cross-national diffusion. This chapter is concerned with the latter type of diffusion process.

As far as the channels of cross-national diffusion are concerned, the literature distinguishes between relational and non-relational channels, which are each emphasized in a different model of diffusion (McAdam and Rucht 1993, 59–60). The relational model of diffusion focuses on direct and personal contacts between adopters and transmitters as the primary dynamic of diffusion. Non-relational models on the other hand attach less significance to personal contact and point to the importance of non-relational dimensions of diffusion, such as those provided by the mass media (McAdam and Rucht 1993, 59). They emphasize the identification of adopters with transmitters in terms of their institutional positions and roles, in terms of their personal identity and in terms of the situation they are facing and/or the problem or issue at stake to explain how diffusion can occur in the absence of interpersonal ties (McAdam and Rucht 1993, 59, 63–4, 66). Both models are consistent with Slaughter's arguments and relevant in the context of NHRI networks, for even though these networks are relational, the professional identities of adopters and transmitters as well as their institutional positions are important to understanding diffusion processes within transgovernmental networks.

The epistemic communities approach also puts forward arguments that are quite similar to the ones advanced by Slaughter. Epistemic communities are defined as networks of experts in certain fields whose members influence politics and international norms through the introduction of their knowledge and expertise into the political process (Haas 1992, 1–35; Haas and Adler 1992, 367–90). The expertise and authority of the individual members involved in an epistemic community are generally recognized, which gives the community substantial opportunities for exerting influence over the policy process. The network members share values, understandings of causal relationships and criteria for evaluating the validity of knowledge in their area of expertise, and they pursue common political goals that are grounded in their shared values and interpretations of the subject matter they study. Since the foreign policy environment today is characterized by the proliferation of issues that have to be addressed at the international level, foreign policy decision makers do not have knowledge in all areas of international politics and are therefore often not able to assess the implications and consequences associated with different foreign policy options. For this reason, there is an increasing reliance on experts' understandings and interpretations of the issue under consideration, which is a major source of influence for experts. When an epistemic community succeeds in establishing its influence within national bureaucracies or international organizations it can institutionalize this influence and diffuse its ideas internationally. Once certain ideas are institutionalized, their influence is likely to continue over extended periods of time. A substantial part of the influence that epistemic communities can exercise is due to their ability to frame issues. Framing means defining a problem by the experts of an epistemic community and placing it in a broader context as well as highlighting its most salient dimensions. Issue frames are defined by Nelson and Oxley by reference to Gamson as "alternative definitions, constructions, or depictions of a policy problem" (Nelson and Oxley 1997, 567–8). These constructions of policy problems entail "framing social and political issues in specific ways", and they "declare the underlying causes and likely consequences of a problem and establish criteria for evaluating potential remedies for the problem" (Nelson, Clawson, and Oxley 1997, 567–8).

Finally, neo-functionalism is an approach developed in the 1950s to explain regional cooperation and integration, particularly in post-World War II Europe (Nugent, 1999, 507–8; Tranholm-Mikkelsen 1991). Neo-functionalism advances a number of arguments, among them the elite socialization argument, which states that elites from different countries who interact and engage in decision-making on a regular basis within the framework of a regional integration process will develop values and attitudes that are supportive of this process and will work to advance it. In other words, cooperation between elites from different countries within a special forum or arena towards a common goal can shape the attitudes of participants, making such forums a space where socialization can take place among elites who can then diffuse and promote the newly acquired values in their respective national settings.

These approaches and arguments bear on the concept of transgovernmentalism and NHRI networks because they too focus on actors organized as non-hierarchical networks that are characterized by the common professional identity of their members and their ability to collect and disseminate information, frame and interpret important issues or problems and propose solutions. This makes these theoretical approaches relevant to the study of networks and lends more support to Slaughter's argument about the significance of soft power in making an actor important and influential on the world stage. In other words, Slaughter's main arguments, if seen within the broader context of the literature on globalization and governance, have intellectual affinities with other theoretical approaches that identify networks of non-state and sub-state actors as important and influential actors in global governance. This lends Slaughter's argument more support and demonstrates the need for more research on the role that networks of NHRIs can play in promoting and advancing international human rights norms and standards.

The Potential Effect of NHRIs

Slaughter's approach, and other similar approaches in the international relations literature, applies to networks of NHRIs, and an important part of the argument of this chapter is that in the area of human rights, transgovernmental networks are especially important. This is so because their structure and the procedural and organizational arrangements that they use address some of the major issues that make the promotion and protection of human rights worldwide difficult and only moderately effective. The recent human rights literature provides several arguments and conclusions that support this position.

By and large, the status of human rights in foreign policy and in the bilateral relations of nation-states is not conducive to the promotion of human rights. As Jack Donnelly explains, promoting human rights internationally is for the most part a low priority for foreign-policy makers, and other foreign policy goals often take precedence (Donnelly 2002, 155–81). This is true even in cases where human rights are a major concern for foreign policy makers. Since foreign policy is geared towards pursuing and realizing the national interest, and the protection of human rights is only one dimension of the national interest, even decision-makers who are concerned with the international status of human rights often have to make trade-offs and give more immediate national interests precedence over the protection of human rights (Donnelly 2002, 155–81). As far as the United Nations human rights regime is concerned, it is not always effective in protecting human rights because it is essentially a promotional regime that lacks implementation competencies and political clout (Donnelly 2002, 155–81). In addition, there are political, legal, and ethical concerns surrounding the question of whether or not national foreign policy can/should be used as an instrument to promote human rights worldwide. Realism, which is influential in some foreign policy circles, posits that power and security are and should be the prime concern of foreign policy. According to this view, moral issues, such as human rights, are not and should not be ends in their own right, and they should not be considered when foreign policy is formulated and implemented because they are not compatible with the pursuit of security.

Moreover, sovereignty, one of the defining organizing principles of the modern international system, is often seen to be at odds with attempts to promote human rights. The argument here is that a state or a group of states cannot legitimately raise concerns about the human rights record of another state as this would not be compatible with the notion of sovereignty and the principle of non-interference. Although increasing concerns about human rights violations in the world has led to a change in the idea of sovereignty to allow for making human rights a legitimate concern in foreign policy, nation-states' preoccupation with their sovereignty still hinders the promotion of human rights at the international level. Finally, relativism, which is the view that moral values and conceptions of human rights are grounded in culture, is also seen to preclude the active promotion of human rights in foreign policy. The argument here is that there is substantial diversity in cultures and traditions today, which entails a corresponding diversity in value systems and basic understandings of moral concepts, such as justice, liberty or equality (Donoho 1991, 345–91). It also entails the existence of different notions concerning the relationship between individuals and the state and between individuals and society at large. Since one cannot argue for the superiority of one culturally-based value-system over another, practices of other cultures have to be accepted or at least tolerated, even if they appear to entail violations of human rights. Criticism of practices of other cultures is, relativists argue, not legitimate and not justified (Donoho 1991, 345–91). The persistence of all of these circumstances and international principles and ideas leads Donnelly to maintain that "(h)uman rights are ultimately a profoundly *national*, not international issue," and to conclude that respect for human rights "is almost always the legacy of persistent national political struggles against human rights violations" pointing out that "(m)ost governments that respect human rights have been created not from the top down but from the bottom up" (2002, 179–80). In other words, according to Donnelly, "(t)he struggle for international human rights is, in the end, a series of national struggles" that can either be encouraged and supported or impeded and inhibited by international action (2002, 180).

Given these limitations to the pursuit of human rights at the bilateral and the international levels, international and regional networks of NHRIs can be potentially influential actors in international human rights politics and can provide the kind of international action that can support national efforts to protect human rights. There are a number of reasons why this is the case. First, NHRIs are government agencies created by the constitution or by the legislative or executive branch of a national government. They are not international actors promoting human rights in a country without being accountable to the legislature of that country. As such, the activities carried out within networks of NHRIs are less likely to raise issues of sovereignty. Networks of NHRIs are thus better suited than many other actors in international human rights politics, such as the UN, other international organizations, foreign national governments or NGOs, to enhance human rights protection internationally. In other words, NHRIs and the networks they form are more likely than other actors to be able to mitigate nations-states' overwhelming concern with issues of sovereignty, which so often interferes with the pursuit of human rights at the international level.

Moreover, networks of NHRIs can mediate between an international human rights regime that has universal claims and national cultural and social idiosyncrasies that are sometimes perceived to be incompatible with universal principles. Donnelly and other students of human rights politics argue that universalism and relativism are not necessarily at odds if one looks at human rights at three different levels of abstraction: The abstract principles, the specific interpretation of the content of these abstract principles, and the application and implementation of those principles (Donnelly 2002; Donoho 1991). For example, while equality is a universal principle, the exact substance and the application of that principle can legitimately vary by culture: some cultures may emphasize equality of opportunity while others may stress equality of outcome. The idea here is "to make the content of rights specific enough to render those rights meaningful and universally understood, but not so specific as to eliminate state consent because of legitimate cultural, political, and social differences" (Donoho 1991, 386). If universalism and relativism are to be reconciled by allowing culture-based variation at some level, networks of NHRIs can play an important role to advance this goal. National and regional networks of NHRIs can diffuse the overarching international human rights principles and create a commitment of member NHRIs to these principles. NHRIs are thus in a good position to translate these principles into local policies and practices that are compatible with local cultures and values.

Finally, unlike national governments or foreign ministries, the UN, NGOs and other international actors, NHRIs can command some political clout and are therefore in a much better position to move beyond the promotion of human rights and towards the implementation of rights.

In short, networks of NHRIs can be significant actors of global governance in the area of human rights. Since the international system is still very much a system of nation-states, any serious and sustained efforts to enhance respect for human rights internationally can only be successful if they involve governments or government agencies. Transgovernmental networks of NHRIs are independent entities that are characterized by distinctive features: a distinctive structure and procedural arrangements and distinctive social processes that take place within them, such as diffusion through socialization, and the interpretation, framing and dissemination of information. At the same time, these networks are composed of governmental agencies, and, unlike other actors who might organize as networks, such as civil society actors or professional associations, they can possess more implementation powers. In that sense, transgovernmental networks of NHRIs can be seen as innovative arrangements of global governance that provide a link between the domestic political setting and international laws and standards. Transgovenmental networks could in the future help reconcile the need for global governance in these areas with the realities of a world of independent nation-states, diverse cultures, and diverging interests. Finally, it is important to note again that appreciating the potential of NHRIs as actors in international politics is possible only if we move beyond the assumption of a unitary actor in world politics and draw on the insights of the literature on global governance, a literature that does not dispute the prominence of nation-states in the international arena, but sheds light on the changing nature of their role in contemporary international relations.

Studying the Impact of NHRI Networks

Are regional and international networks of NHRIs insulated enough from national governments to be effective? Can/do they make a difference in terms of improving the human rights records of governments? And what are the criteria that can be used to evaluate the performance of NHRIs and their potential contribution to the promotion and protection of human rights? These questions are not the focus of this chapter, but they are very important research questions.

As far as the criteria of evaluation are concerned, the Paris Principles, which were designed to set standards that ensure the effectiveness of NHRIs, naturally serve as a starting point for evaluating existing NHRIs. In an overview of criteria for assessing the potential effectiveness of NHRIs, the Australian Human Rights Centre identifies six criteria that are all grounded in the Paris Principles. These criteria are: "independence; defined jurisdiction and adequate powers; accessibility; cooperation; operational efficiency; and accountability" (Australian Human Rights Centre 2000, 272). All of these criteria are, for obvious reasons, necessary conditions for the effectiveness of NHRIs. But are they sufficient conditions? In other words, do networks of NHRIs that enjoy a broad mandate and independence from governments, are endowed with sufficient resources, are accessible to citizens, and accountable to the government and/or the legislature actually have a substantial impact on the human rights record? And how can this impact be measured? And as far as the international and regional networks of NHRIs are concerned, what impact have they had so far?

Beyond describing elements of institutional design that are necessary for NHRIs to be significant and effective actors in human rights politics, the available literature gives little attention to the actual impact of NHRIs and of the networks that they form. This is not surprising, given that NHRIs are relatively novel actors that have just begun to receive more scholarly attention in the last few years. These questions are, in my view, very significant for future research on NHRIs. Since the available research has largely been concerned with describing NHRIs in different countries, future research can be very valuable if it explores this set of questions using the theoretical and conceptual tools provided by the growing literature on global governance. This would allow us to move beyond descriptive analysis and to provide more systematic and more generalized accounts of NHRIs.

Conclusion

This chapter provides an overview of NHRIs and argues that networks of NHRIs have been given little attention so far, even though they can potentially be very significant actors in global governance. I have tried to demonstrate that the literature on globalization and global governance provides a conceptual and theoretical background against which we can study networks of NHRIs and their potential contribution to global governance, and that we need to draw on and integrate the different strands of research in these areas to study NHRIs as international actors. This chapter is mainly concerned with conceptual issues, and it does not attempt to empirically study the work and the impact of networks of NHRIs, which is necessary to provide a complete assessment of the potential of these networks. There is little empirical literature about NHRIs and the networks they form, and some of the available literature takes the form of descriptive analyses on NHRIs in different countries without giving much attention to their network activities. What is therefore needed are empirical studies that can gauge the effect that participation in transgovernmental networks has had on human rights practices and the human rights record in different countries. Any research that focuses on this important question will surely be challenging because separating the influence of network activity from other influences and factors that might affect human rights practices is not an easy task. Such research will need to combine a number of different social science research methods, including interviews with network participants and with local human rights activists to capture the true impact of NHRIs on the status of human rights. Given the continuing violations of human rights in many parts of the world and the potential contribution that transgovernmental networks can make to reduce these violations and balance sovereignty, culture and human rights, research designed to better understand these questions is important and worthwhile and can potentially have significant policy implications.

References

Adler, E. and Haas, P. 1992. Conclusion: Epistemic Communities, World Order, and the Creation of a Reflective Research Program. *International Organization* 46(1), 367–90.

Australian Human Rights Centre. 2000. National Human Rights Institutions: An Overview of the Asia Pacific Region. *International Journal on Minority and Group Rights* 7, 207–77.

Burdekin, B. 2007. *National Human Rights Institutions in the Asia-Pacific Region.* The Raoul Wallenberg Institute Human Rights Library Vol. 27. Leiden and Boston: Martinus Nijhoff Publishers.

Cardenas, S. 2003. Emerging Global Actors: The United Nations and National Human Rights Institutions. *Global Governance* 9(1), 23–42.

Donnelly, J. 2002. *Universal Human Rights in Theory and Practice.* Cornell University Press, 155–81.

Donoho, D. L. 1991. Relativism versus Universalism in Human Rights: The Search for Meaningful Standards. *Stanford Journal of International Law* 27(2), 345–91.

Eldridge, P. 2002. Emerging Roles of National Human Rights Institutions in Southeast Asia. *Pacifica Review* 14(3), 209–26.

Haas, P. 1992. Introduction: Epistemic Communities and International Policy Coordination. *International Organization* 46(1), 1–35.

Haas, P. 1999. Social Constructivism and the Evolution of Multilateral Environmental Governance, in *Globalization and Governance*, edited by A. Prakash and J. Hart. London and New York: Routledge, 103–33.

Huntington, S. 1991. *The Third Wave: Democratization in the Late Twentieth Century*. Oklahoma: University of Oklahoma Press.

Kabir, A. H. M. 2001. Establishing National Human Rights Commissions in South Asia: A Critical Analysis of the Processes and the Prospects. *Asia-Pacific Journal on Human Rights and the Law* 2(1), 1–53.

Koenig-Archibugi, M. 2002. Mapping Global Governance, in *Governing Globalization:Power, Authority and Global Governance*, edited by D. Held and A. McGrew. Malden, MA and Cambridge: Polity Press and Blackwell Publishers Inc., 46–69.

Kumar, C. R. 2006. National Human Rights Institutions and Economic, Social, and Cultural Rights: Toward the Institutionalization and Developmentalization of Human Rights. *Human Rights Quarterly* 28(3), 755–79.

McAdam, D. and Rucht, D. 1993. The Cross-National Diffusion of Movement Ideas. *Annals of the American Academy of Political and Social Science* 528, 56–74.

Mohamad, M. 2002. Towards a Human Rights Regime in Southeast Asia: Charting the Course of State Commitment. *Contemporary Southeast Asia* 24(2), 230–51.

Nelson, T. and Oxley, Z.M. 1999. Issue Framing Effects on Belief Importance and Opinion. *The Journal of Politics* 61(4), 1040–67.

Nelson, T. E., Clawson, R. A. and Oxley, Z. M. 1997. Media Framing of a Civil Liberties Conflict and its Effect on Tolerance. *American Political Science Review* 91(3), 567–83.

Nugent, N. 1999. *The Government and Politics of the European Union.* 4th edition. Durham: Duke University Press.

Pohjolainen, A. 2006. *The Evolution of National Human Rights Institutions: The Role of the United Nations*. The Danish Institute for Human Rights.

Prakash, A. and Hart, J. 1999. Introduction, in *Globalization and Governance*, edited by A. Prakash and J. Hart. London and New York: Routledge, 1–24.

Reif, L. 2000. Building Democratic Institutions: The Role of National Human Rights Institutions in Good Governance and Human Rights Protection. *The Harvard Human Rights Journal* 13(1), 1–69.

Rosenau, J. 2002. Governance in a New Global Order, in *Governing Globalization: Power, Authority and Global Governance*, edited by D. Held and A. McGrew. Malden, MA and Cambridge: Polity Press and Blackwell Publishers Inc., 70–86.

Slaughter, A.-M. 1997. The Real New World Order. *Foreign Affairs* 76(5), 183–97.

Slaughter, A.-M. 2004. *A New World Order*. Princeton and Oxford: Princeton University Press.

Smith, A. 2006. The Unique Position of National Human Rights Institutions: A Mixed Blessing? *Human Rights Quarterly* 28(4), 904–46.
Strang, D. and Soule, S.A. 1998. Diffusion in Organizations and Social Movements: From Hybrid Corn to Poison Pills. *Annual Review of Sociology* 265–90.
Tranholm-Mikkelsen, J. 1991. Neo-functionalism: Obstinate or Obsolete? A Reappraisal in the Light of the New Dynamism of the EC. *Millennium: Journal of International Studies* 20(1), 1–22.

Chapter 4

Universalism Meets Sovereignty at the International Criminal Court

Benjamin N. Schiff

Introduction

The 1648 Peace of Westphalia is conventionally regarded by international relations theorists as the beginning of an international system based on collective acceptance by governments of the institution of sovereignty. Under this institution, governments of territorially defined states possess the exclusive right and duty to maintain internal order and the paramount responsibility to defend their territories from external interference. Internally, individual people are subject to the state's laws. Externally, since states are the relevant actors, individuals have no standing except as agents of states. Westphalian sovereignty is undermined by efforts from outside a state to guarantee its citizens' individual rights or to constrain their behavior apart from the state's own legal framework.

Human rights norms have developed over a very long period of time in ways that both contradict and complement the Westphalian conception. Natural rights theories regard individuals as carriers of inalienable rights regardless of their citizenship status, on the basis that to be human is to have by rights certain basic requirements of life. In contrast, utilitarian theories embed individuals in political contexts, meaning states in the Westphalian system, wherein their rights as against other citizens and against the state are established by a popular agreement, the social contract (Brown 2002, 117–19). These two streams largely converged in the post-World War II world. Acting collectively through international organizations most states have formally acceded to the Universal Declaration of Human Rights and its Covenants, and many have adopted treaty obligations proscribing certain behaviors such as under the Genocide and Torture conventions.

Only with the establishment of the International Criminal Court, however, has a standing international judicial forum been created to implement international criminal law. The International Criminal Court that came into being in 2002 expresses member states' commitments to hold individuals to account for perpetrating the most heinous international criminal violations—genocide, crimes against humanity, and war crimes, and possibly the crime of aggression. The Rome Statute of 1998 that established the International Criminal Court doubly challenges Westphalian sovereignty. First, it regards individuals as agents apart from states. Whether acting on their own or as state officials, inside their own states' territories or on the territory of other states, individual perpetrators can commit acts criminalized under the Statute. Second, it creates obligations for states, thus internally and externally constraining sovereignty. Internally, participating states must implement the Court's statute in domestic law. Externally, participating states are required to cooperate with the Court. Adding to the ICC's apparent challenge to sovereignty, non-governmental organizations played major roles in the negotiation of the Court's Statute and they continue to influence and act as agents of the Court.

The ICC remains, however, only on the cusp of supranationalism. Along with creating the Court, the Statute protects state sovereignty. ICC jurisdiction is complementary to, not paramount over domestic jurisdiction. The United Nations Security Council, dominated by its permanent members, can both refer situations to the Court and suspend its proceedings. The ICC depends on states for information, funds, and enforcement capabilities and states' level of cooperation with the Court is up to them, not the Court. Finally, states seek to "instrumentalize" the Court—to use it for internal and international advantage.

This chapter first briefly reviews the pre-history of the ICC. Then it describes aspects of the Statute that show the tension between sovereignty and supranationalism. It demonstrates the influence of nongovernmental organizations in the development and operation of the court, and reviews the course of early ICC operations. I argue that creation of the ICC conforms to an image of system change in which sovereignty is mitigated by states' conformity to international norms, but states' continued pursuit of sovereign interests mean that ICC operations lag behind international normative aspirations. Still, the overall trajectory of international criminal law in the post-Cold War era is toward a gradual diminution of sovereignty in the Westphalian sense.

ICC Pre-history

The long development of ideas about creating an international criminal jurisdiction can be traced to the mid-nineteenth century rise of humanitarian law and the International Red Cross movement (Schiff 2008, 19–41). In the wake of WWII, victorious western allies articulated universalist human rights values as correctives to the ugly depredations against individuals, groups, and nations that took place during the war. They established the International Military Tribunals at Nuremberg and Tokyo, and subsequently supported the 1948 Universal Declaration of Human Rights. In the same year the Convention Prohibiting the Crime of Genocide was opened for state accession. Early drafts of the Genocide Convention envisioned a court, but its final version left enforcement to the signatory states or to a future "international penal tribunal as may have jurisdiction with respect to those Contracting Parties which shall have accepted its jurisdiction" (UN General Assembly 1948, Article 6).

At about the same time, at the behest of the United Nations General Assembly (UNGA), the International Law Commission (ILC) codified the Nuremberg

Principles that individuals are liable for violations of international law; liability persists even if acts are not criminalized under domestic law; official status does not establish immunity; acting under superior orders does not relieve an individual of responsibility; suspects have the right to a fair trial; and the international crimes are crimes against peace, war crimes, and crimes against humanity or complicity in these crimes (International Law Commission 1950, 191–95). The UNGA set up a committee to develop a draft statute for an international criminal court and requested that the ILC draft a "Code of Crimes Against the Peace and Security of Mankind." The draft statute and code were discussed, reviewed, and reported upon in 1954, following which these activities were suspended due to Cold War political tensions. The effort to connect individual crimes to international jurisdiction halted as the antagonists of the Cold War each feared that opening internal matters to international scrutiny could harm their interests (Schabas 2004, 8–9).

Cessation of the Cold War at the end of the 1980s and new atrocities in the first half of the 1990s returned momentum to the international criminal law project. The UNGA renewed its request to the ILC for a draft ICC statute in 1989. When the United Nations Security Council (UNSC) established international criminal tribunals for the former Yugoslavia and for Rwanda in 1993 and in 1994, their statutes built on the ILC's work, and in 1994 the ILC produced a new draft ICC statute (ILC 1994, Vol. II, Part 2).

Negotiations expanded the 35-page 1994 draft into 173 pages replete with bracketed options, alternative phrasing, and footnotes for consideration by the 1998 Rome Conference on the Statute of the International Criminal Court (Bassiouni 1999, 26). At Rome a group of states called the "like-minded states" (LMS) dominated, supplying most of the working group chairs and the Bureau, the conference's executive body. The LMS sought a court independent of the UN and with broad jurisdiction. Non-Aligned Movement states urged that the Court have jurisdiction over a crime of aggression, the Southern African Development Community pressed for expanded human rights definitions, and Arab and Islamic states sought to prohibit nuclear weapons and include a death penalty in the statute. The newly elected Labor Party government in Britain broke from its big three UN Security Council peers (US, Russia, China), joining Germany, France, and most EU members in the Like Minded States group in calling for a Court not subject to UNSC control (Schabas 2004, 16–17).

The United States was highly influential and most constructive in the negotiations. Its delegation was the largest at the conference. Its legal experts contributed key elements to the Statute and, subsequently, to the Court's Rules of Procedure and Evidence. Many of the compromises negotiated during the conference were aimed at bringing the US into the fold; however, in retrospect, it is doubtful that any statute that met the objectives of the LMS for a highly independent court would have been acceptable to the US which sought a Court subordinate to the UN Security Council.

NGOs provided an important avenue for information exchange throughout the conference, urged the delegates on, and provided position statements and research and analysis used directly in the discussions. Negotiations were most difficult over the tension between the prerogatives of the court and protection of state sovereignty. In the last two days of the conference, crucial breakthroughs accumulated and a document emerged that commanded the support of the vast majority of participating states. An effort to delay final adoption was defeated with 120 votes against, 7 in favor, and 21 abstentions, two hours past midnight on 17 July and the Statute was adopted without a further vote. The US, China, Israel, Iraq, Libya, Yemen and Qatar had voted to delay (Kaul 1998, 57; Schiff 2008, 72).

Sovereignty and the Statute

The ICC inaugurated by the Rome Statute teeters on the fine line between universalism and sovereignty. It asserts existence of a global society united by shared cultures, but restricts the Court's ability to intervene in national jurisdictions. The preamble portrays humanity as a global society. It presents the universalistic image that "all peoples are united by common bonds, their cultures pieced together in a shared heritage." It asserts that this collective "mosaic" of shared heritage is "delicate" and "can be shattered at any time," the violence of the twentieth century, including "unimaginable atrocities that deeply shock the conscience of humanity" showing its fragility. An end to impunity would contribute to deterring atrocious crimes, and since "grave crimes threaten the peace, security and well-being of the world," action against these crimes should lead to a more peaceful, secure and happy world. In establishing a Court thus to improve the world, the preamble launches the Statute as a document of liberal, universalistic institutionalism (ICC 1998, Preamble).

On the other hand, the Statute limits the Court's jurisdiction. The ICC's jurisdiction is complementary to that of national courts. If national courts do not prosecute when they should, the ICC can; but national responsibility comes first (ICC 1998, Article 17; El Zeidy 2002). The preamble declares that the Statute's objectives do not justify the use of force against states, interference in their internal affairs, or other acts inconsistent with the UN Charter.

The 1994 International Law Commission draft statute conformed to UNSC permanent members' preferences that ICC actions would be triggered only by Security Council initiative. NGOs and the Like Minded States, however, sought a Court independent of the Security Council. During the Rome Conference, the LMS sought to find a compromise formula that would keep the US in the Court, but establish ICC independence. Under Statute Article 13b the Security Council can refer situations to the ICC Prosecutor under Chapter VII of the UN Charter, but jurisdiction can also be exercised if a state party to the Statute refers a situation to the Prosecutor (Article 13a) or if the Prosecution initiates an investigation on its own authority, *proprio motu* (Article 13c). Instead of the UN Security Council being the exclusive trigger of an investigation or being required to agree in order that an investigation be pursued, its involvement is limited. It can suspend an ongoing investigation for 12 months (renewable) if the conflict situation is on the UNSC agenda and the Court's involvement is believed to threaten efforts to create peace (Article 16). The suspension clause was intended to mollify US concerns but was not enough to gain its acceptance of the Statute.

The ICC Prosecutor can decide when to launch a preliminary investigation into a conflict situation. "Situation" is a term unique to the ICC. Once a situation is under investigation, the Prosecutor seeks to determine whether crimes under the jurisdiction of the Court may be taking place and to determine who the likely perpetrators are. Formal investigations, other than requested by the UNSC, require a finding by a Pre-Trial Chamber (PTC) of judges that the seriousness of the case justifies the ICC investigation and that no appropriate domestic proceedings are underway. Subsequently the Prosecutor must request from the PTC issuance of summonses or warrants in order to bring suspects to court, and the PTC must confirm charges against a suspect in order for a trial to move from the pre-trial to trial. These limits on the Prosecutor were intended to prevent what US critics called "frivolous" prosecution and also moved the ICC toward the "inquisitorial" model of civil justice, away from a purely "adversarial," common-law model (Schiff 2008, 77–87).

States that accede to the ICC Statute obligate themselves to criminalize ICC crimes in their domestic laws, have procedures in place to arrest and surrender persons sought by the Court, to try such crimes in their own jurisdictions, and to cooperate with the Court by providing information when so requested (ICC 1998, Part 9). Extensive negotiation at the Statute Conference softened cooperation requirements so that states can withhold information or intervene to prevent disclosures that they deem prejudicial to their national security (Article 72). The Statute sets out extensive procedures for consultation in such an event, but in the end the states decide. The most that the Court can do in response is report non-cooperation to the Assembly of States Parties, or, in the event that the case flows from a Security Council referral, to the UNSC (ICC 1998, 87.7).

The Rome Statute creates an international jurisdiction, a supranational organization that reaches beyond the sovereign state to individual crimes and suspects, but defers to states' jurisdiction and is dependent upon their cooperation, threading the needle between internationalism and sovereignty. It requires states that join to bring their domestic legal systems into conformity with Rome Statute standards, but permits states to protect sensitive information. In practice, since the ICC has no enforcement capacity, states can restrict its access to people and information, thus limiting its activities.

Non-governmental Organizations: Shaping and Extending the ICC's Reach

Non-governmental organizations do not figure in the Westphalian state system model, but they significantly affected the development of the ICC and they continue to be influential in its operations. The compelling quality of the norms NGOs espouse impels states' adherence to the rhetoric, if not the reality, of universalist values. Paying respect to such values, according to some commentators, constitutes the first step toward changes in state behavior (Risse and Sikkink 1999). From the Statute Conference onward, the relationship between the ICC and the NGOs has probably been closer, more consistent and more vital than have been analogous relations between NGOs and any other international organization (Schiff 2008, 144–64).

Until the 1990s the idea of the International Criminal Court was primarily developed by international legal experts (Schiff 2008, 14–39). During the 1970s and 1980s international human rights and humanitarian non-governmental organizations multiplied and expanded. The esoteric quest by international lawyers to establish a mechanism for punishing international crimes reached the mainstream of international human rights activism in the 1990s. NGOs commented extensively on the 1994 ILC draft ICC Statute (Amnesty International 1994), and in the fall they successfully pressed the UNGA's Sixth (legal) Committee to recommend that the UNGA resolve to create an ad hoc committee to discuss the draft and move toward a Statute Conference (UNGA 1994). In February 1995, World Federalist Movement (WFM) Executive Director William Pace convened a meeting in New York to establish a Steering Committee of what came to be the NGO Coalition for the ICC (CICC). The committee included representatives from the WFM, the International Commission of Jurists, Amnesty International, the Lawyers Committee for Human Rights, Human Rights Watch, Parliamentarians for Global Action, and No Peace Without Justice (Stoelting 1999) and attracted 25 NGO members. By late 2008, the CICC claimed more than 2,500 affiliates with a steering committee of 15 (CICC 2008a, 2).

The CICC served as an umbrella and coordinating organization for NGOs interested in the creation of the ICC. CICC members now ascribe to three principles: 1) promoting world-wide ratification and implementation of the Rome Statute of the ICC; 2) maintaining the integrity of the Rome Statute of the ICC; and 3) ensuring the ICC will be as fair, effective and independent as possible (CICC 2008b). These general principles permit organizations with broadly varying objectives to participate in the coalition. The CICC coordinates efforts to improve the efficiency of NGOs' contributions to the Court and to pool their influence on major common issues. From the ICC side, it has been extremely useful to have the CICC channel NGO contacts with the Court so that its officials don't have to interact individually with thousands of separate organizations.

While the Statute was under negotiation, CICC member organizations and the CICC secretariat itself produced information materials, lobbied in support of creating an ICC, organized regional meetings with NGO and governmental representatives to promote their ideas about the Court, and produced newsletters and position papers on a multitude of aspects of the ICC and affiliated issues of international law and human rights. Close contact with national delegations meant that many NGO positions were articulated as national positions as well.

The NGO Coalition for the International Criminal Court vastly increased the transparency of the negotiations by providing daily updates of states' positions based on public comments and conversations with delegates. Groups not attending at Rome could receive a daily digest of events called *On the Record* which the CICC helped distribute but did not write (CICC 1998). The Inter-Press Service, a non-profit journalists' association with NGO consultative status at UNESCO published a newspaper called *Terra Viva* supported by contributions from the European Union through the NGO No Peace Without Justice (NPWJ) and the CICC, in which the *CICC Monitor* was an insert (Inter-press Service 1998, 2). These helped maintain negotiating momentum and informed state representatives about developments in areas where they were not directly involved. The daily updates also served as a running "straw vote" on major conference topics, enabling in particular small states and the LMS to recognize the extent of their agreement even as the more powerful states sought to re-open areas of negotiation and divide opposition. The CICC's innovative use of electronic communications made it the fastest and most comprehensive information source for Conference participants. CICC Convener William Pace emerged as one of the Court's major founding influences. NGOs exerted tremendous effort to bolster the majority of countries' drive for a highly independent ICC.

NGOs remained engaged after the Statute was launched. Through the CICC they were in constant contact with the preparatory commission as it developed the Rules of Procedure and Evidence and the Definitions of Crimes. They pushed states to support the emerging organization's budget, campaigned for states' accession to the Statute, and urged member states to adopt domestic implementing legislation. Once the Court came into being, the NGOs became advocates for it in ways that Court officials could not. They continue to campaign for further state accessions, adoption of implementing legislation, expansion of the Court's budget, and to disseminate information about the ICC worldwide.

NGOs have also become vital to the ICC as information sources to the Court and to local populations of areas where crimes under the Court's actual or potential jurisdiction take place. Most of the thousands of communications to the ICC Office of the Prosecutor seeking investigations come from local and international NGOs. NGO programs, many coordinated by the CICC with local organizations, bring local people into contact with Court officials and disseminate information about the Court in conflict areas. NGOs have become active as well in informing victims of the possibilities for being represented before the Court, organizing applications and arranging legal representation (Schiff 2008, 131–3).

NGO involvement with the Court shows the multiplication of actors relevant to, if not transformative of, the Westphalian system. The state system has become more complicated as non-state actors' advocacy roles, information channels, and representative activities complement and complicate states' relations to the international organization and slip through borders to press for domestic legal change.

Situations, Cases and Contradictions

When states join international organizations and accept constraints on their autonomy, they may appear to be permitting a moderation of Westphalian sovereignty, but they do not necessarily contravene it. As liberal institutionalist theories explain, they still pursue interests as they define them (Schiff 2008, 6–7). A truer measure of the effects of international institutions upon sovereignty could be taken when the norms of the institution conflict with the interests of states. A weak test would be when a state, apparently living up to institutional norms, nonetheless sought to bend implementation in the direction of its interests and either succeeded, reaffirming the apparent vitality of Westphalian sovereignty, or failed, pointing to sovereignty's erosion. A strong test of organizational supranationality, hence transformation of Westphalian sovereignty, would be when a state subordinated its interests to institutional norms when the two came into conflict or redefined interests in an entirely new way, as constructivist theories describe (Schiff 2008). Such tests are ongoing for the International Criminal Court. In self-referred situations in Uganda, the Democratic Republic of the Congo (DRC) and the Central African Republic, the weaker form of the test pits state efforts to instrumentalize the Court against the ICC's efforts to retain the appearance, if not the reality, of independence. The stronger test is being applied in the Sudan situation with complicated results. The referral of the situation to the Court appeared to fly in the face of US policy, showing that multilateral norms have some power against even a major power's preferences. On the other hand, the Court has so far been unable fully to carry out its judicial functions against the will of the Sudan (which, while not a party to the Statute is technically bound to comply with it because the situation was referred to the Court by the UN Security Council, and as a member of the UN, Sudan is obligated to comply with UNSC resolutions).

Uganda

In late 2003 lawyers representing Uganda in a dispute with the DRC at the International Court of Justice in The Hague indicated informally to ICC Office of the Prosecutor (OTP) personnel Uganda was interested in referring the Lord's Resistance Army (LRA) conflict situation in northern Uganda to the Court (Schiff 2008, 198). In December, Ugandan President Yoweri Museveni sent a confidential letter to ICC Chief Prosecutor Luis Moreno Ocampo referring the conflict to the Court (Akhavan 2005, 403), and on 29 January 2004, Museveni and Moreno Ocampo announced the referral at a joint news conference in London. Human rights NGOs welcomed the referral but cautioned that the ICC should pursue all relevant crimes regardless of who had committed them, fearing that the joint appearance and Museveni's statements appeared to put the ICC on the government's side (Amnesty International 2004; Human Rights Watch 2004). Observers claimed that crimes were being perpetrated not only by the LRA, but also by members of the government army, the Ugandan People's Defense Forces (UPDF) (Human Rights Watch 2005).

The referral appeared to serve Museveni's political objectives. While the UPDF was free to act inside Uganda, ICC involvement could help gain Sudanese and DRC permission for forays across their borders to attack the Lord's Resistance Army. By calling upon the ICC to act against the LRA, he could shift attention away from UPDF misdeeds. His embrace of the ICC could help legitimate his government, especially in the eyes of European leaders. Moreover, the ICC's appeal for international cooperation in apprehending LRA suspects might help lead to their capture.

Uganda's referral served the ICC Prosecutor's purposes as well. State self-referrals would vastly simplify the prosecutor's task by making situation states' cooperation much more likely than would his proceeding *proprio motu*. Uganda's self-referral could help build the Court's credibility since critics had wondered whether it could gain cooperation from situation states. Self-referral eased the Court's practical problems, but it raised the possibility of ICC instrumentalization.

On 29 July 2004, the Chief Prosecutor opened a formal investigation into the Northern Uganda situation (ICC 2004a), but in deference to ongoing peace efforts pursued the investigation with a "low profile" (Schiff 2008, 202). In November, Museveni announced a partial cease-fire to enable discussions with the LRA about government amnesty offers. The president said that if the LRA leadership reached some kind of settlement with the victim Acholi population, "the state could then withdraw its case and we could inform the ICC that we have a solution to the Kony problem. That is what the ICC wants. No cover-up, no impunity" (*The New Vision* 2004).

In spring 2005, the Prosecutor requested confidentially that Pre-Trial Chamber II issue warrants of arrest for the leader of the LRA, Joseph Kony, and four of his top lieutenants. After long consideration and disputes with the Office of the Prosecutor over provisions for the safety of victims and witnesses, the PTC issued the warrants in mid-October (ICC 2005b). Betty Bigombe, a former Ugandan government minister who had been serving as an intermediary with the LRA, said that the warrants would end mediation efforts: "There is now no hope of getting them to surrender. I have told the court that they have rushed too much" (*The New Vision* 2005).

Although not a party to the Rome Statute, the Sudanese government agreed to cooperate in efforts to apprehend the LRA suspects (IRIN 2005a), apparently seeking to conform to international norms and to improve its image in the wake of Al Qaeda's rise to notoriety and former residence in Sudan. The LRA leadership departed Sudan, were tracked around northern Uganda, into the DRC and Central African Republic, and apparently divided into several groups. They continued to be dangerous to both civilians and military forces, which they demonstrated by killing eight Guatemalan UN peacekeepers in an ambush in the eastern Congo in late January 2006 (*The New Vision* 2006a). Ugandan government spokesmen referred to the LRA as no longer a serious force, but continued UPDF military efforts failed. Humanitarian agencies continued to describe effects of the long-running conflict as among the direst in the world (Civil Society Organizations for Peace in Northern Uganda 2006).

ICC proponents argued that the Court's involvement had positive results. Sudan was cooperating against the LRA, and with its freedom of operations increasingly constrained the LRA had lost any hope of victory. ICC involvement raised international awareness, and prompted some lower-level LRA leaders to accept the government's amnesty offer (Akhavan 2005, 416–20). Critics argued to the contrary that the ICC arrest warrants "may indeed have jeopardized the security of civilians, sparking increases in LRA violence and attacks on humanitarian organizations" (Civil Society Organizations for Peace in Northern Uganda 2006. 12). As 2006 progressed, however, the situation began to change.

Uganda's 2000 amnesty law was amended in April 2006 to bring Ugandan law into conformity with ICC Statute obligations. In May, however, Museveni appeared to offer Kony a friendly inducement, again demonstrating his proclivity to use the Court for leverage, riding roughshod over the ICC's legal obligations. "The President said much as Kony and four of his cohorts had been indicted by the International Criminal Court, if he got serious about peaceful settlement, the Government of Uganda would guarantee him safety" (*The New Vision* 2006b), again asserting sovereignty over supranational obligations.

Chief Prosecutor Moreno Ocampo immediately responded,"The governments of Uganda, Sudan and Democratic Republic of Congo are obligated to give effect to the arrest warrants, and we are confident they will honour their commitment to do so" (BBC 2006), and Court spokesperson Sandra Khadouri said, "It's the government of Uganda that referred the situation to the International Criminal Court in December 2003... they are now under obligation and made a commitment" (Nyakairu 2006). Having previously asserted that the prosecution's timing was flexible, Moreno Ocampo had hardened his position. "'The defendants could challenge the admissibility of the arrest warrants,' he told journalists. 'But the prosecutor can do nothing. The case is in the hands of the judges'" (Anderson 2006a).

The joint Museveni-Moreno Ocampo news conference of 2004 highlighted the threat of apparent instrumentalization by the government of the Court and President Museveni appeared to regard the ICC's involvement as a bargaining chip for his dealings with the LRA. As of fall 2008, the matter remained unresolved as negotiations broke down and Kony remained at large and the LRA continued sporadic attacks against civilians. As a weak test of sovereignty versus supranationality, the Uganda case showed that the Court could attain a degree of at least symbolic independence, rejecting Museveni's claims that he could order the ICC warrants lifted. However, since the situation remained unresolved, the best that can be said of the ICC's practical involvement is that it appeared to help constrain the LRA, although it did not lead efficaciously to either the alleged perpetrators' apprehensions or to peace.

Congo

The Democratic Republic of the Congo (DRC) government was among those whose ratification in April 2002 started the 60-day clock ticking to bring the Statute into effect. In July 2003, the then-newly appointed Chief Prosecutor announced he would "closely follow the situation in the DRC," responding to reports that international crimes were being committed in the internal conflict there. In September he publicly contemplated seeking Pre-Trial Chamber authorization to initiate an investigation *proprio motu* but said he would prefer to work with the Congolese authorities. Moreno Ocampo urged President Joseph Kabila to refer the DRC situation to the Court, and in April 2004, Kabila did so (ICC 2004b).

Like Museveni's, Kabila's referral to the Court appeared motivated by political calculations. He had entered politics after the assassination of his father in January 2001 and had little record until then of participation in the conflicts ravaging the country (Burke-White 2005, 565). Compared to other DRC political and military leaders, Kabila had little to fear from the Court. "The ICC was exploited right from the start. It suited Kabila as a weapon against his adversaries," said a lawyer from the region quoted anonymously in 2004 (Cruvillier 2004). The vice presidents and ministers of the transitional government represented a broad spectrum of DRC political parties and former enemies. Because of the others' reputations and records—and the continuing violence in the northeast after 1 July 2002—ICC involvement threatened them. Their indictment would likely impair their political chances or even remove them from electoral contention, strengthening Kabila.

Because of the weakness of the Congolese judicial and police systems, Kabila could not be sure that the local justice system would operate effectively against his powerful adversaries, nor that the courts would be or appear impartial. The ICC could provide a surer route to trials. His willingness to engage international justice could improve his international standing particularly with the European Union and France, which had strongly encouraged him to accept ICC jurisdiction.

The referral appears to have had some cautionary effect. In a 2003 interview, Thomas Lubanga Dyilo, head of the Union of Congolese Patriots (UPC), an Ituri-region political and (allegedly) militia organization, said that "the Court has been a pressure on the political actors who were killing people ... these people are very afraid today to commit such slaughter," and another regional leader, Xavier Ciribanya said, "many here in the East are afraid the Court will come .... We all now are thinking twice. We do not know what this Court can and will do" (Burke-White 2005, 588).

Lubanga came to Kinshasa, the DRC's capital, in August 2003 to participate in peace talks, but continued to reside there "under virtual house arrest" although claiming that he was in control of his forces (Anderson 2006b). On 11 March 2005 he was placed under formal house arrest by order of President Kabila with three others accused of genocide and crimes against humanity under the DRC military code. He was also accused by the United Nations of having masterminded the killing in an ambush of nine Bangladeshi MONUC peacekeepers in the Ituri district on 25

February. On 29 March the DRC authorities issued another arrest warrant against Lubanga, alleging crimes of murder, illegal detention and torture (ICC 2006a).

Lubanga's detention presented the ICC Prosecutor's office an opportunity to avoid the problems associated with organizing the arrest of a suspect. Even if the transfer appeared opportunistic, however, the Prosecutor argued that it was compelled by events. Under DRC law, Lubanga could be held for up to a year. After the year, which would have ended in mid-March 2006, the case would require review and a judge would have to renew the detention. The ICC Prosecutor feared Lubanga would be released because DRC authorities had not compiled a record that would justify continued detention (ICC 2006b), and on 13 January 2006, he requested that the Pre-Trial Chamber issue an arrest warrant for Lubanga (ICC 2006c). The PTC examined the OTP's application and issued the warrant on 10 February for crimes of recruiting, enlisting, and deploying child soldiers in combat in Ituri. Lubanga was turned over to officials of the Court, flown to the Netherlands on a French military aircraft, and appeared before the Pre-Trial Chamber in open court for the first time on 22 March 2006. NGOs questioned the narrowness of the charges against Lubanga, arguing that atrocities committed under his command were much broader than just the employment of child soldiers, and in particular that the failure to charge him with gender crimes in connection with massive numbers of rapes undermined victims' faith in justice. The Prosecutor argued that focused charges on crimes that could be most convincingly documented for trial would speed the proceedings and serve most effectively to counter impunity.

The Lubanga case moved very slowly as the ICC developed procedures for dealing with document sharing between the prosecution and defense, victim participation, and myriad other problems. In the summer of 2008, the case was suspended at the trial stage when the Court found that the Prosecution had failed to share potentially exculpatory information with the defense due to the confidentiality of information provided by NGOs and UN agencies. The problem was resolved in November, with a trial date set for late January 2009 (ICC 2008a).

Meanwhile, two further suspects were transferred to the Court on charges stemming from violence in the Congo. At the Prosecutor's request, warrants were issued secretly in July 2007 for Congolese Patriotic Resistance Front in Ituri (FRPI) leader Germaine Katanga and National Integrationist Front (NFI) leader Mathieu Ngudjolo Chui for attacks in Ituri, 2002–2003. Katanga was surrendered to the Court by DRC authorities on 18 October 2007, and Chui was surrendered to the ICC on 7 February 2008 (ICC 2008b). A fourth warrant was made public in April, 2008, issued in 2006 for Bosco Ntaganda in connection with events in Ituri 2002–2003 where he was deputy Chief of the General Staff for Military Operations of the Patriotic Forces for the Liberation of the Congo (FPLC). Ntaganda has not been apprehended, however, but subsequently re-emerged as central to violence in late 2008 in Kivu state, working for rebel General Laurent Nkunda (Clifford 2008).

From the standpoint of sovereignty, DRC apprehension of Lubanga, Katanga and Chui and their transfers to the Court showed the ICC's potential for action with the cooperation of the situation state. The arrests did not cut against the interests of the DRC government, so are not a strong test of supranationality, but they do demonstrate that the ICC is apparently a useful adjunct to a state seeking to prosecute violations of international criminal law but lacking the wherewithal to do so—a demonstration of complementarity in action.

Central African Republic

The third self-referral came in a letter from the Central African Republic in December 2004, which was followed by documentation in June 2005 of alleged crimes that had taken place from 2002 to 2003 prominently including mass rapes. During the upheavals at the time, then-President of the CAR, Félix Patassé had enlisted support from Jean-Pierre Bemba and his militia, the Movement for the Liberation of the Congo (MLC). In September 2006, CAR authorities asked that the ICC Prosecutor explain why action had not been taken on their referral. In May 2007, the OTP asked Pre-Trial Chamber III for authorization to conduct an official investigation, and in May 2008, the OTP applied for a warrant of arrest for Bemba.

Continuing to play a major role in Congolese politics following his involvement in the CAR from 2002 to 2003, Bemba became one of four vice-presidents in the DRC transitional government from 2005 to 2006. He came in second in the 2006 presidential election won by Joseph Kabila. In March 2007, his militia fought with government forces in Kinshasa, and the DRC's chief prosecutor issued a warrant for his arrest for treason. He fled to Portugal and also bought a house in Belgium. Belgium arrested Bemba at the ICC's request and transferred him to The Hague on 8 July 2008 (International Herald Tribune 2008; ICC 2008c).

As in the Congo situation, the Bemba arrest and transfer demonstrates the potential efficacy of the ICC when states cooperate with it. In providing the possibility of putting on trial for international crimes individuals whose trials would be extremely difficult or perhaps impossible in the states where the crimes were committed, the ICC is serving the supranational function for which it was designed. But like the Congo cases, while this one demonstrates the potential efficacy of international cooperation through an international organization, explainable under liberal institutionalist theories, it does not challenge Westphalian sovereignty. The organization is carrying out the interests of its member states.

Sudan

In contrast to Uganda's instrumentalization of ICC involvement and the DRC's and CAR's fuller cooperation, the ICC's involvement in Sudan provided three tougher tests of supranationality. First, because of US opposition to the Court, the referral of the situation by the Security Council to the ICC demonstrated the power of normative constraints even upon a major international actor, although the US did gain significant concessions for its abstention on the vote. Second, Sudan's refusal to cooperate with the Court showed that the Court's range of independent action is quite limited. Third, there remains the possibility that the Court's actions will help pressure Sudanese officials to moderate their actions in the internal conflict in Darfur.

On 31 March 2005, the UNSC referred the Darfur, Sudan, situation to the ICC (UNSC 2005). In the weeks prior to the Security Council's decision, the US strongly opposed the referral and pressed for alternatives. Frank about US motives, Ambassador-at-Large for War Crimes Issues Pierre-Richard Prosper said, "We don't want to be party to legitimizing the ICC" (Hoge 2005). Prosper had sought to convince Security Council members that a special Sudan Tribunal should be created under African Union auspices using the facilities of the International Criminal Tribunal for Rwanda in Arusha (Aita 2005). NGOs, governments friendly to the ICC, and international media protested that the US threatened to sacrifice the welfare of hundreds of thousands of Sudanese, preserve perpetrators' immunity, undermine principles of justice, and subvert humanitarian values all on the altar of its ideological antipathy to the Court (Cryer 2006).

On 31 March, the Security Council referred the situation to the ICC with eleven affirmative votes, no negative votes, and Algeria, Brazil, China and the US abstaining (UNSC 2005). Acting US Permanent Representative Ambassador Anne Patterson's statement to the Security Council demonstrated that while new US Secretary of State Condoleeza Rice had apparently convinced President George Bush to take a pragmatic position on the referral, ICC opponents, such as the soon-to-be nominated Permanent Representative to the UN, John Bolton, had extracted their pound of flesh in the form of caveats and conditions that sought to make life harder for the Court.

US fingerprints are all over Security Council Resolution 1593. The Resolution announces that all states shall cooperate with the Court under the UN Charter, while noting that for Rome Statute non-parties, their obligation arises only from the Charter and not from the Rome Statute (UNSC 2005, para. 2). Other than Sudanese, people from non-party states involved in referral-related activities in the Sudan would themselves be subject only to jurisdiction of their own ("the sending") states and not to the ICC unless they explicitly accepted the ICC's jurisdiction (UNSC 2005, para. 6). The Council decreed that none of the expenses of the referral would be paid by the UN, but would be borne by voluntary contributors and the parties to the Rome Statute (UNSC 1593, para. 7) contrary to the ICC Statute that appears to assign to the UN financial responsibility for referrals by the UNSC (Cryer 2006).

US Ambassador Patterson embraced international justice norms when she "strongly supported bringing to justice those responsible for the crimes and atrocities that had occurred in Darfur and ending the climate of impunity there" (UN Security Council 2005), but argued that the resolution actually supported the US view of limited ICC jurisdiction, setting the precedent that "absent consent of the State involved, any investigations or prosecutions of nationals of non-party States should come only pursuant to a decision by the Council" (UN Security Council 2005), a position clearly at odds with the jurisdictional regime of the

Rome Statute under which such a person could be subject to the Court if the alleged crime took place on the territory of a State Party to the Rome Treaty (ICC 1998, Article 12.2.a).

The good news for the ICC and for supranationalism and for international criminal law norms was that the US had abstained. The US's desire to support humanitarian interests, counter impunity in the Sudan, and avoid the approbation of other states overcame its objections to the Court. The bad news for the Court was that, with the referral, the ICC faced a huge challenge: Sudan had not agreed to its jurisdiction, and although bound under the UN Charter to fulfill Security Council Resolutions, the government showed no sign it would cooperate with the Court.

The good news from the standpoint of impunity in the Sudan was that the Security Council referral denoted an international commitment to pursuing the perpetrators of large-scale crimes. Countering impunity and supporting humanitarian law, or at least appearing to do so, were only two of the outside powers' multiple objectives in Sudan. The US, UK, Russia and China were all interested in the oil concessions Khartoum controlled, and the US and UK were in close contact with the government on measures to monitor and counter suspected Al Qaeda terrorist operations in the area.

Immediately after the Security Council announced the referral on 3 April 2005, President Omar Hassan Ahmad al-Bashir and the Sudanese cabinet condemned the Resolution (Sudan Tribune 2005). The government subsequently created a Special Criminal Court to prosecute crimes committed in Darfur, and in June, Justice Minister Ali Mohamed Oman Yasmin stated that the government considered the new court "a substitute to the International Criminal Court" (IRIN 2005).

On 1 June 2005, Moreno Ocampo informed the Pre-Trial Chamber and the President of the ICC that he had decided to go ahead with the formal investigation. On 27 February 2007, the Prosecutor submitted to PTC I an application for summonses for Ahmad Muhammad Harun, former Minister of State for the Interior and head of the "Darfur Security Desk," allegedly involved in recruiting the Janjaweed who "knowingly contributed to the commission of crimes against humanity and war crimes, including murder, rape, torture, inhumane acts, pillaging and the forcible transfer of civilian populations," and Ali Kushayb, a local commander allegedly responsible for leading Janjaweed attacks (ICC 2007a). The request for summonses, rather than warrants of arrest, implicitly invited Sudanese cooperation in turning the two suspects over. The Prosecutor's application noted, however, that should Sudan not assist the ICC's efforts, the PTC would be justified in issuing warrants for arrest, which it did in April (ICC 2007b, 2007c).

In the summer and fall of 2008, the standoff between the Court and Sudan intensified following the Prosecutor's request to PTC I for a warrant on grounds of genocide, crimes against humanity and war crimes for Sudan's President Al-Bashir (ICC 2008c). Not only Sudan objected to the move. The Organization of the Islamic Conference, African Union, and some commentators, including human rights advocates, argued that the Prosecutor's efforts would inhibit peace efforts in Darfur, appeared to be grandstanding, and were unlikely to hold up in Court

(Rozenberg 2008). Other observers congratulated the Prosecutor for appearing to act against the impunity of a head of state accused of suborning international crimes. In November, Al-Bashir announced a cease-fire in Darfur. Some observers speculated that this was an effort to persuade the UNSC to suspend the warrant. Should a cease-fire actually occur, some credit could perhaps fall to the pressure exerted by the ICC. Still awaiting a response from the PTC regarding the request for the warrant for Al-Bashir, the Prosecutor meanwhile announced that he had requested warrants for rebel leaders accused of organizing the killings of UN peacekeepers (ICC 2008d).

The Sudan situation demonstrated US disinclination to act on behalf of its anti-ICC position in ways that would put it directly at odds with norms of anti-impunity. Thus the free exercise of external Westphalian sovereignty was constrained. Internal to Sudan, however, the ICC's writ ran small. Resisted by a government that denied the legitimacy of the UNSC referral and rejecting the demand that the Sudanese hand over the two officials for whom warrants had been issued, Sudan was also organizing resistance among regional organizations against the ICC delivering a warrant for its head of state.

Conclusions

The International Criminal Court is the organizational manifestation of a growing international commitment to ending impunity and upholding international criminal law norms. Its Statute establishes individual culpability for genocide, crimes against humanity and war crimes and opens the possibility for the exercise of jurisdiction over the crime of aggression. Its jurisdiction and procedures moderate its supranationalism by establishing the principle of complementarity and retaining states' rights to determine the degree of their cooperation with the Court.

In practice, the ICC has demonstrated some successes, as in the Congo and CAR situations, when enabled by state cooperation to act against transgressors. It has been manipulated by the partial cooperation of Uganda. Although the United States appeared opposed to the Sudan referral, the compelling quality of international sentiment in favor of justice norms and in reaction to apparent massive criminality in Darfur appears to have forced a US backdown, in the form of abstention on UNSC Resolution 1593. The ICC has been stymied as Sudan exercises sovereign prerogatives in violation of obligations under the United Nations Charter, although the Court's actions may nonetheless have constrained Sudanese actions.

Since World War II and following the Universal Declaration on Human Rights, international criminal law norms have taken major steps toward institutionalization, among which the creation of the ICC is the most recent and concrete. For the first time in history there is a standing international court available to try transgressions that offend the conscience of humanity. As might be expected of any new judicial forum, the Court has yet to gain full international support or demonstrate complete competence in its areas of operation.

The 1998 Rome Statute and the ICC have created a much more direct link between individual behavior and international society than has ever existed before, created international standards by which to measure domestic reactions to mass criminality, and offered a permanent forum to complement state institutions that may be too weak or compromised fairly to try perpetrators of humanity's most heinous crimes. Protections to sovereignty built into the Statute enabled the Court to be established in an international system in which sovereignty remains a major institution. Successful creation and operation of the Court, however, demonstrates progressive softening of sovereignty as an institution, and its coexistence with increasingly pervasive global norms.

References

Aita, J. 2005. *African Union Tribunal Proposed for War Crimes in Darfur: US Suggests Alternative to ICC for Prosecution of Violators* [Online: US Department of State web site]. Available at: http://www.america.gov/st/washfile-english/2005/February/http://www.america.gov/st/washfile-english/2005/February/20050209175854atiayduj0.6344873.html [accessed: 4 December 2008].

Akhavan, P. 2005. The Lord's Resistance Army Case: Uganda's Submission of the First State Referral to the International Criminal Court. *American Journal of International Law* 99(2), 403–20.

Amnesty International 1994. *Memorandum to the International Law Commission: Establishing a Just, Fair and Effective Permanent International Criminal Tribunal*. IOR 40/07/94 [Online]. Available at: http://asiapacific.amnesty.org/library/Index/ENGIOR400071994?open&of=ENG-332ENGIOR400071994?open&of=ENG-332 [accessed 5 January 2009].

Amnesty International 2004. *Uganda: First Steps to Investigate Crimes Must Be Part of Comprehensive Plan to End Impunity*. Index Number: AFR 59/001/2004 [Online]. Available at: http://www.amnesty.org/en/library/info/AFR59/001/2004 [accessed: 4 December 2008].

Anderson, J. 2006a. World Court Faces Biggest Challenge. *Institute for War and Peace Reporting* AR No. 67 [Online, 16 June]. Available at: http://www.iwpr.net/?p=acr&s=f&o=321675&apc_state=henh?p=acr&s=f&o=321675&apc_state=henh [accessed: 4 December 2008].

Anderson, J. 2006b. ICC Enters Uncharted Territory. *Institute for War and Peace Reporting* TU No 445 [Online, 24 March]. Available at: http://www.iwpr.net/?p=tri&s=f&o=260514&apc_state=henptri [accessed: 4 December 2008].

Bassiouni, M. C. 1999. Historical Survey 1919–1998. *ICC Ratification and National Implementing Legislation, Nouvelles Ètudes Pénales*. Saint-Agne, France: Association International de Droit Pénal, 1–44.

BBC 2006. New Overture to Uganda's Rebels [Online, 17 May]. Available at: http://news.bbc.co.uk/go/pr/fr/-/2/hi/africa/4990086.stm [accessed: 4 December 2008].

Beaumont, P. 2006. Sudan's Gosh Holds Talks in London on Darfur and Terror. *Sudan Tribune* [Online, 14 March]. Available at: http://www.sudantribune.com/spip.php?article14517 [accessed: 4 December 2008].

Brown, C. 2002. *Sovereignty, Rights and Justice: International Political Theory Today*. Cambridge: Polity Press.

Burke-White, W. 2005. Complementarity in Practice: The International Criminal Court as Part of a System of Multi-level Global Governance in the Democratic Republic of Congo. *Leiden Journal of International Law* 18(3), 557–90.

Civil Society Organizations for Peace in Northern Uganda 2006. *Counting the Cost: Twenty Years of War in Northern Uganda*. Available from Oxfam [Online]. Available at: http://www.oxfam.org/en/policy/report-CSOPNU-nuganda-060330 [accessed: 4 December 2008].

Clifford, L. 2008. ICC Risks Losing the Plot in Congo. *Institute for War and Peace Reporting* 21 November 2008 [Online]. Available at: http://www.iwpr.net/?p=acr&s=f&o=347941&apc_state=henh [accessed: 30 November 2008].

Coalition for the International Criminal Court (CICC) 1998. *The Rome Treaty Conference Monitor* 1 [Online, 15 June]. Available at: http://www.icc-cpi.int/legaltools/download.hp?p=L0QuIElDQyBwcmVwYXJhdG9yeSB3b3Jrcy80LiBVbml0ZWQgTmF0aW9ucyBEaXBsb21hdGljIENvbmZlcmVuY2UvMTk5OC8xOTk4MDYxNV9OR09fSU5URVJQUkVTUlNFUlZJQ0VldGFsKEUpLnBkZg== [accessed: 1 December 2008].

Coalition for the International Criminal Court (CICC) 2008a. *ICC Monitor* 37 [Online] Available at: http://www.iccnow.org/documents/monitor37_english.pdf [accessed: 1 December 2008].

Coalition for the International Criminal Court (CICC) 2008b. Membership Request Form [Online] Available at: http://www.iccnow.org/?mod=membership [accessed: 4 December 2008].

Cryer, R. 2006. Sudan, Resolution 1593, and International Criminal Justice. *Leiden Journal of International Law* 19(1), 195–222.

Cruvillier, T. 2004. ICC Joins the Congolese Chess Game. *International Justice Tribune* 8 [Online]. Available at http://www.justicetribune.com/index.php?page=v2_article&id=2697 [accessed: 6 December 2004].

El Zeidy, M. 2002. The Principle of Complementarity: A New Machinery to Implement International Criminal Law. *Michigan Journal of International Law* 23(4), 869–975.

Glasius, M. 2005. *The International Criminal Court: A Global Civil Society Achievement*. New York: Routledge.

Hoge, W. 2005. US Lobbies UN on Darfur and International Court. *NY Times* [Online, 29 January]. Available at: http://www.nytimes.com/2005/01/29/international/29nations.html [accessed: 4 December 2008].

Human Rights Watch 2004. ICC: Investigate All Sides in Uganda—Chance for Impartial ICC Investigation into Serious Crimes a Welcome Step [Online, February 4]. Available at: http://www.iccnow.org/documents/02.04.2003-HRW-Uganda.pdf [accessed: 4 December 2008].

Human Rights Watch 2005. *North Crisis Worsened by UPDF* [Online, September 22] Available at: http://www.hrw.org/en/news/2005/09/22/north-crisis-worsened-u.pdf [accessed: 2 December 2008].

ICC 1998. *Rome Statute* [Online]. Available at: http://www.icc-pi.int/legaltools/download.php?p=L0IuIEJhc2ljIElDQyBkb2N1bWVudHMvUm9tZSBTdGF0dXRlICgwMS0wNy0yMDAwKShFKS5wZGY= [accessed: 2 December 2008].

ICC. 2004a. *Prosecutor of the International Criminal Court Opens an Investigation into Northern Uganda* [Online]. Available at: http://www.icc-cpi.int/pressrelease_details&id=33&l=en.html [accessed 2 December 2008].

ICC 2004b. *Prosecutor Receives Referral of the Situation in the Democratic Republic of Congo* [Online]. Available at: http://www.icc-cpi.int/pressrelease_details&id=19&l=en.html [accessed: 2 December 2008].

ICC 2005a. *Letter from Luis Moreno Ocampo to Judge Claude Jorda, Presiding Judge, Pre-Trial Chamber I* [Online, 1 June]. Available at: http://www.icc-cpi.int/library/cases/ICC-02-05-2_English.pdf [accessed: 2 December 2008].

ICC 2005b. *Pre-Trial Chamber II. Decision on the Prosecution's Application for Warrants of Arrest under Art 58* ICC-02/04 [Online, 8 July]. Available at: http://www.icc-cpi.int/library/cases/ICC-02-04-01-05-1-US-Exp_English.pdf [accessed: 2 December 2008].

ICC 2006a. *Pre-Trial Chamber I. Decision Concerning Pre-Trial Chamber I's Decision of 10 February 2006 and the Incorporation of Documents into the Record of the Case against Mr. Thomas Lubanga Dyilo* ICC-01/04-01/06-8-Corr [Online, 17 March]. Available at: http://www.icc-cpi.int/library/cases/ICC-01-04-01-06-8-US-Corr_English.pdf [accessed: 2 December 2008].

ICC 2006b. *PTC I. Redacted Version of the Transcripts of the Hearing Held on 2 February 2006 and Certain Materials Presented During that Hearing* [Online]. Available at: http://www.icc-cpi.int/library/cases/ICC-01-04-01-06-48_English.pdf [accessed: 2 December 2008].

ICC 2006c. *PTC I. Warrant of Arrest* [Online, 10 February]. Available at: http://www.icc-cpi.int/library/cases/ICC-01-04-01-06-2_tEnglish.pdf [accessed: 2 December 2008].

ICC 2007a. *Pre-Trial Chamber I, Prosecutor's Application under Article 58* ICC-02/05-56 27-02-2007 1/94 EO PT [Online]. Available at: http://www.icc-cpi.int/library/cases/ICC-02-05-56_English.pdf [accessed: 2 December 2008].

ICC 2007b. *Pre-Trial Chamber I, Situation in Darfur, Sudan, Warrant of Arrest for Ahmad Harun* ICC-02/05-01/07-2-Corr [Online, 27 April]. Available at: http://www.icc-cpi.int/library/cases/ICC-02-05-01-07-2-Corr_English.pdf [accessed: 2 December 2008].

ICC 2007c. *Pre-Trial Chamber I, Situation in Darfur, Sudan, Warrant of Arrest for Ali Kushayb* ICC-02/05-01/07-3-Corr [Online, 27 April]. Available at: http://www.icc-cpi.int/library/cases/ICC-02-05-01-07-2_English.pdf [accessed: 2 December 2008].

ICC 2008a. *Stay of Proceedings in the Lubanga Case is Lifted— Trial Provisionally Scheduled for 26 January 2009* [Online: ICC press release]. Available at: http://www.icc-cpi.int/press/pressreleases/445.html [accessed: 29 November 2008].

ICC 2008b. *Combined Factsheet, Situation in the Democratic Republic of the Congo Germain Kaatanga and Mathieu Ngudjolo Chui* [Online]. Available at: http://www.icc-cpi.int/library/organs/otp/ICC-OTP-FS-20080207_ENG.pdf [accessed: 29 November 2008].

ICC 2008c. *Summary of the Prosecutor's Application under Article 58* ICC-02/05-152 14-07-2008 [Online]. Available at: http://www.icc-cpi.int/library/cases/ICC-02-05-152-ENG.pdf [accessed: 2 December 2008].

ICC 2008d. *Summary of the Prosecutor's Application under Article 58* ICC-02/05-162 20-11-2008 [Online]. Available at: http://www.icc-cpi.int/library/cases/ICC-02-05-162-ENG.pdf [accessed: 2 December 2008].

International Herald Tribune 2008. *Jean-Pierre Bemba, Former Congo Warlord, Arrested in Belgium* [Online, 25 May]. Available at: http://www.iht.com/bin/printfriendly.php?id=13183970 [accessed: 29 November 2008].

International Law Commission 1950. *Yearbook of the International Law Commission*, Volume II [Online]. Available at: http://untreaty.un.org/ilc/publications/yearbooks/1950.htm [accessed: 2 December 2008].

International Law Commission 1994. *Yearbook of the International Law Commission*, Volume II, Part 2 [Online]. Available at: http://untreaty.un.org/ilc/publications/yearbooks/1994.htm [accessed: 2 December 2008].

Inter-press Service 1998. *Terra Viva No. 1* [Online]. Available at http://www.icc-cpi.int/legaltools/download.php?p=L0QuIElDQyBwcmVwYXJhdG9yeSB3b3Jrcy80LiBVbml0ZWQgTmF0aW9ucyBEaXBsb21hdGljIENvbmZlcmVuY2UvMTk5OC8xOTk4MDYxNV9OR09fSU5URVJQUkVTU1NFUlZJQ0VldGFsKEUpLnBkZg== [accessed: 2 December 2008].

IRIN 2005a. *UGANDA: Army to Hunt for LRA Rebels Inside Sudan* [Online]. Available at: http://www.globalsecurity.org/military/library/news/2005/10/mil-051011-irin04.htm [accessed: 29 November 2008].

IRIN 2005. *Sudan: Judiciary Challenges ICC over Darfur Cases* [Online]. Available at: http://www.irinnews.org/report.aspx?reportid=55068 [accessed: 2 December 2008].

IRIN 2006. *LRA Leaders not Entitled to Amnesty—Minister* [Online]. Available at: http://www.irinnews.org/report.aspx?reportid=58805 [accessed: 2 December 2008].

Kaul, H. 1998. Special Note: The Struggle for the International Criminal Court's Jurisdiction. *European Journal of Crime, Criminal Law and Criminal Justice* 6(4), 48–60.

Silverstein, K. 2005. Official Pariah Sudan Valuable to America's War on Terrorism Despite Once Harboring Bin Laden, Khartoum Regime has Supplied Key Intelligence, Officials Say. *Los Angeles Times* [Online]. Available at: http://articles.latimes.com/2005/apr/29/world/fg-sudan29 [accessed: 2 December 2008].

The New Vision 2004. ICC may Drop LRA Charges [Online]. Available at: http://www.newvision.co.ug/D/8/12/400006 [accessed :2 December 2008].

The New Vision 2005. LRA Talks Over, says Bigombe [Online]. Available at: http://www.newvision.co.ug/D/8/12/460057 [accessed: 2 December 2008].

The New Vision 2006a. Kony Flees into Congo [Online]. Available at: http://www.newvision.co.ug/D/8/12/480338 [accessed: 2 December 2008].

The New Vision 2006b. Museveni gives Joseph Kony Final Peace Offer [Online]. Available at: http://www.newvision.co.ug/D/8/12/498862 [accessed: 2 December 2008].

Nyakairu, F. 2006. International Criminal Court Opposes Museveni Peace Offer to Kony. *The Monitor* [Online]. Available at: http://allafrica.com/stories/200605180694.html [accessed: 19 May 2006]

Risse, T. and Sikkink, K. 1999. The Socialization of International Human Rights Norms into Domestic Human Practices: Introduction, in *The Power of Human Rights: International Norms and Domestic Change*, edited by T. Risse, S. Ropp, and K. Sikkink. New York: Cambridge University Press, 1–38.

Rozenberg, J. 2008. Why the World's Most Powerful Prosecutor Should Resign, Part 3. *Telegraph UK* [Online]. Available at: http://www.telegraph.co.uk/news/newstopics/lawreports/joshuarozenberg/2700862/Why-the-worlds-most-powerful-prosecutor-should-resign-Part-3.html [accessed: 30 November 2008].

Schabas, W. 2004. *Introduction to the International Criminal Court*, 2nd edition. New York: Cambridge University Press.

Schiff, B. 2008. *Building the International Court.* New York: Cambridge University Press.

Stoelting, D. 1999. NGOs and the ICC. *World Order Under Law*. Downloaded 2006 from http://www.morganlewis.com/PDFs/21CC52F7-B792-40C0-813FE3CCBC45F981_PUBLICATION.PDF [no longer online].

Sudan Tribune 2005 Sudan's Cabinet Rejects UN Resolution on ICC Trials [Online, 4 April]. Available at: http://www.sudantribune.com/article.php3?id_article=8865 [accessed: 30 November 2008].

UN General Assembly 1948. *Convention on the Prevention and Punishment of the Crime of Genocide*. Resolution 260 A (III) of 9 December 1948.

UN General Assembly. 1994. *Establishment of an International Criminal Court*. Resolution 49/53.

UN Security Council 2005. *Resolution 1593 Press Release* [Online]. Available at: http://www.un.org/News/Press/docs/2005/sc8351.doc.htm [accessed: 4 December 2008].

US House of Representatives 2005. *Committee on International Relations, Subcommittee on Africa, Global Human Rights and International Organizations, 109th Congressional 1st Session. 1 November 2005 Serial No. 109—115. Sudan: Losing Ground on Peace?* [Online]. Available at: http://www.foreignaffairs.house.gov/archives/109/24374.pdf [accessed: 4 December 2008].

Chapter 5
The Responsibility to Protect: Embracing Sovereignty *and* Human Rights

Cristina G. Badescu

> If humanitarian intervention is, indeed, an unacceptable assault on sovereignty, how should we respond to Rwanda, to Srebrenica—to gross and systematic violations of human rights that offend every precept of our common humanity? (Annan 2000, 48)

This much-cited quotation captures the dilemma of the humanitarian intervention debate, and, in turn, the conundrum of the two allegedly opposing sets of norms in international law: sovereignty and human rights. On the one hand, the fundamental international law principle of sovereignty inhibits intervention into the internal affairs of states, and on the other hand, there is a growing concern that the international community should react to massive and systematic violations of human rights by any state. At the 54th session of the UN General Assembly in 1999, the former UN Secretary-General, Kofi Annan, challenged member states to "prevent another Rwanda" and urged them to reach consensus on the issue of humanitarian intervention.[1] In response to his challenge, in 2000, the Government of Canada established an independent commission, the International Commission on Intervention and State Sovereignty (ICISS),[2] to focus on solving the humanitarian intervention conundrum. The ICISS report, *The Responsibility to Protect*, was released in December 2001, together with a supplementary volume detailing the extensive research on the topic.

The responsibility to protect, known by its acronym, R2P, was labeled "new thinking" (e.g., Weiss 2007, 88) because it recognized the changing nature of threats in today's world, the changing character of contemporary war, and the new ways of thinking about state sovereignty, human rights, and domestic jurisdiction. R2P acknowledged the inadequacy of existing norms in addressing such threats and thus the need for "new rules of the game" (Thakur 2005, 122) to replace them. R2P has also been characterized as a "new declaratory commitment to protect

1 In his address to the General Assembly, Kofi Annan requested the international community to "find common ground in upholding the principles of the UN Charter, and acting in defence of our common humanity."

2 Hereafter, the International Commission on Intervention and State Sovereignty will be referred to as the ICISS, or the Commission.

endangered populations" (Wheeler 2005, 12), and as a "normative innovation" (Brunnee and Toope 2006, 2). The UN Secretary-General, Ban Ki-Moon (2008), has called R2P "a solemn commitment by the international community...[and] a profound moral imperative in today's world," and has also created two new positions, closely related to the application of the R2P.[3] A new Global Centre for the Responsibility to Protect was launched mid-February 2008, with a declared mission to move R2P from principle to practice.

And yet, there is no consensus on what R2P represents and no agreement on the stage R2P has reached in its normative evolution towards becoming a new norm of international law. Much skepticism continues to surround R2P from different perspectives. There is no doubt, however, that in historical terms, the evolution of the R2P is an impressive example of an idea moving from the level of concept, as stated in the ICISS report of December 2001, to an official endorsement by heads of state in September 2005 at the United Nations World Summit. This acceptance by UN member states of an international responsibility to protect is significant because it confers upon the international organization a permissive right to carry out civilian protection tasks in peace and security missions.[4] Their backing marks a milestone in the evolution of the R2P principle, as it expresses the possibility of having states called upon to react militarily to stop genocides and mass atrocities, as part of their "international responsibility to take collective action." Even if the inclusion of the R2P in a General Assembly resolution is not paramount to a legal obligation, it provides the foundation for taking action when political will exists. It also translates into universal acknowledgment of the existence of the R2P principle by all 192 member states. The fact that the internal situation of member states has become a legitimate discussion topic in the UN arena advances the framework of an articulated principle, which now places expectations on member states to react, when serious triggers occur.

This chapter focuses on the "responsibility to protect" (R2P), and explains how this principle redefines sovereignty in an attempt to reconcile it with the need to respect human rights. It is in the context of the movement toward a broader understanding of the term sovereignty and a greater concern for human rights that R2P emerged. Given that Chapter 1 covers the evolving, post-Cold War relationship between state sovereignty and human rights issues at length, this chapter does not analyze the two, but instead discusses the relationship R2P envisaged between sovereignty and human rights. As such, after a brief description of what R2P entails, the focus will be placed on exploring the extent to which R2P encompasses a workable relationship between sovereignty and human rights, as designed in the 2001 ICISS report and subsequently embraced by the United Nations in September 2005.

---

3 That of the Special Representative of the Secretary General for the Prevention of Genocide and Mass Atrocities (Francis Deng) and that of Special Advisor on matters relating to R2P (Ed Luck), with the latter specifically assigned to translating R2P into practice.

4 See United Nations, *World Summit Outcome Document*, A/60/L.1, 15 September 2005, paras 138 and 139.

R2P: Explaining the Conceptual Domain

The R2P report addresses the large and growing gap between the codified practice of international behavior as articulated in the UN Charter, whose explicit language emphasizes the importance of state sovereignty, and actual state practice, starting with the 1990s, which underlines the limits of sovereignty and the need to protect human rights (ICISS 2001a, 15). There is general agreement that one of the major contributions of the R2P report to the intervention debate belongs to the conceptual domain (e.g., Acharya 2002; Evans 2004; Thakur 2006). The novelty of the R2P approach to humanitarian intervention comes from the way in which the ICISS had phrased the underlying inquiry of the report, focused on reaching consensus on what to do when faced with genocide, ethnic cleansing, mass crimes, and crimes against humanity.

The R2P report changed the conceptual language from "humanitarian intervention" to "responsibility to protect" in order to move away from the impasse reached by the "right to intervene" debate. The ICISS sought to overcome the sovereignty-humanitarian intervention dichotomy through a reinterpretation of sovereignty. The Commission hoped that the new language replacing the controversial "humanitarian intervention" terminology would bring about constructive engagement on the part of the opponents, as it had happened in the past, for instance with the Brundtland Commission's concept of "sustainable development." The new language also signals a change in focus from the prospective interveners to the civilians in need of protection, in addition to placing the emphasis on the duty of others to protect those who are suffering and need support (ICISS 2001a, 17). This occurred in a context in which broader security concepts were shifting from national to human security.

The central normative tenet of the ICISS report is that state sovereignty entails responsibility and, therefore, each state has a responsibility to protect its citizens from mass killings and other gross violations of their rights. However, if that state is unable or unwilling to carry out that function, the state abrogates its sovereignty, and the responsibility to protect falls to the international community. The ICISS, then, identified two key aspects of the R2P: state sovereignty as responsibility, and international responsibility in instances of genocide, ethnic cleansing, mass crimes, and crimes against humanity. Another conceptual contribution of the R2P report was to design the responsibility to protect umbrella as encompassing three distinct components, namely the "responsibility to prevent", the "responsibility to react" and the "responsibility to rebuild". The report includes separate chapters on the continuum of the obligations to prevent gross violations of human rights from arising, the responsibility to react to them when they occur, and the responsibility to rebuild after any intervention, thus clarifying that R2P entails more than solely humanitarian intervention. Other contributions of the ICISS report encompass the principles that must be satisfied before the most coercive form of reaction—military intervention—takes place.

The key assessment of the ICISS report is that sovereignty is best thought of not in terms of control—or viewed as an absolute term of authority—but rather in terms of responsibility. Theoretically, and to the extent suggested by the state practice of humanitarian interventions in the 1990s practically as well, this reinterpretation of sovereignty emphasizes the importance placed on respecting human rights. This approach is also strengthened by the increased impact of international human rights norms and the concept of human security in the international discourse (ICISS 2001a, 4–6, 13). The reconceptualization of sovereignty from control to responsibility has several implications: first, state authorities are responsible for protecting their citizens' lives and safety and for promoting their welfare; second, national political authorities are responsible both internally, to their citizens, and externally, to the international community, through the UN; and, third, the agents of the state are accountable for their actions, namely for their acts of commission and omission (ICISS 2001a, 13). Francis M. Deng (1996) was the first to articulate the concept of sovereignty as responsibility to protect the people of a given territory, an approach which explicitly challenged what was regarded as the key principle of nonintervention. Many other scholars in the field subsequently adopted this idea (e.g., Teson 1997; Barkin 1998; Welsh 2002) and described sovereignty as responsibility as a new principle of international order (Etzioni 2006).

Extensive consultations around the world involving scholars and practitioners with very different views on intervention and state sovereignty defined a "long and grueling year of meetings" (ICISS 2001a, viii). Without doubt, gathering a very broad range of opinions was an essential requirement for a report that sought to identify new common ground on intervention. During the consultations that helped shape the report, the ICISS reached broad agreement among participants from both North and South countries that the "responsibility to protect people from killing and other grave harm was the most basic and fundamental of all the responsibilities that sovereignty imposes—and if a state cannot or will not protect its people.then coercive intervention for human protection purposes…may be warranted" (ICISS 2001a, 69). Thus, contrary to popular misconception, the Commission did not find widespread support for an unlimited, absolute view of sovereignty. Instead, both developed and developing countries agreed during consultations that "sovereignty implies a dual responsibility: externally, to respect the sovereignty of other states, and internally, to respect the dignity and basic rights of all the people within the state" (ICISS 2001a, 8). The participating delegations also shared the view that "the defence of state sovereignty, by even its strongest supporters, does not include any claim of the unlimited power of a state to do what it wants to its own people" (ICISS 2001a, 8).

The ICISS report found grounding for intervention under existing international law. As the report itself explains, R2P is grounded in a variety of legal foundations, such as the Genocide Convention, the Geneva Conventions, human rights treaty provisions, the International Criminal Court statute, in growing state practice, and the Security Council's own practice (2001a, 50). Concurrently, R2P also reflects an international context which has changed significantly since 1945, as a result of the "emerging practices of states, regional organizations and the Security Council itself" (ICISS 2001a, 7–8). The erosion of the absolute principle of national sovereignty is rooted in today's reality of global interdependence. In line with such transformations, human rights cease to be a purely domestic matter (ICISS 2001b, 146). The supplementary research volume of the report gives extensive details on the emerging challenges to the traditional concept of sovereignty. The R2P report explains the transformation from rights to responsibilities, which are associated with the new interpretations of state sovereignty.

The Need to "Strike a Balance" between Sovereignty and Human Rights

Basic assumptions intrinsic to the two contrasting legal concepts of sovereignty and human rights make military intervention for human protection purposes a challenging concern each time serious violations requiring such action occur. The tension between the two—despite being sometimes described as overplayed (e.g., Chesterman 2001; Acharya 2002)—is a constant in any discussion on humanitarian intervention and in all debates on finding ways to react to gross violations of human rights. This tension is also the foundation for the majority of arguments put forward by most critics of actions to protect civilians from egregious crimes occurring in other parts of the world. The obvious resolution would be to find a workable balance between the two norms.

For the most part, the sovereignty debates question whether the concept is absolute or not, whether it implies solely a legitimate authority, or if it also requires the power to perform that authority, and discuss the extent to which existing norms on sovereignty hinder the solution to key pressing issues today. Disagreements over the norm of state sovereignty also involve debating the interplay and the various degrees of importance assigned to the two major aspects of sovereignty, internal and external, and assess the current relevance of the so-called "demise" of the state. Sovereignty is frequently connected with the nonintervention principle. And yet, despite the fact that nonintervention is one of the most basic norms of international law, states have intervened in the affairs of other states in the past, for various reasons, including strategic interests, security of their territory, and humanitarian motives. As a result of the substantial evolution of the conditions under which sovereignty is exercised, an extensive literature on changing norms of sovereignty has appeared (e.g., Jackson 1990; Lyons and Mastanduno 1995; Krasner 1999). This literature covers the emerging challenges to the traditional interpretation of sovereignty, such as the broadened concept of international peace and security threats, the collapse of state authority, the importance placed on popular sovereignty, and new demands for self-determination (ICISS 2001b, 6–12). At present, sovereignty is no longer regarded as sacrosanct (e.g., Chopra and Weiss 1992).

Just as the meaning of sovereignty as an international legal concept has evolved the human rights regime has evolved as well. A phenomenon of the twentieth century, the focus on individual human rights has materialized into a proliferation of human rights agreements since the Second World War (Krasner 1999, 109). The last five decades show an increased recognition of the importance of adopting a human rights perspective in all policy areas, at all levels, along with the gradual acceptance of individual criminal responsibility for gross violations of human rights. Such developments encourage some legal scholars to argue that respecting human rights has gradually became one of the main concerns of the international community in the post-Cold War era. As such, obligations to respect human rights have started to imply the right to take action to enforce it (e.g., Cassese 1999, 26). And yet, the debate over universal human rights versus cultural relativism remains a constant challenge for all efforts to find the balance between sovereignty and human rights.

Being a member of the international society does imply that a state has to respect human rights. When a state fails to do so, the international community has the responsibility to take action to protect the rights of those affected by internal strife, and this includes, as last resort, military intervention for humanitarian purposes. The language of human rights that has been used to justify the increased number of humanitarian interventions in the 1990s supports the norm of sovereignty as responsibility. It is also illustrative of how "the old rules [of international legal sovereignty] do not suffice" (Cohen 2004, 24) and of the consequential need to rethink them.

Even so, reaction to large-scale violations of human rights remains limited by the explicit language of the UN Charter highlighting the respect owed to state sovereignty. Most criticisms of the current legal system governing intervention regard it as morally inadequate, for privileging the principle of sovereignty. The UN itself faces a major difficulty, namely finding ways to reconcile its foundational principle of member states' sovereignty and the primary mandate to maintain international peace and security, "to save succeeding generations from the scourge of war," with the equally compelling mission to promote the rights and welfare of people within those states (e.g., Evans 2004). This quandary has been described in the relevant literature as an "unacceptable gap" (e.g., Makinda 1996, 2002; Buchanan 2003, 2004; Teson 2003; Frank 2003). The purpose of the following section is to examine whether R2P, in the format expressed in the 2001 ICISS report, properly addresses this gap, and how it meets the main objections to humanitarian intervention. Such analysis will also assess the extent to which the R2P report strikes a workable balance between the two norms of state sovereignty and respect for human rights.

The R2P Balance: Addressing the Main Objections to Humanitarian Intervention

R2P's Response to Relativism

The ICISS was designed to reconcile both the tension, in principle, between sovereignty and humanitarian intervention, and the opposing perspectives on intervention in the policy world. The composition of the commission was a reflection of these goals.[5] The commission was inclusive and balanced, as suggested by the commissioners' dissimilar backgrounds and positions on the sovereignty-intervention debate. It represented both industrialized and developing countries' perspectives, and it was also diverse as per continent-inclusions and civilizations (Thakur 2006, 248). Furthermore, the ICISS was an independent body, and produced its report after extensive consultations and round tables held on all continents and in the major capitals around the world, as suggested by the supplementary research volume of the R2P report. The ICISS report's deference to both norms is a reflection of the consultation process involving participants with various backgrounds and from different continents.

This was the context in which military intervention for humanitarian purposes was canvassed by the ICISS, and only in respect to extreme cases (ICISS 2001a, 32), where issues of cultural relativism *do not* arise. The R2P's insistence that humanitarian intervention is to be "an exceptional and extraordinary measure" represents a key feature of the R2P report, designed to address the main objections *vis-à-vis* the potential for abuse of humanitarian intervention justifications (e.g., Acharya 2002, 374; Thakur 2006, 254). That is, the R2P report describes the use of force to protect human rights as an extreme measure, justified only in cases of egregious circumstances. As such, some scholars have praised the report for advancing "standards and benchmarks with admirable caution" (e.g., Malone 2003, 1001). R2P emphasizes that the rights described in humanitarian law and human rights law apply to all human beings, because they *are* universal. As opposed to rights such as freedom of expression or assembly, which might be more controversial, and less clear-cut as a consequence, "there can be no argument that the rights to freedom from arbitrary killing, genocide and torture apply equally to all people in every situation, in every corner of the globe" (ICISS 2001b, 145).

Genocide and ethnic cleansing of the type seen in Rwanda, Bosnia and Kosovo are the "most egregious expressions of discriminations and the ones that entail large enough losses of life to constitute…a trigger for humanitarian intervention" (ICISS 2001b, 145). In the words of the R2P report, the two key triggers are: "A. large scale loss of life, actual or apprehended, with genocidal intent or not…the product either of deliberate state action, or state neglect or inability to act, or a failed state situation; or B. large scale 'ethnic cleansing', actual or apprehended, whether carried out by killing, forced expulsion, acts of terror or rape" (2001a, xii).

Such thresholds suggest that the claim according to which sovereignty—understood as the sole defense the weak states have against the more powerful ones—is negatively affected by the reconceptualization of "sovereignty as responsibility" seems exaggerated. The ICISS report specifically emphasizes these two thresholds for intervention, whose primary purpose should be halting or averting human suffering (ICISS 2001a, 35). Thus, the commission discards any other triggers for military intervention that might, potentially, be used abusively to

5 The composition of the commission was balanced, starting with the two co-chairs, and it included UN officials, former foreign ministers, generals, journalists and scholars.

support the national interests of the interveners, while disguised as "humanitarian" endeavors. Accordingly, using force for the alteration of borders or for supporting a particular group's claim to self-determination, as well as for the overthrow of regimes, is not considered a genuine aim for humanitarian interventions (ICISS 2001a, 35).

Independent Statehood

While some have criticized the R2P approach for being too state-centered (e.g., Makinda 2004),[6] the sovereignty as responsibility thesis generally encourages others to announce the demise of the state,[7] given its acceptance of outside intervention in the internal affairs of a state. The R2P approach to sovereignty does pose important challenges to the traditional concept of sovereignty; however, it does not announce its demise. That is, the challenges covered in the R2P report are not tantamount to an abandonment of the discourse of state sovereignty. R2P actually reinforces the importance of state sovereignty, while acknowledging the changes in how sovereignty is accepted and perceived on the international stage and in evolving customary law. The Commission's focus on state sovereignty is in line with the relevant scholarly literature, which argues that the sovereignty discourse[8] remains the dominant one in international politics and international law (e.g., Werner and De Wilde 2001; Cohen 2004).

R2P reaffirms the nonintervention principle as default through its focus on independent statehood, and this is the primary way in which it meets any objection to humanitarian intervention. According to the report, "nonintervention…is the norm from which any departure must be justified…[and] exceptions to the principle of nonintervention should be limited" (2001a, 31–2). According to R2P, the responsibility to intervene in a state where extreme violations of human rights are taking place comes from the failure of that state to meet its responsibilities as a sovereign member of the international community. As such, the ICISS report encapsulates the shift in the culture of sovereignty from one of impunity to one of accountability and responsibility of states in light of their obligation to protect. The essence of this shift, however, entails reformulating, not abandoning, the

6 Samuel Makinda (2004) argues that despite recognizing, on the surface, the role of NGOs, the R2P report actually marginalizes the role of other relevant actors in the international society, such as NGOs, by placing too much emphasis on the state.

7 There is a variety of positions within this one side of the argument about the demise of the state: for instance, what Kurt Mills (1998) understands by the transformation suffered by the sovereign state as a result of the focus on human rights is different from what another proponent of the demise of the state thesis, David Chandler (2002), understands by the end of sovereign equality.

8 The sovereignty discourse evolved significantly from the imperial concept of sovereignty to that of popular sovereignty, according to which sovereignty now resides in the political will of a population, rather than in the will of its ruler or government.

default position of sovereignty and its correlate, the principle of nonintervention. The Commission's proposals respect what is important in sovereignty, namely the nonintervention principle as a basis for the international society, to protect against outside interference. As Ramesh Thakur appropriately noted, "the continuing validity of the nonintervention norm needed restatement and got it in R2P" (2006, 257).

The R2P report emphasizes that the main "responsibility to protect" lies with the state, which is illustrative of the role of the state as the primary level of action (2001a, xi, 17, 69). The focus of the ICISS on the prerogatives of the sovereign state rightly mirrored the continuing relevance of the sovereignty norm. The R2P report states that it is based on "the principles inherent in the concept of sovereignty… the impact of emerging principles of human rights and human security, and the changing state and intergovernmental practice" (2001a, 12). This is in line with the arguments of many scholars who suggest that, for the foreseeable future, the instruments providing security and welfare for their citizens will be offered by nation states (e.g., Beetham 1998; Howard-Hassmann 2005).

According to R2P, it is *only* when states fail to prevent or put an end to the gross human rights violations taking place within their borders that the responsibility to protect falls on the international community, as a second tier of responsibility (ICISS 2001a, 69).[9] To further highlight the enduring importance of states, the expectation to pick up the responsibility to protect innocent civilians elsewhere falls on *other states*; the international community, however, is not an abstract concept, but one which depends on its members—the society of states. As Shashi Tharoor aptly suggests, "the UN is both a stage on which member states have the starring roles and work out their relationships, partnerships and rivalries; and an actor implementing the decisions made on the stage by the member states" (cited in Thakur 2006, 344). In addition, if the UN is at a deadlock, which makes a Security Council authorization for intervention in instances "crying out for action" impossible, the responsibility for action falls, ultimately—and again—on states, which are part of regional organizations, or which form the so-called "coalitions of the willing."

Equality of States

Apart from emphasizing independent statehood, another way in which the R2P report meets the main objections to humanitarian intervention is by focusing on

9 Henry Shue best captures the need for this in an appropriate synopsis: "…to claim, on the one hand, that one believes that Hutu and Tutsi alike, like all persons, have a basic right not to be killed arbitrarily (genocidally or otherwise), but to claim, on the other hand, that it is the job of 'their' state to protect them, in accord with the customary international division of labour—each state, its own police—is not to be serious about implementing rights in the real world. If we do not believe that anyone beyond their own state can reasonably be asked to bear the responsibility of protecting these people against the single most serious threat to their lives—their own state—we do not believe in any practically meaningful way that they have a basic right not to be killed" (2004, 21).

the equality of states. And yet, critics of R2P have suggested that the "sovereignty as responsibility" thesis has negative consequences for sovereign equality. That is explained by the fact that sovereignty is the only shield that weak states have against the intrusive powerful ones, and so undermining state sovereignty results in generalized world disorder (e.g., Ayoob 2002; Chandler 2002). Critics of the approach to sovereignty as responsibility argue that a shift towards human rights replaces sovereign equality "with an abstract universality that can never be realized within the confines of contemporary society…[since] human rights can be nothing more than an empty concept" (Chandler 2002, 137). Others have suggested that "…if we assume that a constitutional, cosmopolitan legal order already exists, which has replaced or should replace international law and its core principles of sovereign equality, territorial integrity, nonintervention…with cosmopolitan right…and intervention as the enforcement of that right…we risk becoming apologists for imperial projects" (Cohen 2004, 3).

Such critics are correct to suggest that states relate to each other as equals through international law, and that sovereign equality is essential for the application of international law (see Chandler 2002, 136–7). However, the reconceptualization of sovereignty as responsibility does not translate, as some scholars wrongly imply, into a "redistribution of sovereign power; or [to put it differently, into] an acceptance of sovereign inequality" (Chandler 2002, 122). According to the R2P report, the redefinition of sovereignty does not imply a dismissal of sovereign equality—states continue to remain equal (2001a, 7). The principle of "sovereign equality" has constantly been updated as a result of the key transformative developments in international relations, which included sovereign states giving up their "sovereign" right to go to war, aggressive war becoming illegal, colonialism being deemed a violation of the principle of self-determination, sovereign states beginning to cooperate in a multiplicity of international institutions, and states accepting to be limited by human rights principles, renouncing thus their impermeability to international law in this domain (see Cohen 2004, 20).

As such, sovereignty is not an untouchable concept, but one which also encompasses responsibilities, in both internal functions and external duties (ICISS 2001a, 13), including responsibilities towards one state's own citizens. This affects a failed state, for instance, where the government is lacking authority and, therefore, the state lacks capacity to protect its citizens and needs help from outside. The fact that the sovereign status of this state is claimed and recognized by the international community, even under these circumstances, suggests that sovereignty, as a status, is never lost and therefore not "less equal" in this particular instance than in others. States that are involved in gross violations of their citizens' rights do, indeed, lose some of their "sovereign" attributes, but not in regard to their status as sovereign states; rather, they lose some of the rights and powers that come with it. While this is in agreement with the new rules of state sovereignty, it is not an indication of the abolition of sovereign equality.

Scholars have argued long ago that sovereignty is best tested in moments of crisis and in exceptional circumstances (e.g., Morgenthau 1948). More recently,

Werner and De Wilde suggested that the most fervent defenses of state sovereignty occur in times when "the freedom and independence of states is believed to be at stake" (2001, 284). Such arguments reinforce the idea that instances when a state's ability to rule and its autonomy are threatened, strengthen, rather than weaken, the claims to sovereignty. In light of the central question of this chapter, one can easily take up this argument and move it one step further. If one embarks on a theoretical exercise, "the next level" is represented by instances when gross violations of human rights are taking place, as a result of internal strife. This particular context is one clear example of sovereignty being at stake. Nonetheless, it is also an instance when state sovereignty is a claimed status, which is accepted and perceived as such by the international community. The very fact that the sovereign state represents the first tier of responsibility to stop gross human rights violations is the first indicator of the continuing importance of sovereignty, particularly in moments of crisis. It also illustrates that states are treated as equal, since the broad assessment regarding the "first tier responsibility" of sovereign states applies to *all* states.

Another major criticism against the practice of humanitarian intervention relates to some states being "more equal than others." This argument emerged from the syllogism that no major intervention is likely to occur, for instance, against the most powerful states, such as the five permanent members of the Security Council. This raises the important question of double standards, which, unfortunately, cannot be overridden since it is a matter of political reality. The R2P report acknowledges that the regime will be applied selectively: "the reality that interventions may not be able to be mounted in every case where there is justification for doing so, is no reason for them not to be mounted in any case" (2001a, 37). Nonetheless, such selectivity is just a realistic characteristic of today's world, and it signals no departure from the past when nonintervention was allegedly sacred, but never treated as such.

The emphasis of the R2P report on the sovereign state is accurately justified by considerations of risk of abuse with regard to humanitarian intervention, but also by practicalities regarding enforcement mechanisms for the human rights regime. It is precisely the prominence of sovereign states in enforcing human rights that deserves further consideration at this point.

Enforcement of the Human Rights Regime

The R2P report placed considerable emphasis on states because it correctly assessed that the most problematic of the various governance tasks in human rights is enforcement, and therefore, states' compliance is key in a context in which international institutions, such as the UN, have limited capacity to compel enforcement. The same focus on states was later on reflected by the embracement of R2P in the 2005 General Assembly resolution, and also present in subsequent Security Council resolutions of 2006 referencing the principle. Ultimately, states are the only actors capable of ensuring respect for international law and compliance with the human rights regime. That is, international law cannot be put into practice without states' consent. And yet, the enforcement of the human rights regime remains a critical problem, and the mechanisms in place appear insufficient and weak,[10] as suggested by the gross human rights violations that are presently taking place in various parts of the world, and by the lack of mobilization and political will to address them.

Despite the many controversial dimensions of the international human rights regime, one conclusion on which all opposing parties seem to agree is that international legislation is effective only if the law-making parties also consider provisions for enforcement and compliance. This generally occurs either by involving existing institutions, such as the International Court of Justice, or by generating treaty-specific bodies. So far, however, the international human rights regime has not forced the creation of effective enforcement mechanisms for compliance. The reason for this is a very obvious one: state sovereignty. The international legal system is founded on the concept of sovereignty and international obligation depends, after all, on the will of particular sovereign states. Indeed, individual states have to be willing to enforce international human rights norms.

In most cases, states are not willing to accept international supervision, and this applies not only to the obvious category of states with a bad record of respect for human rights, but also to states with a positive record, such as the United Kingdom and the United States. The enforcement of human rights by the international community relies on the sovereign will and the foreign-policy goals of states, which tend to give a relatively low priority to issues of human rights (e.g., Brown 1999; Ayoob 2002; Chesterman 2003). Furthermore, as Robert Jackson (2004) argues with respect to the responsibilities of statecraft, great power brings greater privilege, but also greater responsibility on the world stage. According to this view, states such as the US and the UK, for instance, have heavier responsibilities than others. This is an appealing argument, especially given the need for states to play a leading role in the enforcement of the human rights regime. However, as suggested above, it might well be the case that the very same states with "greater responsibilities" lack the political will to react.

Focusing on the role of individual states is important, given that sovereign states decide whether to ratify international human rights treaties in the first place, and whether they go through with implementation afterward. While some of the powers that used to be performed by states have moved upward to regional and international organizations, others have shifted toward NGOs, and even individuals. Even so, while international organizations and NGOs push for compliance, it is *individual states* that have to put human rights norms into practice. Indeed, if one examines the success of the European human rights regime as compared to the modest accomplishments of the other regional regimes, it is clear that the first owes its achievements, to a great extent, to the voluntary acceptance of the regime by its member states. European states are nationally committed to respecting human

10 The European human rights regime is the exception, with strong and effective mechanisms of compliance and enforcement in place.

rights, and are, thus, very supportive of international procedures *vis-à-vis* human rights. Undoubtedly, the European regime has strong enforcement mechanisms; however, the power of the European states' deliberate compliance to the human rights regime is also critical.

Having rules about the responsibility to protect and using the R2P language in diplomatic circles are hardly enough. What matters most is to get the necessary political commitment right, in order to implement the R2P guidelines. It is in regard to such issues that another merit of the ICISS report emerges; one chapter of the R2P report—Chapter 8—deals exclusively with key considerations regarding implementation. This chapter acknowledges that without mobilizing the political will when action is needed, "the debate about intervention for human protection purposes will largely be academic" (2001a, 70). And so, if the R2P rhetoric is not matched by reality, R2P's contribution risks being reduced solely to a theoretical one, generally associated with reports and declarations. The ICISS report recognizes that paper rights are meaningless for victims of atrocities, without ways to impose compliance; the problem, however, is that human rights and humanitarian law "say little about the role of other states in insuring compliance" (2001b, 146).

The R2P report emphasizes that *national* commitment to respect human rights is both an essential component of a strong human rights regime, and the source of the political will that lies behind strong regimes. The most important steps of the human rights regime, namely the move towards implementation and enforcement, require a significant qualitative increase in states' commitments to human rights. R2P rejects the views advanced by some opponents of the "sovereignty as responsibility" principle, according to which human rights treaties and conventions fundamentally violate the essential sovereign attributes of a state. As Stephen Krasner (1999) aptly points out, states voluntarily enter into conventions on human rights, as equal actors on the world stage, and therefore willingly authorize external monitoring procedures that might come with signing such conventions. This is in itself a validation of a state's international legal sovereignty, and therefore contradicts the criticism according to which human rights are in direct opposition to state sovereignty.

Conclusion

This chapter took a closer look at the correlation between sovereignty and human rights, as advanced by R2P. One of the most notable contributions of the R2P report toward solving the sovereignty-human rights dilemma is its rejection of the argument that intervention and sovereignty are essentially irreconcilable concepts, which should therefore be perceived as contradictory. The ICISS report suggests that sovereignty and intervention should be viewed as complementary, rather than at odds. It proposes to solve the frustrating, traditional conflict of placing human rights and state sovereignty in permanent opposition to each other by arguing that human rights and state sovereignty can be intertwined. The report contradicts the assumption that respect for human rights runs counter to sovereignty practice, mainly in developing countries (e.g., Ayoob 2002), explaining instead how the two components are actually interrelated. Within the three types of sovereignty, namely internal, external, and what is generally referred to as "individual" or "popular" sovereignty (Annan 2000; Makinda 2004), the last one rests on the recognition of human rights (ICISS 2001b, 8–11). That is, individual sovereignty is based on the claim that all individuals are equal and entitled to the same fundamental freedoms and rights.

The reinterpretation of sovereignty as responsibility, which focuses on what sovereignty obliges versus what it endows, is one of the key values of R2P. The essence of this new approach to sovereignty is not so much control as responsibility. Such responsibility is owed by the state to its citizens, to the international community, and to the institutions representing it. As such, it becomes more difficult for states to hide behind the concept of sovereignty in order to conduct widespread violations of their populations' human rights.

I have dubbed the relationship between sovereignty and human rights put forward by the R2P report as balanced, because it expresses deference to both state sovereignty and protection of human rights. The ICISS report identified the problems related to the traditional meaning of sovereignty and made recommendations accordingly, in a successful effort to accommodate universal respect for human rights, in regard to extreme humanitarian emergencies. Should it have placed more emphasis on sovereignty at the expense of human rights, the balance would have inclined toward a no-longer morally sustainable, absolutist, state-focused approach. Instead, R2P's depiction of sovereignty implies a very clear-cut, dual responsibility: internally, toward one state's population, and externally, toward other states, as a member of the society of states. The focus of the R2P report on relativism, independent statehood, and the equality of states had the double purpose of putting forward a workable balance between sovereignty and human rights, and of addressing the main objections to humanitarian intervention.

The envisaged relationship between the two norms appears apposite from human rights considerations as well. Should the R2P report have focused more on the human rights module in light of the constantly increasing public discourse emphasizing human rights and human security, the balance would not have remained a workable one. More importantly, it would not have been politically achievable. Limiting the sovereignty emphasis would have given rise to selectivity and abuse *vis-à-vis* intervention for humanitarian purposes, and it would have clearly failed to capture the endurance of the sovereignty norm. Also, more emphasis on human rights would have given more leverage and fed the worries of those convinced that "[h]e who invokes humanity wants to cheat" (Carl Schmitt cited in Cohen 2004, 4). Furthermore, the latter scenario would have never been accepted by developing countries and by some of the permanent members of the Security Council that are still deeply committed to the traditional meaning of sovereignty, such as Russia and China.

In sum, the most important characteristic of the balance between sovereignty and human rights advanced in the R2P report results from the focus on the durability of state sovereignty. The ICISS report's emphasis on the state and its reinterpretation of sovereignty as responsibility are justified by two key motives: the need to appease the claims regarding the potential for abuse of humanitarian intervention, and the practicalities related to the enforcement mechanisms of the human rights regime. Without doubt, the meaning of the responsibility to protect, as expressed in the ICISS report, and in subsequent formulations of the R2P at the UN, encompasses deference to both sovereignty *and* human rights.

References

Abbott, K. W. and Snidal, D. 2000. Hard and Soft Law in International Governance. *International Organization* 54 (3), 421–56.

Acharya, A. 2002. Redefining the Dilemmas of Humanitarian Intervention. *Australian Journal of International Affairs* 56 (3), 373–81.

Annan, K. 2000. "*We the Peoples": The Role of the UN in the 21st Century*, A/54/2000, Millennium Report of the Secretary-General.

Ayoob, M. 2002. Humanitarian Intervention and State Sovereignty. *The International Journal of Human Rights* 6 (1), 81–102.

Barkin, S. 1998. The Evolution of the Constitution of Sovereignty and the Emergence of Human Rights Norms. *Millennium* 27 (2), 229–52.

Beetham, D. 1998. Human Rights as a Model for Cosmopolitan Democracy, in *Re-Imaging Political Community: Studies in Cosmopolitan Democracy*, edited by D. Archibugi et al. Cambridge: Polity Press, 58–71.

Brown, C. 1999. Universal Human Rights: A Critique, in *Human Rights in Global Politics*, edited by T. Dunne and N. Wheeler. Cambridge: Cambridge University Press, 103–27.

Brunnee, J. and Toope, S. J. 2006. Norms, Institutions and UN Reform: The Responsibility to Protect. *Behind the Headlines. Canadian Institute of International Affairs* 63 (3), 1–22.

Buchanan, A. 2003. Reforming the International Law of Humanitarian Intervention, in *Humanitarian Intervention: Ethical, Legal and Political Dilemmas*, edited by J. L. Holzgrefe and R. Keohane. Cambridge: Cambridge University Press, 130–73.

Buchanan, A. 2004. *Justice, Legitimacy, and Self-determination: Moral Foundations for International Law*. Oxford: Oxford University Press.

Cassese, A. 1999. *Ex iniuria ius oritur*: Are We Moving Towards International Legitimation of Forcible Humanitarian Countermeasures in the World Community? *European Journal of International Law* 10 (1), 23–30.

Chandler, D. 2002. *From Kosovo to Kabul: Human Rights and International Intervention.* London: Pluto Press.

Chesterman, S. 2001. *Just Wars or Just Peace: Humanitarian Intervention and International Law*. Oxford: Oxford University Press.

Chesterman. S. 2003. Hard Cases Make Bad Law: Law, Ethics and Politics in Humanitarian Intervention, in *Just Intervention*, edited by A. F. Lang Jr. Washington, D.C.: Georgetown University Press, 65–84.

Chopra, J. and Weiss T. 1992. Sovereignty is no Longer Sacrosanct: Codifying Humanitarian Intervention. *Ethics and International Affairs* 6, 95–118.

Cohen, J. L. 2004. Whose Sovereignty? Empire Versus International Law. *Ethics & International Affairs* 18 (3), 1–24.

Deng, F. M. et al. 1996. *Sovereignty as Responsibility: Conflict Management in Africa.* Washington, D.C.: The Brookings Institute.

Etzioni, A. 2006. Sovereignty as Responsibility. *Orbis* 50 (1), 71–85.

Evans, G. 2004. *The Responsibility to Protect: Rethinking Humanitarian Intervention.* Paper presented at the 98th Annual Meeting, The American Society of International Law, Panel on "Rethinking Collective Action," Washington, D.C.

Frank, T. 2003. Interpretation and Change in the Law of Humanitarian Intervention, in *Humanitarian Intervention: Ethical, Legal and Political Dilemmas*, edited by J. L. Holzgrefe and R. Keohane. Cambridge: Cambridge University Press, 204–31.

Fraser, M. 2005. Sovereignty, International Law and Global Cooperation, in *Globalization and the Rule of Law,* edited by S. Zifcak. London: Routledge, 163–83.

Howard-Hassmann, R. 2005. The Second Great Transformation: Human Rights Leapfrogging in the Era of Globalizations. *Human Rights Quarterly* 27 (1), 1–40.

International Commission on Intervention and State Sovereignty. 2001a. *The Responsibility to Protect: Report of the International Commission on Intervention and State Sovereignty*. Ottawa: International Development Research Centre.

International Commission on Intervention and State Sovereignty. 2001b. *The Responsibility to Protect: Report of the International Commission on Intervention and State Sovereignty*. Supplementary Volume. Ottawa: International Development Research Centre.

Jackson, R. 1990. *Quasi-states: Sovereignty, International Relations and the Third World.* Cambridge: Cambridge University Press.

Jackson, R. 2004. Sovereignty as a Doctrine of Moderation, in *Power and Responsibility in World Affairs: Reformation versus Transformation*, edited by C. J. Nolan. Westport, CT: Praeger, 57–78.

Krasner, S. D. 1999. *Sovereignty: Organized Hypocrisy.* Princeton: Princeton University Press.

Krasner, S. D. 2001. Problematic Sovereignty, in *Problematic Sovereignty: Contested Rules and Political Possibilities*, edited by S. D. Krasner. New York: Columbia University Press, 1–23.

Lyons, G. M. and Mastanduno, M. (eds). 1995. *Beyond Westphalia? State Sovereignty and International Intervention.* Baltimore: Johns Hopkins University Press.

Makinda, S. M. 1996. Sovereignty and International Security: Challenges for the United Nations. *Global Governance* 2 (2), 149–68.

Makinda, S. M. 2002. The Global Covenant as an Evolving Institution. *The International Journal of Human Rights* 6 (1), 113–26.

Makinda, S. M. 2004. Debating Sovereignty and Intervention. *The Australian Journal of Political Science* 39 (2), 430–6.

Malone, D. 2003. Humanitarian Intervention: Ethical, Legal and Political Dilemmas. *The American Journal of International Law* 97 (4), 999–1002.

Mills, K. 1998. *Human Rights in the Emerging Global Order: A New Sovereignty?* London: Macmillan.

Morgenthau, H. 1948. *Politics Among Nations: The Struggle for Power and Peace.* New York: Knopf.

Philpott, D. 1995. Sovereignty: An Introduction and Brief History. *Journal of International Affairs* 48 (2), 353–68.

Secretary General, United Nations, Office of the Spokesperson 2008. *Secretary-General's Message on the Opening of the Global Centre for the Responsibility to Protect.* Available at: http://www.un.org/apps/sg/sgstats.asp?nid=3000 [accessed 30 June 2008].

Shue, H. 2004. Limiting Sovereignty, in *Humanitarian Intervention and International Relations,* edited by J. Welsh. Oxford: Oxford University Press, 11–28.

Teson, F. R. 1997. *Humanitarian Intervention: An Inquiry into Law and Morality.* 2nd edition. Irvington-on-Hudson, New York: Transnational.

Teson, F. R. 2003. The Liberal Case for Humanitarian Intervention, in *Humanitarian Intervention: Ethical, Legal and Political Dilemmas*, edited by J. L. Holzgrefe and R. Keohane. Cambridge: Cambridge University Press, 93–129.

Thakur, R. 2005. Freedom from Fear: Effective, Efficient, and Equitable Security, in *Irrelevant or Indispensable? The United Nations in the 21st Century*, edited by P. Heinbecker and P. Goff. Waterloo: Wilfrid Laurier University Press, 115–30.

Thakur, R. 2006. *The United Nations, Peace and Security: From Collective Security to the Responsibility to Protect.* Cambridge: Cambridge University Press.

Weiss, T. G. 2007. *Humanitarian Intervention: Ideas in Action,* Cambridge: Polity Press.

Welsh, J. 2002. From Right to Responsibility: Humanitarian Intervention and International Society. *Global Governance* 8 (4), 503–19.

Werner, W. and De Wilde, J. 2001. The Endurance of Sovereignty. *The European Journal of International Relations* 7 (3), 283–313.

Wheeler, N. 2005. *A Victory for Common Humanity? The Responsibility to Protect after the 2005 World Summit*. Paper Presented at a Conference on "The UN at Sixty: Celebration or Wake?" Faculty of Law, University of Toronto, 6–7 October 2007.

Chapter 6
Human Rights and Soft Law: Alternative Paths for New Challenges

Daniel B. Braaten[1]

Introduction

Globalization presents tremendous opportunities as well as challenges for human rights. The long-term impact of globalization on human rights may be positive as it may propel economic development, increase democracy, and enhance respect for the rule of law; on the other hand the short-term impact has the potential for negatively affecting human rights (Howard-Hassmann 2005). Part of the fear that economic globalization may have a harmful effect on human rights stems from the fact that transnational corporations (TNCs), have greatly expanded in economic power over the past several years. Accompanying this expansion in economic power is a global reach and real time functioning for TNCs that potentially allows them to operate outside the bounds of state based regulation (Ruggie 2004). This phenomenon has aroused concern amongst human rights advocates that the global integration of markets may have a detrimental effect on human rights (Brysk 2002). This then leads to the question of effective regulation of TNCs for their potential negative impact on human rights.

The regulation of corporate violations of human rights presents a variety of legal questions, such as to what extent international human rights law is applicable to TNCs (Clapham 2006; Steinhardt 2005), and to what extent TNCs are able to evade domestic regulation (Subedi 2003). The main problem is the traditional locations of authority for the governance of human rights, nation-states and international law, appear unable and unwilling to handle all of the issues surrounding TNCs and human rights. The main response to this issue has been advocacy for enforcement of rights through existing international institutions such as the WTO (Meyer 2003), or for the direct binding of corporations to international human rights law ("Beyond Voluntarism" 2002).

A common long-term goal for many advocates of human rights is for the increased legalization of human rights in international relations, which would entail not only subjecting more of international relations to human rights standards

1 The author would like to thank Noha Shawki and Michaelene Cox for their helpful comments. An earlier version of this chapter was presented at the International Studies Association Conference, San Francisco, March 2008.

but also increased enforcement of human rights through domestic and international courts (Forsythe 2006). This "hard law" approach to protecting human rights is laudable and has yielded considerable progress. On the other hand, the emphasis on hard law solutions may obscure the utility and practicality of non-binding or "soft law" approaches to protecting human rights. This may be especially true for newly emerging issues like business and human rights.

The focus of this chapter then will be on how "soft law" can be used to regulate TNCs and human rights. The argument that I put forward is that globalization has empowered both NGOs and TNCs to take on greater public roles. This process has altered the business and human rights agenda by increasing the number of relevant actors participating in the policymaking process. The inclusion of NGOs and TNCs in the policymaking process means that states must take into account the interest of non-state actors in the formation of international regulation thus decreasing some of their authority and challenging strict conceptions of state sovereignty. This pluralist policymaking environment favors soft law and decreases the likelihood of developing binding hard law measures. In essence, for the new challenges that TNCs represent for human rights soft law measures are, for the time being at least, the most politically feasible. This does not mean, however, that TNCs are completely unregulated since soft law measures are not just a substitute for hard law but have value in their own right and maybe in some cases superior than hard law approaches as means of protecting human rights. As Amartya Sen has argued:

> Public recognition and agitation (including the monitoring of violations) can be part of the obligations—often imperfect-generated by the acknowledgment of human rights. Also, some recognized human rights are not ideally legislated, but are better promoted through other means, including public discussion, appraisal and advocacy (2004, 319–20).

The rest of the chapter will flesh out these arguments in more detail. Specifically, it will proceed as follows: the first section will address how globalization has helped create a pluralist policymaking environment favoring soft law approaches and how that led to the tabling of the Draft Norms on the Responsibilities of Transnational Corporations and Other Business Enterprises with Regard to Human Rights (2003), otherwise referred to as "UN Norms." The second section will address the question of what soft law is and why soft law initiatives are created at the international level. The third section goes further into the issue of business and human rights focusing specifically on the structure and operation of the UN Global Compact (GC). Finally, the conclusion will evaluate how soft law approaches, specifically the GC, have faired in regulating TNCs and human rights.

Human Rights and the Global Public Domain

Globalization has redistributed a considerable amount of power from states to non-state actors such as TNCs (Matthews 1997). The transfer of power from national governments to corporations creates a whole new range of issues regarding human rights. The potential detrimental effects of TNCs derive from many sources: such as, forcing changes in domestic production that lead to exploitation of workers, the disruption to the environment and local communities that is often an externality of extractive industry activity, and providing support to corrupt and repressive host state governments.[2] The background condition for these issues is the challenge that TNCs represent to state sovereignty and the ability of states to regulate and control the flow of goods and services that cross their borders. As Susan Strange argued, "Where states were once the masters of markets, now it is the markets which, on many crucial issues, are the masters over the governments of states" (1996, 4).[3]

These effects and others have contributed to a growing backlash against the further integration of the world economy. According to John Ruggie there are three forces driving the globalization backlash, the unequal distribution of the benefits of globalization, the imbalance in global rule making, and a crisis in global identity (2003). These three factors along with the high profile violation of human rights by large transnational corporations[4] have converged to create a movement among NGOs and activists to hold large private economic actors accountable for their human rights impact. The public role of non-state actors such as TNCs and NGOs has increased considerably over time (Rondinelli 2002; Keck and Sikkink 1998). The increased interdependence of globalization has opened a political space where non-state actors such as NGOs and TNCs are able to have a seat at the table, along with national governments, when determining certain public policies. This space allows each actor to push their particular policy preferences meaning that states must concede some of their decision-making authority to accommodate the interests of these new actors.

This new political space has been described in a number of different ways. Sandrine Tesner identifies what she describes as a "metaspace" where non-state actors such as TNCs operate "separate and above that of the nation-state" (Tesner 2000, 26). According to Wolfgang Reinicke, it is global public policy networks

2 The operation of TNCs is not on balance purely negative for human rights and can possibly be beneficial and lead to improvements in the protection of human rights. See for examples, Spar 1998, Spar 1999, and Meyer 1998.

3 For an overview of the debate on the impact organizations like TNCs have on state sovereignty see Risse 2002.

4 Some of the more high profile cases include Shell's operations in Nigeria (Manby 1999) and Nike's use of subcontractors in developing countries (Conner 2001). For a broader perspective on the negative impact TNCs have on human rights see Interim report of the Special Representative of the Secretary-General on the issue of human rights and transnational corporations and other business enterprises 2006.

that have occupied the new political space, which are characterized by "loose alliances of government agencies, international organizations, corporations and elements of civil society…to achieve what none can accomplish on its own" (1999–2000, 44). John Ruggie provides the fullest explication of this new phenomenon, which he terms "the new global public domain," and is defined as "an increasingly institutionalized transnational arena of discourse, contestation, and action concerning the production of global public goods, involving private as well as public actors" (2004, 504). The various descriptions of this new political space focus on several similar elements: most important is the idea that non-state actors are becoming an important player in the public policy process, or as Ruggie claims, the production of global public goods.

With the addition of non-state actors the global policymaking process has taken on a highly pluralist nature with a variety of different actors with different, and often divergent, preferences. According to Abbott and Snidal, pluralist interactions are comprised of *demandeur* groups who try to increase the cost of violations and seek new normative arrangements and *resister* groups who try to block them (2000). According to this logic, NGOs as *demandeurs* will seek regulatory approaches, which legally bind corporations to follow international human rights standards (Raustiala 2005). On the opposite side business as *resister* groups will try to block those demands and push for self-regulatory measures. States, in an effort to maintain their sovereignty, have also generally resisted the efforts to increasingly bind TNCs to international human rights law as well as using domestic law to hold TNCs to international standards (Forsythe 2006).

This pattern is broadly consistent with the economic ideology of neo-liberalism, which advocates minimum government intervention in the marketplace.[5]

The interaction among *demandeurs* and *resisters* in the global public domain is reflected in the debate surrounding the UN Norms. The UN Norms have been described as the only nonvoluntary corporate social responsibility arrangement that has been accepted at the international level (Weissbrodt and Kruger 2003). The UN Norms, while maintaining that states still have the primary responsibility for protecting human rights, set out standards for businesses to follow, within their spheres of activity and influence, in numerous areas from security of persons to protection of workers rights to preservation of the environment. The UN Norms also require businesses to adopt internal compliance mechanisms and submit to periodic monitoring by the UN and other entities on their application of the provisions encompassed in the document (Ruggie 2007).

When the UN Sub-Commission on the Promotion and Protection of Human Rights approved the UN Norms many of the main international human rights NGOs expressed their approval. In fact a caucus of nearly 200 NGOs and civil society organizations issued a statement in support of the UN Norms (Osorio

5 As clarification the resistant is not advocating outright rejection of any regulation of TNCs for any negative social impact they may have but resistance to using domestic law to apply international standards.

2004). In addition, fifteen human rights NGOs, including Amnesty International, Human Rights Watch, Christian Aid and Oxfam GB among others, sent out a joint press release stating that they plan on using the Norms in their work protecting and promoting human rights (Human Rights Watch 2003). Business organizations, on the other hand, had the complete opposite reaction to the UN Norms than did the various human rights NGOs. For example, the International Chamber of Commerce (ICC) and the International Organization of Employers (IOE), in a statement to the member states of the UN Commission on Human Rights criticized the norms as vague and unclear. They also claimed the UN Norms would lead to the "privatization" of human rights by shifting the regulation of human rights from governments to business (International Chamber of Commerce 2004). There was significant resistance from states as well regarding the development of the UN Norms with the US leading countries such as the UK, Saudi Arabia, Egypt and India in an attempt to remove the issue from the agenda of the UN Commission on Human Rights altogether (Osorio 2004; Williams 2004). This attempt failed however as the full UN Commission on Human Rights did decide to examine the issue.

During the 60th session of the UN Commission on Human Rights in 2004 the UN Norms were put on the agenda. The Commission however, while recognizing that the issue was an important one, decided against adopting the proposal and claimed that the norms had no legal standing. The Commission did, on the other hand, request that the Secretary-General examine the issue of business and human rights, which led to the appointment of John Ruggie as special representative to the Secretary-General with a two-year mandate (which was extended) to thoroughly investigate the problem (Ruggie 2007).[6] The response by the Commission on Human Rights to effectively table the UN Norms reflects the pluralist nature of the policymaking process with regards to business and human rights. With both TNCs and States resisting efforts to directly bind businesses to human rights standards NGOs were not able to exert enough influence to overcome that resistance. The political realities are such that a soft law approach appears to be the only politically viable option. Ultimately the *demandeurs* were able to prevent a complete dismissal of the subject, which indicates that their position did have some influence and further indicating that the monopoly on decision-making authority that states once possessed has diminished.

6 The mandate of the special representative was to "identify and clarify" international standards regarding business and human rights and to submit "views and recommendations" that the UN Commission on Human Rights (now Human Rights Council) can look at (Ruggie 2007). The special representative has submitted a final report to the Council outlining a three-part framework on which to base the issue of business and human rights. The framework acknowledges that the main duty to protect human rights against abuses by business resides with the state, but corporations also have a responsibility to respect human rights and finally that there needs to better access for remedies for victims of human rights abuses (Ruggie 2008).

Soft Law: What and Why

In a review of various definitions of soft law Ulrika Morth identifies two main components of soft law, that the rules are not legally binding, and that it comes in many different forms (2004). The multiple forms of soft law derive from the interplay of the various structures of law with the substance or content of law (Shelton 2000). What this implies is that law can be placed on a continuum in which on the one side it comprises binding specific regulations with judicial enforcement and on the other pole non-binding promotional standards with non-judicial means of enforcement. The best articulation of this continuum was developed in a special issue of *International Organization*, where Abbott et al. developed a continuum of legalization in which the poles of the continuum represented hard and soft law. The continuum consisted of three categories: obligation describes the level at which the actor is bound by the particular rule or rules, precision illustrates to what extent the rules are defined, and delegation, which describes how the rules are interpreted, administered, and enforced (2000). Using this continuum, Abbot et al. identify soft law initiatives as having a non-legal obligation, vague as far as specification and precision is concerned, and relying on diplomacy or politics for interpretation, administration, and enforcement. Hard law initiatives, in contrast, are characterized as having binding legal obligations, defined and elaborated rules, and the delegation of administration, interpretation, and enforcement to third party authorities (2000).

When comparing soft law versus hard law it is easy to see why NGOs and activists advocate for hard law approaches since their goal is to increase the costs of violations to deter human rights abuses, hence the emphasis on enforceable legal penalties as opposed to simply relying on condemnation. The difficulty for NGOs in working with governments and international institutions to develop hard law regulation is that TNCs also play a role in the policy making process and usually are able to exercise more influence than NGOs. While hard law regulatory measures directly binding TNCs may be the preference for NGOs and activists, they are not the preference for business or states, thus creating a conflict among actors in the global public domain. One can see the divergent preferences among NGOs, TNCs and states in the debate over the UN Norms: whereas NGOs generally favored the UN Norms, TNCs and most states opposed them. With the preferences between NGOs and TNCs at odds regarding hard law regulation, and governments generally siding with business, it appears that agreement among all groups on direct hard law regulation of TNCs and human rights is unlikely in the immediate future (Ruggie 2001). It is in situations such as these where a soft law approach may be preferable to hard law.

According to Abbott and Snidal, interactions among actors who have divergent preferences are characterized by high contracting costs, such as high uncertainty and bargaining problems, because coming to an agreement is difficult since the distance actors must travel to find a compromise is significant. These factors are what make soft law initiatives more attractive since the contracting costs are lower

(2000). From the perspective of TNCs the uncertainty that surrounds their liability for real or potential violations of human rights is too great to acquiesce to binding regulation with significant legal penalties. Two concepts in particular create a significant amount of concern for TNCs, complicity and sphere of influence. Complicity revolves around the point at which a company may be held responsible for the actions committed by a third party (i.e. the use of private or government security forces). Sphere of influence refers to the various stakeholders that the company has a responsibility to (i.e. shareholders, employees). These issues are usually addressed with regards to a company's operation in a country with a repressive government known to commit human rights abuses or their management of their supply chain, which may involve hundreds of subsidiaries and contractors across many countries. The vague and potentially far reaching nature of these concepts give business organizations pause when considering the legally binding nature of initiatives such as the UN Norms (International Chamber of Commerce 2004). Another virtue of soft law from the perspective of states is that it has low "sovereignty costs" meaning states do not lose sufficient authority over decision-making processes (Abbott and Snidal 2000). The benefits of the soft law approach are that it can reduce sovereignty and contracting costs, thus getting an agreement, while maintaining some of the benefits of hard law by filling in the gaps in the particular regulatory environment and pointing the way to more acceptable binding rules. More specifically, soft law provides a framework for negotiations over common interests and values, which may set the stage for greater precision and specificity in the future (Chinkin 1989).

The Global Compact is an initiative that was able to reduce uncertainty for TNCs through its voluntary requirement. Although NGOs, have been, and are, critical[7] of the GC there are still a significant number of human rights NGOs that are members including Human Rights First, International Alert and Oxfam International (UN Global Compact 2008f). It is this (admittedly tenuous) compromise that has made the GC the main regulatory response by the UN to the problem of TNC impact on human rights. The question now becomes whether the GC has been effective as a soft law initiative? Has it filled the regulatory gap by developing specific standards for TNCs, especially in the areas of complicity and sphere of influence, and has it helped reduce uncertainty among the participants and thus pointing the way towards a hard law agreement?

---

7 Much of the NGO criticism of the Global Compact revolves around its non-binding voluntary nature, which they view as irrevocably dooming the initiative too little more than window-dressing (Utting 2002). For example, Ramesh Singh, the chief executive of ActionAid claims that GC "at the moment is so voluntary that it really is a happy-go-luck club" (quoted in Capdevila 2007). For thorough and specific criticism of the GC and its structure, see Human Rights First 2004.

Effectiveness of the Global Compact

The Global Compact: Process and Structure

The Global Compact is a voluntary multi-stake holder initiative composed of business, civil society, and labor organizations as well as six UN agencies. Its membership includes over 3,500 businesses and over 1,000 civil society organizations including, NGOs, labor unions, business associations, cities, and academic institutions (UN Global Compact 2008c). The GC is a horizontally integrated organization comprised of ten principles regarding human and labor rights, environmental protection and anti-corruption. The ten principles are all derived from various multilateral agreements including the Universal Declaration of Human Rights, The International Labour Organization's Declaration on Fundamental Principles and Rights at Work, The Rio Declaration on Environment and Development, and the United Nations Convention Against Corruption. The two main goals of the Global Compact are to get businesses to internalize these ten principles into their operations and to facilitate problem solving between the different participants to develop best practices for businesses to follow (Kell and Ruggie 1999; Ruggie 2002; Kell 2003).

The GC attempts to fulfill these goals through four methods: leadership, dialogue, learning, and outreach. Leadership acknowledges that for change to occur in business practice it must start from the top, that is, CEO commitment to the principles. The multi-stakeholder structure incorporates dialogue into the GC by creating an institutional forum for the various participants to work together. The GC is a learning network meaning that it not only purports to develop best practices for business but also to spread those practices to all its participants. Finally, outreach is achieved through projects at the local, country, regional, and sectoral level (Kell 2003).

Despite its relatively recent history the GC has already undergone significant restructuring. Although its main goals and methods remain the same, the governance of the GC has changed including the addition of various integrity and accountability measures. The institutional structure of the GC is comprised of six entities each charged with different tasks: a Leaders Summit, Local Networks, a Local Network Forum, a Global Compact Board, The Global Compact Office and Inter-Agency Team, and a Global Compact Foundation. The Leaders Summit is held triennially to review the progress of the GC and provide future direction. Local Networks are comprised of stakeholders at the local level that work on projects developing and implementing the principles. The Local Network Forum allows members of various local networks around the world to meet and share experiences. The Global Compact Board is composed of twenty members representing the main constituency groups of the GC and to providing continuous advice for the operation as a whole. The Global Compact Office is responsible for the management of the GC brand and implementation of its integrity measures while the Inter-Agency team is responsible for coordinating and internalizing the

GC principles within the UN as a whole. Finally, the Global Compact Foundation is responsible for retaining voluntary contributions from businesses and other sources for non-core related activities, which are funded through government sources (UN Global Compact 2005).

Arguably the more significant change that the GC has instituted in its brief history is the introduction of two integrity measures to help ensure accountability among the participants, especially business entities. One of the common criticisms leveled against the Global Compact is that it allows TNCs that have poor human rights records to "bluewash" themselves through association with the UN (Bruno and Karliner 2000). Despite its voluntary nature, the members of the GC realized that there needed to be some measures available to insure the integrity of the initiative and the UN in general.

The first integrity measure is the Communication on Progress annual reports (COPs). COPs require all GC participants to communicate on an annual basis about their progress in implementing the principles and undertaking partnership projects. Specifically, a COP must contain a statement of continued support for the GC and its goals from the CEO or senior executive, a description of actions the company has taken in implementing the principles and partnership projects, and a measurement of outcomes from those actions (UN Global Compact 2008g). The significant aspect of the COP policy is that after two years of non-communication a company will be declared inactive and removed from the GC website. As of January 2008 over 900 companies were delisted (UN Global Compact 2008b). While delisting companies is not meant as a form of regulation it does protect against "bluewashing" and punishes non-compliant companies in the sense that they will not gain the reputation benefits of the GC unless they are attempting to live up to their obligations.

The second integrity measure implemented by the GC has the potential to impose more severe reputational costs on companies, however there are several procedural hurdles that need to be overcome before it can be used. The second measure is simply a means for dealing with allegations of systemic or egregious abuses of the GCs principles and goals. Complaints against companies that have allegedly engaged in systemic and egregious abuses can be brought to the Global Compact Office (Office) where they will determine if the complaint is frivolous or not. If the complaint is not determined to be frivolous then the Office will request that the company respond to the complaints and include any actions taken to address the complaints.

The main goal of the Office in this situation is to engage in a dialogue with the company and the accuser to try to rectify the situation, but if the company refuses to engage in a dialogue within three months it may be listed as "inactive" and if the accusations against the company are so egregious that they are determined to be detrimental to the reputation of the GC, the Office reserves the right to in effect "delist" the company (UN Global Compact 2007c). While neither of these integrity measures are meant to substitute as compliance mechanisms they are meant to impose some costs on companies that are only seeking the reputation benefits of aligning themselves with the UN while failing to live up to the principles of the GC.

The structure and the process of the GC are oriented to developing best practices for businesses to implement in accordance with the 10 principles and to spread those principles throughout all companies and communities. The structure and the process of the GC is set up to provide specificity with regards to TNC activity and its impact on human rights, labor standards, the environment, and corruption. The make up of the GC overall fits with one of the main benefits of soft law, which is to fill in regulatory gaps, and it does this through the refinement and specification of standards for TNC activity through learning networks and partnership activity. The next question then is how is this process proceeding, i.e. how is the regulatory gap being filled and what standards and best practices are being developed in the area of TNC impact on human rights?

The Global Compact and Human Rights: Overall

The first two principles of the GC state that:

1. Business should support and respect the protection of internationally proclaimed human rights
2. Make sure they are not complicit in human rights abuses (UN Global Compact 2008e).

As was mentioned earlier, two of the issues that create uncertainty for business with regards to any type of binding hard law regulation in the area of human rights are complicity and sphere of influence. While Principle 2 specifically mentions the issue of complicity, businesses are also called upon to "develop an awareness of human rights and to work within their sphere of influence to uphold these universal values" (UN Global Compact 2008e). These two points do not do much to get at the nuances of concepts like complicity and sphere of influence, however the GC does contain specific processes, such as multi-stakeholder problem solving and partnership projects, which are aimed at specifying and refining those concepts, along with trying to minimize the negative impact TNCs may have on human rights.

The GC openly acknowledges the difficulty that presents itself for corporate activity in a globalized world regarding specific issues such as underage children working in factories, or operating in countries where gender discrimination is part of local or national law, or operations in countries where unions are outlawed (UN Global Compact 2008c). Dealing with these specific problems, and many others, represents the difficulty in trying to determine the parameters of concepts such as complicity and sphere of influence. However, determining practical ways to deal with these specific issues represents a potential benefit of the GC and a measure of its effectiveness.

The GC's approach to human rights and business is two-fold, to raise awareness about the impact businesses can have on human rights (both positive and negative) and develop practical ways in which businesses can support human rights and avoid complicity in human rights abuses (UN Global Compact 2008c). In fulfillment of this last step the GC has developed some practical tools for business to integrate human rights into their standard operating procedures. For example the GC in partnership with the Business Leaders Initiative on Human Rights, and the Office for the High Commissioner of Human Rights has developed a guideline for businesses on how to integrate human rights principles into their operations.

The guideline is a technical manual for implementing human rights standards into an established business management system. The guideline outlines seven management areas where businesses can implement human rights standards and how to actually put them into practice. The seven areas include: strategy, policies, processes and procedures, communications, training, measuring impact and auditing, and reporting (UN Global Compact 2006). The guideline is significant because it draws its recommendations from the experiences of several large firms who have attempted various methods for integrating human rights into their practices.

The GC has also produced a very comprehensive series of publications with case studies and policy reports on specific areas of concern. For example, the recent version of this series includes a detailed examination of the concepts of complicity and sphere of influence. The report acknowledges that the concept of a sphere of influence is not defined in international human rights law and its precise definition is determined through the interaction of companies, NGOs, and governments, however it acknowledges that the general understanding of the concept includes "the individuals to whom the company has a certain, political, contractual, economic or geographic proximity," and also situates the core of the businesses operation at the center of the sphere (UN Global Compact 2008a, 17). The report goes onto refine who is actually in a company's sphere of influence and also identify what particular type of human rights issues may emerge in the various sections within the sphere.

With regards to complicity the report acknowledges that complicity in human rights abuses "means that a company is participating in or facilitating human rights abuses committed by others, whether it is a state, a rebel group, another company or individual" (UN Global Compact 2008a, 19). The report also identifies four general situations in which a company may be complicit in human rights abuses. If there is a causal link, even indirectly, between a company's assistance to another entity and their violation of human rights then the company would be considered complicit in those violations. If a company is involved in a joint venture and knew, or should have known, about the violations committed by its partner then it can be considered complicit. If a company benefits from the opportunities created by human rights violations, even without providing any type of assistance to the perpetrators, that company may be considered complicit as well. Finally, if a company is silent or inactive in the face of serious violations of human rights it may also be considered complicit in those violations (UN Global Compact 2008a). As with the guideline for implementing human rights into business practices these publications derive their substance from the experiences of businesses trying to deal with these concepts in their everyday experiences.

Although these publications have helped to specify and refine specific concepts such as complicity and sphere of influence and have developed practical methods for implementing human rights into everyday practices, human rights are one of two areas (the other being corruption) where participants have made the least amount of progress (UN Global Compact 2008c). In order to provide more direction for the GC in the area of human rights the Global Compact Board approved the creation for a working group on human rights, chaired by the former UN High Commissioner for Human Rights Mary Robinson, with a mandate to provide advice on how business can implement human rights principles, among other functions (UN Global Compact 2007b). The establishment of the working group acknowledges that while the GC has been effective in developing and refining standards, implementation of those standards has lagged.

The Global Compact and Human Rights: Local

Overall the GC has contributed to the refinement and specification of important concepts such as complicity and sphere of influence as well as developing practical methods for businesses to implement human rights standards. Although these advances are derived from the practices of GC member companies and have been publicized, the actual operational impact has so far not kept pace. Two of the more significant developments stemming from the restructuring of the GC in 2005 were the creation of Local Networks and the COPs annual reports. Both of these components provide a way to evaluate the operational impact of these principles developed through the GC process.

There are over 75 GC Local Networks around the world composed of both local and international stakeholders who focus on advancing the principles of the GC at the local or national level. Since 2006 and 2007, there have been 49 reports from various local networks submitted to the GC outlining activities and initiatives that the network has undertaken over the past year (UN Global Compact 2008d). Seven of these networks addressed issues regarding business and human rights.[8] The most comprehensive approach with regards to advancing human rights was undertaken by the Colombian network.

The Colombian network is composed of 220 companies and civil society members. One of the main programs implemented by the Colombian network involves taking a full look at the complexities present for companies doing business in Colombian, including the country's ongoing conflicts, its lack of governmental capacity, and social deterioration in certain areas (UN Global Compact 2007a). One of the main components of the program is the in-depth learning module, which specifically deal with business operations in conflict zones and the management

8 The seven networks are located in South Africa, Colombia, India, Japan, Germany, Ukraine, and the United Arab Emirates.

and prevention of displacement of peoples as a consequence of a company's operations (UN Global Compact 2007a). The Colombian program is impressive in its scope and provides a model for other networks in that it addresses the specific human rights situations businesses face in Colombia and how to deal with them.

Along with the development of Local Networks the COPs annual reports also provide examples of how specific companies have advanced the principles of the GC. A search of the GC COP database shows that there have been over 4,000 COPs submitted to the GC from companies in over 100 countries. Over 1,700 of the COPs address human rights with roughly 1,500 of them providing a description as to how the company in question plans on implementing the GC principles in its operations. It is important not to overstate the detail of the COPs that have been submitted, as many are quite banal in their explanations regarding how companies are integrating human rights into their operations.[9] However, some of the reports have a great deal of specificity and detail. One of the more specific and thorough reports is from Hewlett-Packard, which identifies how the company has implemented human rights and labor rights principles into their operation.

Specifically the Hewlett-Packard report states that the company commits itself to the principles outlined in the Universal Declaration of Human Rights despite the fact that managers interviewed for the report did not especially understand what was contained within the concept of human rights (McElhaney and Hill 2003). This does not mean that Hewlett-Packard did not take human rights issues seriously it is just simply that they have internalized practices that respect human rights because they consider them good business practices. Some of those specific arrangements involve areas such as privacy and supply chain management. For example, the company requires its top 40 suppliers to adhere to the company's code of conduct. The downside of this process however, is that the code requires suppliers to abide by local laws with regards to labor issues, but does contain provisions on the use of forced labor and discrimination that may not be covered by local law (McElhaney and Hill 2003). The Hewlett-Packard report is an example of a company working to implement human rights principles into its operation and also highlights the difficulties involved with that process.

Conclusion

Soft law approaches are beneficial when the parties to the policy making process have significantly divergent preferences. Soft law arrangements reduce uncertainty for participants and help fill in areas where regulation is scarce. Further they also point the way to hard law initiatives that all participants can agree on. In the area of business and human rights the main players involved have widely divergent preferences, with NGOs favoring hard law regulation while TNCs generally favor

9 The last search was done on 15 December 2008. GC COP database can be found at http://www.unglobalcompact.org/COP/cop_search.html.

self-regulation or voluntary initiatives. States have been generally unwilling to place "their" TNCs directly under international law preferring domestic regulation instead. It is interesting to note in terms of the impact this has on state sovereignty that with the inclusion of non-state actors into the policy-making environment states have had to acknowledge the preferences of a variety of different actors therefore weakening their decision-making authority. On the other hand this inclusion of various actors with different policy preferences often leads to soft law regulatory outcomes, which actually reduce the sovereignty costs to states.

The UN as the centerpiece of the international human rights regime has developed two initiatives, one a hard law approach the other a soft law approach, to try to exercise some regulation over the issue, which has lacked any significant governance structures. The two initiatives are the UN Norms on the Responsibilities of Transnational Corporations and Other Business Entities with Regards to Human Rights and the Global Compact. The Norms have been met with significant resistance from the business community as well as some governments. While NGOs have been critical of the Global Compact it still enjoys significant participation from civil society actors as well as businesses. However, while participation in the GC from all the various stakeholders is important it is also necessary to determine if the GC is living up to the promises of a soft law initiative such as filling in regulatory gaps and pointing the way for more binding regulation in the future.

Regarding the first category, the GC appears to be serving a useful function especially in the refinement and specification of concepts such as complicity and sphere of influence. Through its multi-stake holder dialogues and learning networks the GC has been looking at those two concepts and trying to determine exactly when and where businesses should be held accountable for any potential negative impact on human rights that accrue from their activity. The downside of course is that even a cursory overview of the GC's Local Network reports and COPs annual reports shows the difficulty in dealing with these concepts when it comes to implementing human rights principles into a business's basic operations.

The second major benefit of soft law initiatives, aside from providing at least some cover for an issue area that lacks any serious regulatory framework, is that they may point the way to more binding regulation. The pathway to binding regulation is developed through the reduction of uncertainty courtesy of the interactions among the various participants in the soft law initiative. As far as pointing to any binding regulation for TNCs and human rights the GC appears to be a ways off. Using the three-category continuum of legalization developed by Abbott et al. (2000) one can see that the GC has not moved very far in the direction of hard law regulation. The only category in which the GC has potentially moved towards hard law is in the area of precision. For example, the work the GC has done trying to determine the parameters of complicity and sphere of influence are making it clearer what the responsibilities of business are in protecting human rights. The other two categories of the continuum, obligation and delegation, have not advanced toward the hard law side.

Globalization represents a double-edge sword for human rights. The long-term benefits that accrue from globalization such as economic growth and development may also help foster an environment in which human rights are afforded greater respect. On the other hand the short-term impact of globalization can be volatile and disruptive creating an environment in which inequality and exploitation occur. TNCs are the visible face of globalization and over the past decades they have greatly expanded in strength and capacity. The question of effective regulation of business and human rights is contentious with NGOs favoring binding hard law regulations, which TNCs and states resist. In a pluralist policymaking environment such as this the political reality is that binding hard law regulating business and human rights is unlikely. The alternative is a soft law approach as embodied in the Global Compact. Since soft law approaches help to reduce uncertainty and limit sovereignty and contracting costs they also can point the way to what hard law regulation may look like.

References

Abbott, K. W. et al. 2000. The Concept of Legalization. *International Organization* 54(3), 401–19.

Abbott, K. W. and Snidal, D. 2000. Hard and Soft Law in International Governance, *International Organization* 54(3), 421–56.

Beyond Voluntarism: Human Rights and the Developing International Legal Obligations of Companies. 2002. Versoix, Switzerland: International Council on Human Rights Policy.

Bruno, K. and Karliner, J. 2000. *Tangled Up in Blue: Corporate Partnerships at the United Nations*. San Francisco: Transnational Resource & Action Center [online]. Available at: http:///www.corpwatch.org/article.php?id=996 [accessed: 12 March 2008].

Brysk, A. 2002. Introduction: Transnational Threats and Opportunities, in *Globalization and Human Rights*, edited by A. Brysk. Berkeley: University of California Press, 1–18.

Capdevila, G. 2007. UN: Global Compact with Business 'Lacks Teeth'—NGOs, *Inter Press News Services* [online, 6, July 2007]. Available at: www.corpwatch.or g/article.php?id=14549 [accessed: 10 March 2008].

Chinkin, C. M. 1989. The challenge of soft law: Development and change in international law. *The International and Comparative Law Quarterly* 38(4), 850–66.

Clapham, A. 2006. *Human Rights Obligations of Non-State Actors*. Oxford: Oxford University Press.

Conner, T. 2001. Nike's Labor Practices in the Three Years Since CEO Phil Knight's Speech to the National Press Club Global Exchange. *Global Exchange* [online]. Available at:www.globalexchange.org/campaigns/sweatshops/nike/stillwaiting.html [accessed: 10 March 2008].

Draft Norms on the Responsibilities of Transnational Corporations and Other Business Enterprises with Regard to Human Rights. 2003.UNDoc.E/CN.4/Sub.2/2003/12/Rev.2 2003.

Forsythe, D. 2006. *Human Rights in International Relations*. Cambridge: Cambridge University Press.

Howard-Hassmann, R. 2005. The Second Great Transformation: Human Rights Leapfrogging in the Era of Globalization. *Human Rights Quarterly* 27(1), 1–40.

Human Rights First 2004. *Human Rights First Raises Concerns About the UN Global Compact* [online, 11 June 2004]. Available at: www.humanrightsfirst.org/workers_rights/issues/gc/index.htm [accessed: 10 March 2008].

Human Rights Watch 2003. *Nongovernmental Organizations Welcome the New UN Norms on Transnational Business* [online, August 13]. Available at: www.hrw.org/press/2003/08/un-jointstatement.htm [accessed: 10 March 2008].

International Chamber of Commerce 2004. *Joint Views of ICC and the IOE on the Draft 'Norms on the Responsibilities of Transnational Corporations and Other Business Enterprises with Regard to Human Rights* [online, March 2004]. Available at: www.business-humanrights.org/Links/Repository/179848/link_page_view [accessed:10 March 2008].

Keck, M. E. and Sikkink, K. 1998. *Activists Beyond Borders*. Ithaca: Cornell University Press.

Kell, G. 2003. The Global Compact: Origins, Operations, Progress, Challenges. *Journal of Corporate Citizenship* 11(Autumn), 35–49.

Kell, G. and Ruggie, J. G. 1999. Global Markets and Social Legitimacy: The Case of the "Global Compact." *Transnational Corporations* 8(3), 101–20.

Manby, B. 1999. *The Price of Oil: Corporate Responsibility and Human Rights Violations in Nigeria's Oil Producing Communities*. New York: Human Rights Watch.

Matthews, J. 1997. Power Shift. *Foreign Affairs* 76(1), 50–67.

McElhaney, K. A. and Hill, N. 2003. Business and Human Rights: The Case of Hewlett-Packard, *UN Global Compact* [online]. Available at: http://www.unglobalcompact.org/COP/case_search.html?detail=Hewlett Packard+Company&back=/COP/case_search.html&case=7e301562-f900-0010-8faa-da6efee902d1 [accessed: 15 March 2008].

Meyer, W. H. 1998. *Human Rights and International Political Economy in Third World Nations: Multinational Corporations, Foreign Aid, and Repression*. Westport: Praeger.

Meyer, W. H. 2003. Activism and Research on TNCs and Human Rights: Building a New International Normative Regime, in *Transnational Corporations and Human Rights*, edited by J. G. Frynas and S. Pegg. New York: Palgrave Macmillian, 33–52.

Morth, U. 2004. Introduction, in *Soft Law in Governance and Regulation*, edited by U. Morth. Cheltenham, UK: Edward Elgar Publishing Limited, 1–9.

Osorio, R. 2004. The 60th Commission on Human Rights: Norms on the Responsibilities of Transnational Corporations and Other Business Enterprises with Regard to Human Rights. Centre for Applied Studies in International Negotiations [online, April 2004]. Available at: www.casin.ch/web/pdf/normstncshumanrights.pdf [accessed: 8 December 2008].

Raustiala, K. 2005. Form and Substance in International Agreements. *American Journal of International Law* 99(3), 581–614.

Reinicke, W. H. 1999–2000. The Other World Wide Web: Global Public Policy Networks. *Foreign Policy* (Winter 116), 44–57.

Risse, T. 2002. Transnational Actors and World Politics, in *Handbook of International Relations*, edited by W. Carlsnaes, T. Risse and B. Simmons. London: Sage Publications Ltd, 255–74.

Rondinelli, D. A. 2002. Transnational Corporations: International Citizens or New Sovereigns? *Business and Society Review* 107(4), 391–413.

Ruggie, J. G. 2001. Global_governance.net: The Global Compact as Learning Network. *Global Governance* 7(4), 371–8.

Ruggie, J. G. 2002. The Theory and Practice of Learning Networks: Corporate Social Responsibility and the Global Compact. *Journal of Corporate Citizenship* (Spring 5), 27–36.

Ruggie, J. G. 2003. Taking Embedded Liberalism Global: The Corporate Connection, in *Taming Globalization: Frontiers of Governance*, edited by D. Held and M. Koeing-Archibugi. Cambridge: Polity Press, 93–129.

Ruggie, J. G. 2004. Reconstituting the Global Public Domain: Issues, Actors and Practices. *European Journal of International Relations* 10(4), 499–531.

Ruggie, J. G. 2006. *Interim Report of the Special Representative of the Secretary-General on the Issue of Human Rights and Transnational Corporations and Other Business Enterprises*, 2006 UN Doc. E/CN.4/2006/97, 22 February.

Ruggie, J. G. 2007. Business and Human Rights: The Evolving International Agenda. *American Journal of International Law* 101(4), 819–40.

Ruggie, J. G. 2008. *Protect, Respect, and Remedy: A Framework for Business and Human Rights*, Report of the Special Representative of the Secretary-General on the Issue of Human Rights and Transnational Corporations and Other Business Enterprises. UN Doc. A/HRC/8/5, 7 April.

Sen, A. 2004. Elements of a Theory of Human Rights. *Philosophy & Public Affairs* 32(4), 315–56.

Shelton, D. 2000. Introduction: Law, Non-Law, and the Problem of "Soft Law," in *Commitment and Compliance: The Role of Non-Binding Norms in the International Legal System*, edited by D. Shelton. Oxford: Oxford University Press, 1–20.

Spar, D. 1998. The Spotlight and the Bottom Line: How Multinationals Export Human Rights, *Foreign Affairs* 77(2), 7–12.

Spar, D. 1999. Foreign Investment and Human Rights. *Challenge* 42(1), 55–80.

Steinhardt, R. 2005. Corporate Responsibility and the International Law of Human Rights: The New *Lex Mercatoria*, in *Non-State Actors and Human Rights*, edited by P. Alston. Oxford: Oxford University Press, 177–227.

Strange, S. 1996. *The Retreat of the State.* Cambridge: Cambridge University Press.

Subedi, S. 2003. Multinational Corporations and Human Rights, in *Responding to the Human Rights Deficit*, edited by K. Arts and P. Miyho. Hague: Kluwer Law International, 171–85.

Tesner, S. 2000. *The United Nations and Business: A Partnership Recovered.* New York: St. Martin's Press.

UN General Assembly 2006. *Towards Global Partnerships.* UN Doc. A/Res/60/215, 29 March.

UN Global Compact 2005. *Global Compact's Next Phase* [online, 6 September 2005]. Available at: http://www.unglobalcompact.org/AboutTheGC/stages_of_develop ment.html [accessed: 1 March 2008].

UN Global Compact, Business Leaders Initiative on Human Rights, Office of the UN High Commissioner for Human Rights 2006. *Guide for Integrating Human Rights into Business Management* [online, May 2006]. Available at: http://www.unglobal compact.org/Issues/human_rights/Tools_and_Guidance_Materials.html [accessed: 1 March 2008].

UN Global Compact 2007a. *Colombia Annual Activity Report 2007* [online]. Available at: http://www.unglobalcompact.org/NetworksAroundTheWorld/gc_networks_report_on_activities.html [accessed: 11 March 2008].

UN Global Compact 2007b. *Terms of Reference: Global Compact Human Rights Working Group* [online, 10 September 2007]. Available at: http://www.unglobalcompact.org/Issues/human_rights/index.html [accessed: 1 March 2008].

UN Global Compact 2007c. *Note on Integrity Measures* [online, 26 November 2007]. Available at: http://www.unglobalcompact.org/AboutTheGC/integrity.html# [accessed: 1 March 2008].

UN Global Compact, Office of the UN High Commissioner for Human Rights, 2008a. *Embedding Human Rights in Business Practice II* [online, January 2008]. Available at: http://www.unglobalcompact.org/Issues/human_rights/Tools_and_Guidance_Materials.html [accessed: 1 March 2008].

UN Global Compact 2008b. *Update: Over 900 Global Compact Participants Marked 'Inactive' or Delisted* [online 28 January 2008]. Available at: http://www.unglobalcompact.org/NewsAndEvents/news archives/2008_01_28.html [accessed: 12 March 2008].

UN Global Compact 2008c. *Note on the United Nations Global Compact and Business and Human Rights* [online, 7 February 2008]. Available at: http://www.unglobalcompact.org/Issues/humanrights/index.html [accessed: 10 March 2008].

UN Global Compact 2008d. *GC Networks Report* [online, 15 February 2008]. Available at http://www.unglobalcompact.org/NetworksAroundTheWorld/gc_networks_report_on_activities.html [accessed: 1 March 2008].

UN Global Compact 2008e. *Human Rights* [online]. Available at: http://www.unglobalcompact.org/Issues/human rights/index.html [accessed: 7 March 2008].

UN Global Compact 2008f. *Human Rights Working Group Members* [online]. Available at: http://www.unglobalcompact.org/Issues/human_rights/index.html [accessed: 10 December 2008].

UN Global Compact 2008g. *Policy for 'Communication on Progress'* [online]. Available at: http://www.globalcompact.org/COP/ [accessed: 13 March 2008]

Utting, P. 2002. The Global Compact and Civil Society: Averting a Collision Course. *Development in Practice* 12(5), 644–7.

Weissbrodt, D. and Kruger, M. 2003. Norms on the Responsibility of Transnational Corporations and Other Business Enterprises with Regards to Human Rights. *American Journal of International Law* 97(4), 901–22.

Williams, F. 2004. Company Norms 'must be on UN Rights Agenda.' *Financial Times* [online, 8 April]. Available at: www.FT.com [accessed: 13 December 2008].

Chapter 7
Judging Truth: The Contributions of Truth Commissions in Post-Conflict Environments

Eric Brahm

Introduction

Over the past two decades, the truth commission, a temporary body established after political transitions to investigate a pattern of human rights violations that occurred during the course of an earlier era of civil conflict or repressive government, has become a staple of post-conflict peacebuilding. While data and definitional issues make identifying the total number of cases a challenge (Brahm 2007a), most observers agree that at least two dozen have been established to date (see Table 7.1 below for the most widely cited cases). The victim-centered quality of truth commissions is frequently mentioned as a key benefit based on the idea that having one's suffering acknowledged can be therapeutic. In addition, the broad investigations that truth commissions undertake are recommended for the educational role they can serve in producing an authoritative historical narrative of the violence. The investigations also lead commissions to produce recommendations for institutional reforms that are designed to prevent a recurrence of such atrocities and support the development of a democratic polity. Ultimately, uncovering the past is alleged to contribute to reconciliation. In fact, some early depictions almost suggest that truth commissions can be a cure-all for the ails of post-conflict society.

While the purported effects sound intuitively appealing, there is remarkably little evidence to support these contentions. Only recently has the ability of truth commissions to produce these desirable ends been more openly questioned. Few of these claims have been scrutinized through rigorous scientific inquiry. Rather, truth commissions are frequently promoted on normative grounds and through questionable logic and analogizing. Empirical research has begun to address this, but operationalizing key concepts and isolating what effects can be properly attributed to the truth commission itself remain formidable challenges. Muddled as it is, the picture that is beginning to emerge from this empirical turn is one in which truth commissions do matter, but not to the degree that some of the more careless early promoters suggested.

Given the relative absence of evidence supporting the purported effects of truth commissions, why have they proliferated to such an extent? One important reason is that they are being promoted by a growing network of transnational actors. Propelled in part by the perceived success of South Africa's Truth and

Table 7.1 Truth Commission Cases around the World

Country	Date of Commission*
Bolivia	1982–4
Argentina	1983–4
Uruguay	1985
Zimbabwe	1985
Uganda	1986–95
Philippines	1986
Nepal	1990–1
Chile	1990–1
Chad	1991–2
Germany	1992–4
El Salvador	1992–3
Chile	1992–6
Haiti	1995–6
South Africa	1995–2000
Ecuador	1996–7
Guatemala	1997–9
Nigeria	1999–2002
South Korea	2000–4
Peru	2001–3
Panama	2001–2
East Timor	2002–3
Sierra Leone	2002–3
Ghana	2002–3
Central African Republic	2003
Liberia	2003–
Paraguay	2003–
Democratic Republic of the Congo	2004–
Morocco	2004–5

Where no end date is listed, it is unknown whether the truth commission is still in operation.

Reconciliation Commission (TRC), the truth commission idea has caught on with international organizations, human rights groups, as well as states, both in the global North and South. Private foundations, Northern states, and interstate organizations have backed up this new enthusiasm with resources. Former commissioners from South Africa and a number of Latin American cases have become influential proponents as part of the global human rights movement. By and large, human rights groups have embraced truth commissions, provided they are not alternatives to prosecutions. What is more, the United Nations has recommended truth commissions in the peace negotiations in which it has been involved. Furthermore, the UN has become the focal point of efforts to elaborate truth-seeking obligations under international law. These actors are changing normative expectations of what states owe victims in the aftermath of gross human rights violations.

This chapter will provide an overview of the global experience with truth commissions. I first consider the evidence for what effects truth commissions have on post-conflict societies. The discussion focuses on the most frequently mentioned areas of potential impact: peace, democracy, human rights, victim healing, and reconciliation. As we shall see, the remarkable ascent of truth commissions is based as much on faith as it is on hard evidence that truth commissions affect transitional societies in the way many supporters claim. The relative dearth of evidence suggests the power of an emerging truth-seeking/truth-telling norm in international relations. As a result, the second half of the chapter highlights how a variety of transnational actors are shaping how states see their obligations with respect to the non-judicial investigation of gross human rights violations.

Truth Commission Expectations

Overall, claims regarding the effects of truth commissions are wide-ranging, contradictory, and based upon weak empirical foundations. While it is widely believed that truth commissions have positive consequences for human rights, peace and stability, democracy, reconciliation, and victim healing, these assumptions have rarely been tested and, when they have, a number of methodological and empirical challenges emerge (Brahm 2007b; Mendeloff 2004; Vinjamuri and Snyder 2004; Lutz 2006). For example, any attempt to measure potential impact is complicated by the fact that these concepts are difficult to measure. This is frequently compounded by a failure to adequately distinguish these concepts from one another. Furthermore, correlation is often assumed to be causation without employing adequate controls.

In response to growing criticism of the sloppy rhetoric often used in describing truth commission effects, the language has become more cautious in recent years. Truth commissions are now rarely described as a sufficient condition to produce these ends. There is less agreement on whether they are a necessary condition. Many fudge by arguing that truth commissions are jointly necessary and/or sufficient to bring about these ends with a combination of other post-conflict justice mechanisms. For example, a recent UN report claims that its "experience confirms that a piecemeal approach to the rule of law and transitional justice will not bring satisfactory results in a war-torn or atrocity-scarred nation" and that a comprehensive strategy involving a variety of post-conflict justice measure, including truth commissions, is necessary (United Nations 2004). The admonition is well intentioned and designed to maximize the justice delivered to victims of human rights violations. Yet, this turn in language leaves open the empirical cause-effect question and ignores the reality that very few countries have come close to pursuing a comprehensive approach to post-conflict justice. Again, it is a normative appeal.

In the absence of convincing evidence of positive truth commission benefits, critics have become increasingly vocal. Some fear that truth commissions could be used to evade serious investigation or other forms of post-conflict justice, especially the prosecution of perpetrators. In the words of one activist, in the afterglow of South Africa's TRC, "the international community has become blindly besotted with truth commissions" while abusive governments view them "as a soft option for avoiding justice" (Brody 2001; Tepperman 2002). The Serbian Truth and Reconciliation Commission exemplifies this in that it sought to deflect Serbian responsibility by focusing on abuses by Croats and Bosnian Muslims. Others argue that any positive benefit of truth commissions should be properly attributed to the amnesties that frequently accompany them (Snyder and Vinjamuri 2003).

In point of fact, there is not enough known about most truth commission cases to make sweeping judgments for better or worse. The bulk of the knowledge from which these conclusions are reached comes from a biased sub sample of cases. Only recently have a series of large scale data collection projects emerged that will be able to facilitate cross-national comparison (Brahm et al. 2008; Sikkink and Walling 2007; Kim and Sikkink 2007; Payne et al. 2008). To date, much of what we know about truth commissions comes from anecdotal, impressionistic accounts by participants in the process or from those in international civil society with a broader interest in the transition process. This introduces the potential for bias (or at least that observers may have blinders to certain issues). Existing studies typically focus on the circumstances under which commissions are created and descriptions of their operation. Shortly after the completion of a truth commission, observers often move on to the next transitional society, thereby reducing how much we know about long-term consequences.

Recently assessing the state of research on truth commissions, Mendeloff (2004) concludes that "[t]he literature has done a poor job of specifying the logic of truth-telling arguments, defining and clarifying key concepts, operationalizing key variables, indicating the conditions under which proposed relationships hold, providing compelling empirical evidence to support core assumptions, and testing claims systematically against competing explanations." The remainder of this section highlights the challenge of judging truth commission impact. It does so by examining the currently available evidence for truth commissions contributing to peace, democratization, the protection of human rights, the healing of victims, and the promotion of reconciliation.

Peace and Stability

One potential measure of truth commission impact is whether violence reemerges (Kaye 1997). A commission may shed light on a troubling series of events, dispel myths, and, thereby, help to prevent violence from escalating. Truth commissions may reduce tensions by mitigating the desire for revenge on the part of victims and reducing perpetrators' sense of vulnerability. A quick scan of the countries listed in Table 7.1 suggests that most have not seen a return to violence, at least no on a scale approaching what had occurred prior to the truth commission. Unfortunately, findings in more systematic studies have yielded contradictory results.

The peace-promoting claim has, in fact, come in for frequent criticism. Some studies, for example, find that post-conflict justice, including truth commission investigations, heightens tensions and creates new grievances that may stoke further conflict (Snyder and Vinjamuri 2003). In fact, they argue that the alleged peace-promoting effect of truth commissions is actually the result of an accompanying amnesty or the fact that democracy is well-established by the time the truth commission is created. Others echo the fact that truth commission supporters have often been too quick to claim credit when tensions are reduced in some way (Schiff 2002). Others conclude that, while truth commissions are not harmful, they are largely irrelevant for peace building (Lie et al. 2007). In this statistical study, they find that factors such as whether one side achieves outright victory accounts for whether peace endures. Similar to Snyder and Vinjamuri, however, Lie et al. find that truth commissions are positively associated with sustaining peace in countries that are already democratic.

A major difficulty for qualitative and quantitative research involves isolating causality, an issue that haunts all attempts to gauge truth commission impact. Truth commissions are endogenous to the peacebuilding or democratization process, so it is necessary to control for exogenous factors that could have produced both the truth commission and the dependent variable (here, peace). A peace process almost always precedes a truth commission so the direction of causality is open to question. The studies conducted thus far have their own shortcomings. For example, the Snyder and Vinjamuri study discusses most cases far too briefly to adequately trace the impact of the commissions they examine. In addition, both Snyder and Vinjamuri and Lie et al. essentially treat all truth commissions as the same. They do not account for the diversity of truth commission experience. Still, it appears unlikely that truth commissions can produce peace. However, it is possible that, if a truth commission can promote such ends as democracy and reconciliation, it could help sustain peace.

Democratization

Truth commissions have frequently been connected to democracy promotion (Teitel 2000; Gairdner 1999; Minow 1998; Freeman and Hayner 2003). Recommendations often focus on institutional reforms that, if enacted, would theoretically promote democratic governance. Further, the investigation may reduce the power of anti-democratic forces by discrediting them or prompting their removal from positions of authority. If conducted in an open, democratic fashion, the commission may also indicate to different social groups that the government is committed to giving everyone a voice. Some, in fact, see truth commissions as an element of a conscious government effort to inculcate democratic values (Boraine and Levy 1995; Gutmann and Thompson 2000; Chapman and Ball 2001).

Thus far, empirical research provides contradictory findings. One study focusing on Latin America finds a positive relationship between employing a truth commission and subsequent democratic practice (Kenney and Spears 2005). Moreover, an ongoing commission appears to provide additional benefits. However, because it focuses on one region, the study does not reveal whether this effect is found throughout the world. By contrast, a global survey of 78 countries undergoing a democratic transition found no democracy-promoting effect of truth commissions (Brahm 2006). Another study examines the effect of truth commissions on regime legitimacy, something likely to be directly related to democracy (Botha 1998). Botha finds that countries that have created a strong truth commission are less likely to experience mass protest.

In general, quantitative research has been limited by a number of methodological issues. First, there is again the issue of causality; democratization usually precedes a truth commission. Given the fact that the democratic rules are often set prior to the commission, truth commission recommendations have tended to be narrow and specific, such as creating greater civilian oversight over the military. While each of the studies mentioned uses different statistical techniques that attempt to isolate truth commission effects from antecedent conditions that may have caused both the truth commission and changes in democracy, issues of model specification should make one cautious about attributing causality. Moreover, quantitative research has had to deal with the difficulty of operationalizing democracy. Polity, the most widely used democracy measure, focuses on institutional factors influencing political participation. However, truth commissions have not typically contributed to this aspect because electoral rules are set through other means. Finally, quantitative research struggles with modeling truth commission variation. While most rely on a simple dummy variable, Botha goes farthest in labeling commissions as either strong or weak based on their resources, credibility, and publicity. While a welcome innovation, this likely does not go far enough in reflecting the diversity of truth commission experience around the world.

Comparative case study research has also found no systematic relationship between truth commissions and subsequent democratization (Barahona de Brito et al. 2001; Brahm 2006). Where a relationship exists, the effects are often indirect. In El Salvador, for example, the clearest effect has been in facilitating a purge of the military and judiciary (Brahm 2006). The Salvadoran Commission on the Truth did not do this itself, but its revelations ensured that, when the legislature selected supreme court justices in 1994, none of the standing members were given serious consideration. Overall, however, democracy-promoting reforms were more likely to be enacted in countries that had already achieved significant democratic gains (Barahona de Brito et al. 2001). What is more, they find that enacting democratic reforms depended more on antecedent conditions and broader structural factors than on the nature of the truth commission itself.

Human Rights

Another frequently mentioned measure of truth commission impact is human rights (Kaye 1997; Chapman and Ball 2001; Hayner 1994; Minow 1998; Boraine 2000; Ensalaco 1994; Gairdner 1999). In looking at past human rights abuses, the hope is that society can learn from the experience and prevent a future recurrence of such behavior. Many truth commission recommendations are designed to bolster institutions to better protect human rights. Reforms promoting civilian oversight of security forces, independence of the judiciary, and establishing human rights watchdogs are frequently recommended reforms. However, as in other areas, the evidence for these assertions is limited and they do not provide consistent conclusions.

Cross-national research is ambiguous as to whether truth commissions create better human rights conditions. One study of 78 countries attempting to transition to democracy finds no statistically significant relationship between conducting a truth commission and a state's subsequent protection of the human rights of its citizens (Brahm 2006). Unfortunately, the study suffers from the same issues of operationalization and isolating causation discussed in the previous section. Another study that focused on Latin America found that countries that utilize both trials and truth commissions have a better human rights record than those that only employ trials (Sikkink and Walling 2007). While this suggests truth commissions have an added benefit, the authors do not specify a causal path. What is more, the study does not control for alternative explanations for the patterns they observe.

Case study research indicates that, while significant variation in implementation exists across cases, when enacted, recommended institutional reforms have often had some degree of impact on future human rights practices (Brahm 2006; Brahm forthcoming). Truth commissions appear most effective in charting a reform agenda that, if enacted, may prompt legal reform, create watchdogs, and introduce new training and oversight mechanisms for the judiciary and security services. In El Salvador and Chile, for example, in response to truth commission recommendations, the governments established human rights ombudsmen and reformed how detained suspects were treated, among other human rights measures. Many governments have also followed truth commission recommendations to sign international human rights treaties.

Other claims regarding truth commission impact on human rights seem to suggest a cultural effect. The public exposure of past deeds may educate the population on the importance of human rights and alter norms of socially acceptable behavior. This proposition has received limited analytical scrutiny. One large study found that South Africans who accepted the TRC's conclusions regarding abuses during apartheid were more supportive of human rights (Gibson 2004b). Unfortunately, this question has not been systematically explored in other countries that have employed truth commissions. Anecdotal evidence is mixed. In Argentina, for example, public opinion polls consistently show widespread support for human rights (Sriram 2004), but it is unclear whether or not this is due to the National Commission for the Disappearance of Persons (CONADEP). In general, available data on public attitudes in a number of post-truth commission countries suggest that the development of a culture of human rights is a long-term project. Significant numbers of Salvadorans and South Africans, for example, would support brutal methods if they would reduce crime (Brahm 2006).

Victim Healing

Truth commissions have been touted as a victim-centered approach to post-conflict justice that can have therapeutic benefit (Abrams and Hayner 2002; Hayner 2000, 2001; Minow 1998; Hamber 2001). In particular, by providing a venue for victims to tell their stories and receive official acknowledgment of past suffering, it may contribute to their psychological healing (Minow 1998). However, this proposition is largely untested. Evidence for the healing power of the truth is primarily anecdotal and based on questionable analogizing from clinical situations (Mendeloff 2009, forthcoming). In fact, there is also substantial evidence to suggest that reliving the past may be just as likely to rekindle anger or trigger post-traumatic stress as it is to provide healing (Mendeloff forthcoming; Hamber 1998). Of the data that does exist, individual reaction to appearing before a truth commission has been highly variable and virtually impossible to predict a priori (Hamber 2003; Theissen 1999). Outside of South Africa, systematically collected data on victims is nonexistent for most truth commission countries. Even in South Africa, a lack of longitudinal data makes judging truth commission effects difficult.

No truth commission has provided the degree of support that exists in many clinical settings that might be more likely to facilitate healing. Even in South Africa, where the TRC had a comparatively large budget, victims found almost universal disappointment with the TRC (Backer 2004). Many felt that the commission did little to help with what mattered most to them, finding the remains of loved ones and obtaining reparations (Ross 1999). While this result likely reflects the high expectations surrounding the TRC, existing data from other countries supports the contention that victim reaction is highly variable. A survey of Ghanaian victims who had participated in the National Reconciliation Commission (NRC) found that most gained a sense of relief from their experience and some even felt reconciled (Brahm forthcoming). In East Timor, Commission for Reception, Truth, and Reconciliation (CAVR) staff argued that victims gained comfort from the process, but independent observers argued that it led to retraumatization for some (Silove et al. 2006). More negatively, victims groups in Sierra Leone threatened to boycott the Truth and Reconciliation Commission because of the perception that perpetrators' needs were being given priority (Brahm forthcoming). Victims are often disappointed with the fact that Disarmament, Demobilization and Reintegration (DDR) programs happen right away, but reparations, a frequent truth commission recommendation, are often long delayed. Few countries approach the generosity of Chile's government, which followed the recommendations of the

National Commission on Truth and Reconciliation, popularly known as the Rettig Commission after its chair, to provide victims with a reparations package that included a monthly pension, free health services, and educational scholarships.

Reconciliation

The holy grail of most truth commission promotion is reconciliation. Even more than other concepts discussed above, however, reconciliation is difficult to operationalize (Dwyer 1999; Van Der Merwe 1999). Possibilities range from the simple absence of violence to a situation in which former antagonists share a vision for the future (Gloppen 2005). Despite this difficulty, some argue that the emphasis on reconciliation has persisted as a goal of truth commissions because international donors see it as a "feel-good idea" that does not create winners and losers (Brody 2001).

Reconciliation is discussed both in individual terms, e.g. victim-perpetrator reconciliation, and intergroup reconciliation. At the societal level, some argue that truth commissions may facilitate reconciliation, but not on their own (Hayner 2001). Reconciliation is a long term goal that may require the passage of generations. In the short to medium term, truth commissions can aspire to "peaceful coexistence, cooperation, and tolerance" (Ash 1997; Norval 1999). Given this fact, most argue that commissions may lay the foundation for future reconciliation (Bhargava 2000).

To date, while a number of interesting suggestions have been put forward on how reconciliation might be measured (Weissbrodt and Fraser 1992; Hayner 1999), few research projects have been executed. Anecdotal evidence, however, suggests that few minds are changed by truth commission revelations and that reconciliation is a slow process. For instance, in Chile a reluctance to discuss the past belies the common Chilean insistence that reconciliation has occurred (Hayner 2001). Protests by pro- and anti-Pinochet groups after his arrest in London indicated that divergent views of the past persist in Chile. Conservatives eventually abandoned Pinochet in large numbers not because of past human rights abuses, but due to corruption allegations that emerged. In Guatemala, Rios Montt has continued to enjoy political success since the Commission for Historical Clarification (CEH)'s revelations. In Argentina, whenever new revelations about the past emerge, old wounds are reopened (Sriram 2004). Most of the military continues to deny that anything was done wrong, while the Mothers of the Plaza de Mayo insist that more is still needed to address the past. While these examples give rise to skepticism, because reconciliation is an evolving, long-term process, one should be reluctant to draw definitive conclusions on the contribution of truth commissions to reconciliation for years to come.

Individual level reconciliation will likely move at a different pace than intergroup reconciliation does. Given the variability of victim reaction and of the level of remorse amongst perpetrators, individual level reconciliation will inevitably be highly variable (Freeman and Hayner 2003). In South Africa, a survey of over

3,700 individuals found that Black South Africans were the least individually reconciled group (Gibson 2004a). Overall, the survey found that 44 per cent of South Africans were at least somewhat reconciled with the opposing group. More hopefully in terms of truth commission effects, Gibson finds that individuals who are more accepting of the TRC were more likely to be reconciled. Gibson, however, is careful to note that his cross-sectional data does not allow for strong causal arguments. In addition, he allows for the possibility that an unobserved underlying factor may account for the patterns he observes. Despite these shortcomings, he finds no evidence that the TRC has hampered reconciliation.

Popular perceptions do not always agree. Surveys conducted in South Africa reveal fears that the TRC had negative consequences for the country. In 1998, while the TRC was still operating, two-thirds of South Africans felt the TRC had hurt race relations (Hayner 2001; Tepperman 2002). A closer look at the data, and a subsequent poll conducted in 2002, found that white South Africans were far more pessimistic about reconciliation, whereas half of blacks were hopeful (Brahm forthcoming; Gibson and Macdonald 2001). A similar poll conducted in Ghana shortly after the NRC found that 80 per cent of respondents felt the process had not contributed to national reconciliation (Brahm forthcoming).

The Global Promotion of Truth Commissions

Given the relative absence of evidence to support many of the claims made with respect to truth commissions, to what do we owe the profusion of cases? Part of the answer is surely the efforts of a broad coalition of international actors that is shaping norms of post-conflict justice. Perhaps most important in this diverse network are commissioners and staff, many of whom have followed their truth commission experience by consulting with other post-conflict countries worldwide. While a number of Latin American cases were early exemplars, none surpass the importance of South Africa's TRC in raising the visibility of truth commissions and ensuring that this tool would remain a staple of post-conflict landscapes everywhere. Transnational and local civil society groups, some of whom were established by former truth commission participants, have also frequently been vocal advocates. In addition, foreign governments and foundations have directed large amounts of money to support truth commission efforts in many countries. For its part, the United Nations has also played a crucial role in promoting truth commissions since the early 1990s. As a result, by the turn of the century there was a substantial global epistemic community to support the further spread and refinement of the truth commission idea. While the head of the Chadian truth commission could credibly claim in the early 1990s, that he "had scarcely known that this type of investigation existed in other countries" (Bronkhorst 1995), such an assertion would be incredible today. Yet, as we have seen, truth commission proselytizing has been based more on faith than on concrete evidence that these bodies achieve what we think they do.

Truth Commission "Veterans"

In general, those who have worked on earlier truth commissions have tended to dominate academic and policy discussions about truth commissions. Some of the earliest proponents of the truth commission model in Latin America were individuals associated with Argentina's CONADEP. In the early 1990s, Chile's government explicitly drew upon the earlier experiences of Argentina and Uruguay in determining how to approach the human rights violations of the Pinochet era. Of those participating in Chile's Rettig Commission, Jose Zalaquett, in particular, went on to play an important role in the diffusion of the truth commission idea. After being imprisoned by the Pinochet regime, Zalaquett was exiled and spent much of that time working for Amnesty International, where he served as chair of its executive committee. Therefore, he was well-positioned to advance the truth and reconciliation message after the Rettig Commission completed its work, which he has done in a number of instances around the world.

No truth commission, however, can match the South African TRC in terms of the influence it has had on subsequent practice around the world. In fact, South Africa learned much from earlier truth commission experiences as it was formulating its own commission. Prior to the creation of the TRC Act, two international conferences were held in which international experts and truth commission veterans, including Zalaquett and others from Chile, Argentina, and Eastern Europe, came to South Africa to share their experiences (Boraine et al. 1997; Boraine and Levy 1995).

It is hard to overestimate the contribution of the South African TRC to spreading the truth commission gospel. In many respects, it has become the template from which subsequent truth commissions have been built. The Peruvian truth commission, for instance, resembled the South African TRC in a number of respects. In Nigeria, commissioners from the South African, Chilean and Guatemalan commissions helped recalibrate the truth commission after its mandate was initially drawn in an overly broad fashion (Hayner 2001). South Africa even provided a blueprint for Greensboro, North Carolina's attempt to deal with the legacy of racial violence of the late 1970s.

A number of South African commissioners and staff have been particularly important in promoting truth commissions. None can match the global stature of TRC Chair Desmond Tutu. Already enjoying a high profile as a Nobel Prize winner before serving on the TRC, he has spoken extensively around the world on the benefits of truth commissions. Others have developed what are essentially international consulting firms that have ultimately proven more influential in helping countries wade through transitional justice controversies. Two organizations, in particular, emerged from the South African experience and have been crucial for the global promotion of truth commissions: the International Center for Transitional Justice (ICTJ) and the Institute for Justice and Reconciliation (IJR). The ICTJ is far and away the more high profile of the two and will be discussed further in the next section. The Institute for Justice and Reconciliation has more quietly been advancing the cause of transitional justice by explicitly utilizing lessons from South Africa's experience to suggest a path for other post-conflict African societies.

The Role of Civil Society

Human rights and victims' groups have long been interested in uncovering the truth of past human rights abuses. From the earliest cases, local civil society groups have used transnational linkages to exchange information. In fact, according to Hayner (2001, 250), "it is generally nationals—non-governmental advocates, victims' groups, and members of the government or opposition—who have been pushing for these truth bodies." When governments have not acted, NGOs have sometimes taken matters into their own hands to investigate violations (Bickford 2007). Where truth commissions are established, civil society is often an important source of support to the investigation. They may have collected evidence that could be used. NGOs also frequently publicize truth commissions to increase the population's engagement in the process. What is more, the provision of victim support services often falls to civil society groups.

With relatively few exceptions, global civil society has come to embrace the truth commission. For example, meetings of academics, policymakers, and activists have endorsed truth as the centerpiece of peace making (Carnegie Commission on Preventing Deadly Conflict 1997; Justice and Society Program of The Aspen Institute 1989; Henkin 1998). The American Association for the Advancement of Science (AAAS) has given scientific and technical assistance to a number of commissions, including South Africa, Haiti, and Guatemala (Chapman and Ball 2001). Many human rights organizations, such as Amnesty International and Human Rights Watch, were initially cool toward truth commissions out of fear they would distract from prosecutions. However, both have come to advocate truth commissions as one element of a comprehensive justice strategy that includes other measures such as trials and reparations.

Few NGOs, however, have been more important in developing ideas on truth commissions, and transitional justice generally, than the International Center for Transitional Justice (ICTJ). Within six months of opening its first office in New York City in 2001, the ICTJ was working in more than a dozen countries. Initially led by South African TRC commissioner Alex Boraine and supported by Paul van Zyl, executive secretary of the TRC, and leading truth commission expert Priscilla Hayner, the organization now has nearly a dozen offices around the world and a staff of approximately 100 individuals. In its consultations with governments and civil society groups, the ICTJ promotes a comprehensive approach to transitional justice that not only includes truth commissions, but also prosecution, reparations, reconciliation processes, and institutional reform. To date, it has worked in over 35 countries, including two dozen active projects as of late 2008. Increasingly, the ICTJ has worked with the UN in promoting transitional justice strategies in post-conflict states (Office of the United Nations High Commissioner for Human Rights 2006).

Foundation Support

Private foundations have demonstrated their support for truth commissions with expanded funding. The Ford Foundation, in particular, has been one of the largest and longest promoters of truth commissions around the world. It has helped fund commissions. For example, in February 1987, Uganda's Commission of Inquiry into Violations of Human Rights (CIVHR) was saved by an infusion of $93,300 from the Ford Foundation (Hayner 1994).

Ford's work has also had a broader impact on the practice of truth commissions. Most importantly, it sponsored a 2000 meeting at which the ICTJ was first envisioned. It then provided a multi-million dollar grant to start the ICTJ. Ford has also contributed to establishing best practices by supporting a joint ICTJ- New York University School of Law "Lessons Learned" project on South Africa's TRC and Guatemala's CEH. The project worked with commission insiders to identify methodological and operational lessons that could benefit future truth commissions (Quinn and Freeman 2003).

State Support

States are also increasingly embracing the truth commission idea. The Clinton administration was an early advocate. For example, at the time, the State Department described truth commissions and similar bodies as "'new and diverse ways of providing accountability for human rights abuses, which can lead to a negotiated settlement of a conflict" (Green 1996). In January 1995, then-US Secretary of State Warren Christopher argued that truth commissions in Central America had contributed to reconciliation in once war-torn countries.

Governments are not only showing rhetorical support for truth commissions, but are devoting more resources to the cause. When Uganda's CIVHR was threatened again with a shut down in 1991, the Dutch government provided over $400,000 to help it complete its investigation. El Salvador's Commission on the Truth was funded entirely by voluntary contributions from UN member-states, primarily the United States and a number of European countries. The ICTJ's 2002–3 Annual Report also reveals that British aid officials asked it to evaluate the creation of a truth commission in Nicaragua. Over time, the balance between domestic and foreign sources of funding has become increasingly weighted toward the latter. Finally, state support also extends to the general promotion of transitional justice. For example, most governments in Western Europe have contributed to the ICTJ as has Japan and Canada. Truth commissions are attractive because they are less expensive than trials and have the potential to examine a larger number of instances of abuse.

Intergovernmental Organization Support

As the locus of many international cooperative efforts, international truth commission promotion activities are frequently centered on intergovernmental organizations. In general, international legal developments have supported the spread of truth commissions. Since the end of the Cold War, a number of treaty bodies, regional courts, as well as international and domestic tribunals have affirmed a victim's "right to know" about past abuses that have effected them (Orentlicher 2004). Some of the earliest action was at the regional level. For example, in 1988, the Inter-American Court ruled in the Velasquez Rodriguez case that the state has a duty to investigate the fate of the disappeared and disclose information to families. Similarly, the African Charter on Human Rights and Peoples' Rights guarantees a "right to receive information."

Given its global reach and its central role in peace promotion activities, the United Nations' embrace of the truth commission has been tremendously important for the spread of the idea. The UN has nearly two decades of truth commission experience. Its first encounter with the truth commission was during the Salvadoran peace process. As UN-sponsored negotiations between the Salvadoran government and the rebels continued into the early 1990s, the Chilean truth commission proved influential in the parties' decision to incorporate one into the Salvadoran peace agreement. At the time, the depth and breadth of the UN mission in El Salvador was unprecedented, no less so with respect to the truth commission. The UN and its member states provided the resources and manpower for the Salvadoran commission. The experience was formative for the UN as it would go on to advocate a truth commission in virtually every peace process in which it has been involved since then. In Haiti and Guatemala, for example, the commissions were heavily influenced by the Salvadoran experience.

UN interest in truth commissions, often as part of a broader transitional justice strategy, has continued apace. In early 1999, for instance, the UN-commissioned Group of Experts recommended a truth commission for Cambodia. Peace talks in places such as East Timor, Sierra Leone, and Liberia resulted in truth commissions. In East Timor and Sierra Leone, so-called hybrid courts focused on the masterminds of the violence while truth commissions worked to reintegrate lower level offenders back into society. The Timorese case was also groundbreaking in that, since the Security Council gave the UN Special Representative in East Timor exclusive legislative authority in the territory in 1999, the UN formally created the East Timorese CAVR.

Conclusion

Truth commissions remain popular while still being so poorly understood for a number of reasons. First, peace negotiators and new governments hardly have time to wait for long-term studies to be completed. Political transitions provide an opportunity to address the past that may quickly evaporate as other urgent issues come to the fore. Second, the truth commission is a response to a widely felt need to examine the past and to do so in a victim-centered way. As such, a normative argument could be made that, even if truth commissions make little positive contribution, they are still worth doing if victims find value in them. As we have seen, however, the evidence is ambiguous on this point. Perhaps the best hope for grounding truth commission promotion in more sound empirics is via donor governments and foundations, who want accountability for how their money is spent. Their efforts could promote more rigorous data collection that would help to answer these important questions.

The promotion of post-conflict justice tools such as truth commissions is an overt challenge to state sovereignty. With international law developing apace and global civil society applying the rhetorical pressure, states increasingly have to justify why they do not enact measures to address a history of human rights abuses. Some critics, however, worry that truth commissions may serve to insulate abusive governments from accountability (Brody 2001). The growing use of international and internationalized tribunals and the creation of the International Criminal Court suggest that prosecuting perpetrators is not as remote a possibility as it was in the past. By contrast, truth commissions may be viewed by governments as a soft option of post-conflict justice; a showy display of concern for human rights that is cheaper and less threatening to the powerful. To be sure, it remains rare that perpetrators are punished for their deeds. However, this is the result of a lack of political will rather than the presence of a truth commission.

It would be a mistake to assume that the spread of truth commissions has not influenced state behavior. Truth commissions have often had profound political, moral, and financial implications for post-conflict societies. Their investigations generate pressure from victims groups and global civil society for further measures to address the past. As has occurred in places such as Argentina, Chile, and Chad, evidence uncovered by truth commissions sometimes contributes to subsequent prosecutorial efforts. Commission reports typically recommend reforms to prevent future abuses and reparations as recognition of victims' suffering. As such, the reports provide a benchmark against which government performance can be gauged. Although this has not been frequent, development aid and other assistance could be made contingent upon government action on truth commission recommendations. As such, the significance of truth commissions should not be dismissed out of hand.

In shaping post-conflict justice norms, the international community has a delicate role to play in providing information and expertise, while not forcing a policy on a country. Only a minority of scholars believe truth commissions can threaten the stability of post-conflict governments. However, until stronger evidence emerges, this argument should not be dismissed. A more likely danger is that truth commission promotion could become a victim of its success. As truth commission experience continues apace, international human rights groups and the United Nations have contributed to the increasing standardization of truth commission practice (Lutz 2006). Perversely, the growth of truth commissions may, in fact, reduce their utility for post-conflict societies. Warnings of applying a one-size-fits-all approach abound. As one scholar put it, the international community should "resist the tendency, so pronounced in the case of truth commissions, for politicians and negotiators to extrapolate a 'formula' that can be applied, with a few changes, to any and all situations" (Roht-Arriaza 2006, 12). It would be a shame if the form, but not the spirit, of truth commissions would become ensconced as an international norm.

References

Abrams, J. S. and Hayner, P. B. 2002. Documenting, Acknowledging and Publicizing the Truth, in *Post-Conflict Justice*, edited by M. C. Ardsley Bassiouni. NY: Transnational Publishers, 283–93.

Ash, T. G. 1997. True Confessions. *The New York Review of Books* 44(4), 33–8.

Backer, D. 2004. *The Human Face of Justice: Victims' Responses to South Africa's Truth and Reconciliation Commission Process*, Ph.D. dissertation, Department of Political Science, University of Michigan.

Barahona De Brito, A., Gonzalez Enriquez, C. and Aguilar, P. 2001. *The Politics of Memory: Transitional Justice in Democratizing Societies.* Oxford: Oxford University Press.

Bhargava, R. 2000. Restoring Decency to Barbaric Societies, in *Truth V. Justice: The Morality of Truth Commissions*, edited by R. I. Rotberg and D. Thompson. Princeton, NJ: Princeton University Press, 45–67.

Bickford, L. 2007. Unofficial Truth Projects. *Human Rights Quarterly* 29(4), 994–1035.

Boraine, A. 2000. Truth and Reconciliation in South Africa: The Third Way, in *Truth V. Justice: The Morality of Truth Commissions*, edited by R. I. Rotberg and D. Thompson. Princeton: Princeton University Press, 141–57.

Boraine, A. and Levy, J. 1995. *The Healing of a Nation?* Cape Town: Justice in Transition.

Boraine, A., Levy, J. and Scheffer, R. 1997. *Dealing with the Past: Truth and Reconciliation in South Africa*, Cape Town: IDASA (Institute for a Democratic Alternative for South Africa).

Botha, B. M. 1998. *Truth Commissions and Their Consequences for Legitimacy*, Ph.D. dissertation, Department of Political Science, University of Houston.

Brahm, E. 2006. *Truth and Consequences: The Impact of Truth Commissions in Transitional Societies*, Ph.D. dissertation, Department of Political Science, University of Colorado at Boulder.

Brahm, E. 2007a. *Defining the Truth Commission Universe.* Paper to the Western Political Science Association: Annual Meeting, Las Vegas, NV, 8–10 March 2007.

Brahm, E. 2007b. Uncovering the Truth: Examining Truth Commission Success and Impact. *International Studies Perspectives* 8(1), 16–35.

Brahm, E. (forthcoming) An Overview of Truth Commissions and Other Investigative Bodies as Post-Conflict Justice Tools, in *Fighting Impunity and Promoting International Justice,* edited by M. C. Bassiouni. International Institute of Higher Studies in Criminal Sciences.

Brahm, E., Dancy, G. and Kim, H. 2008. *Truth Commission Database Project: What Is a Truth Commission and How Can We Understand It?* Annual Meeting of the International Studies Association, San Francisco, CA, 26–29 March 2008.

Brody, R. 2001. Justice: The First Casualty of Truth? *The Nation* 30 April.

Bronkhorst, D. 1995. *Truth and Reconciliation, Obstacles and Opportunities for Human Rights.* Amsterdam: Amnesty International Dutch Section.

Carnegie Commission on Preventing Deadly Conflict. 1997. *Preventing Deadly Conflict: Final Report with Executive Summary.* Washington, D.C.: The Commission.

Chapman, A. R. and Ball, P. 2001. The Truth of Truth Commissions: Comparative Lessons from Haiti, South Africa, and Guatemala. *Human Rights Quarterly* 23(1), 1–43.

Dwyer, S. 1999. Reconciliation for Realists. *Ethics & International Affairs* 13(1), 81–98.

Ensalaco, M. 1994. Truth Commissions for Chile and El Salvador: A Report and Assessment. *Human Rights Quarterly* 16(4), 656–75.

Freeman, M. and Hayner, P. B. 2003. Truth-Telling, in *Reconciliation after Violent Conflict: A Handbook*, edited by D. Bloomfield. Stockholm: International Institute for Democracy and Electoral Assistance, 122–39.

Gairdner, D. 1999. *Truth in Transition: The Role of Truth Commissions in Political Transition in Chile and El Salvador*. Bergen, Chr. Michelsen Institute Development Studies and Human Rights.

Gibson, J. L. 2004a. *Overcoming Apartheid: Can Truth Reconcile a Divided Nation?* New York: Russell Sage Foundation.

Gibson, J. L. 2004b. Truth, Reconciliation, and the Creation of a Human Rights Culture in South Africa. *Law & Society Review* 38(1), 5–40.

Gibson, J. L. and MacDonald, H. 2001. *Truth—Yes, Reconciliation—Maybe: South Africans Judge the Truth and Reconciliation Process*. Cape Town Institute for Justice and Reconciliation.

Gloppen, S. 2005. Roads to Reconciliation: A Conceptual Framework, in *Roads to Reconciliation,* edited by E. Skaar, S. Gloppen and A. Suhrke. Lanham: Lexington Books, 17–50.

Green, E. 1996. Truth Commissions in Latin America. *Issues in Democracy* 1(3). ISIA Electronic Journals.

Gutmann, A. and Thompson, D. 2000. The Moral Foundations of Truth. Commissions, in *Truth V. Justice: The Morality of Truth Commission,* edited by R. I. Rotberg and D. Thompson. Princeton, NJ: Princeton University Press, 22–44.

Hamber, B. 1998. Truth: The Road to Reconciliation? *Cantilevers: Building Bridges for Peace* 3(1), 5–6.

Hamber, B. 2001. Does the Truth Heal? A Psychological Perspective on Political Strategies for Dealing with the Legacy of Political Violence, in *Burying the Past: Making Peace and Doing Justice after Civil Conflict*, edited by N. Biggar. Washington, D.C.: Georgetown University Press, 155–74.

Hamber, B. 2003. Does the Truth Heal? A Psychological Perspective on Political Strategies for Dealing with the Legacy of Political Violence, in *Burying the Past: Making Peace and Doing Justice after Civil Conflict*, edited by N. Biggar. Washington, D.C.: Georgetown University Press, 155–74.

Hayner, P. B. 1994. Fifteen Truth Commissions--1974 to 1994: A Comparative Study. *Human Rights Quarterly* 16(4), 597–655.

Hayner, P. B. 1999. In Pursuit of Justice and Reconciliation: Contributions of Truth Telling, in *Comparative Peace Processes in Latin America*, edited by C. J. Arnson. Washington, D.C.: Woodrow Wilson Center Press, 363–83.

Hayner, P. B. 2000. Past Truths, Present Dangers: The Role of Official Truth Seeking in Conflict Resolution and Prevention, in *International Conflict Resolution after the Cold War,* edited by P. C. Stern and D. Druckman. Washington, D.C.: National Academy Press, 338–82.

Hayner, P. B. 2001. *Unspeakable Truths: Confronting State Terror and Atrocity.* New York: Routledge.

Henkin, A. H. 1998. *Honoring Human Rights: From Peace to Justice—Recommendations to the International Community.* Washington, D.C.: Aspen Institute Justice and Society Program.

Justice and Society Program of the Aspen Institute. 1989. *State Crimes: Punishment or Pardon.* Queenstown, MD: The Aspen Institute.

Kaye, M. 1997. The Role of Truth Commissions in the Search for Justice, Reconciliation and Democratisation: The Salvadorean and Honduran Cases. *Journal of Latin American Studies* 29(3), 693–716.

Kenney, C. D. and Spears, D. E. 2005. *Truth and Consequences: Do Truth Commissions Promote Democratization?* Paper to the Annual Meeting of the American Political Science Association: Washington, D.C., 1–4 September 2005.

Kim, H. and Sikkink, K. 2007. *Do Human Rights Trials Make a Difference?* Paper to the Annual Meeting of the American Political Science Association. Chicago, IL, 30 August-2 September, 2007.

Lie, T. G., Binningsbø, H. M. and Gates, S. 2007. *Post-Conflict Justice and Sustainable Peace.* World Bank Policy Research Working Paper 4191, Post-Conflict Transitions Working Paper No. 5.

Lutz, E. 2006. Transitional Justice: Lessons Learned and the Road Ahead, in *Transitional Justice in the Twenty-First Century: Beyond Truth Versus Justice*, edited by N. Roht-Arriaza and J. Mariezcurrena. New York: Cambridge University Press, 325–41.

Mendeloff, D. 2004. Truth-Seeking, Truth-Telling and Post-Conflict Peacebuilding: Curb the Enthusiasm? *International Studies Review* 6(3), 355–80.

Mendeloff, D. (forthcoming). Trauma and Vengeance: Assessing the Psychological and Emotional Effects of Post-Conflict Justice. *Human Rights Quarterly* 31(3).

Minow, M. 1998. *Between Vengeance and Forgiveness: Facing History after Genocide and Mass Violence.* Boston: Beacon Press.

Norval, A. 1999. Truth and Reconciliation: The Birth of the Present and the Reworking of History. *Journal of Southern African Studies* 25(3), 499–519.

Office of the United Nations High Commissioner For Human Rights. 2006. *Rule-of-Law Tools for Post-Conflict States: Truth Commissions*. New York: United Nations.

Orentlicher, D. F. 2004. *Independent Study on Best Practices, Including Recommendations, to Assist States in Strengthening Their Domestic Capacity to Combat All Aspects of Impunity*. New York: United Nations.

Payne, L. A., Olsen, T. D. and Reiter, A. G. 2008. *Does Transitional Justice Work?* Paper to the Annual Meeting of the International Studies Association. San Francisco, CA, 26–29 March 2008.

Quinn, J. R. and Freeman, M. 2003. Lessons Learned: Practical Lessons Gleaned from inside the Truth Commissions of Guatemala and South Africa. *Human Rights Quarterly* 25(4), 1117–49.

Roht-Arriaza, N. 2006. The New Landscape of Transitional Justice, in *Transitional Justice in the Twenty-First Century: Beyond Truth Versus Justice*, edited by N. Roht-Arriaza and J. Mariezcurrena. New York: Cambridge University Press, 1–16.

Ross, A. J. 1999. *The Body of the Truth: Truth Commissions in Guatemala and South Africa*, Ph.D. dissertation, Department of Geography, University of California, Berkeley.

Schiff, B. N. 2002. Do Truth Commissions Promote Accountability or Impunity? The Case of the South African Truth and Reconciliation Commission, in *Post-Conflict Justice*, edited by M.C. Bassiouni. Ardsley, N.Y.: Transnational Publishers, 325–43.

Sikkink, K. and Walling, C. B. 2007. The Impact of Human Rights Trials in Latin America. *Journal of Peace Research* 44(4), 427–45.

Silove, D., Zwi, A. B. and Le Touze, D. 2006. Do Truth Commissions Heal? The East Timor Experience. *The Lancet* 367(9518), 1222–4.

Snyder, J. L. and Vinjamure, L. 2003. Trials and Errors: Principle and Pragmatism in Strategies of International Justice. *International Security* 28(3), 5–44.

Sriram, C. L. 2004. *Confronting Past Human Rights Violations: Justice vs. Peace in Times of Transition.* New York: Frank Cass.

Teitel, R. G. 2000. *Transitional Justice.* New York: Oxford University Press.

Tepperman, J. D. 2002.Truth and Consequences. *Foreign Affairs* 81(2), 128–45.

Theissen, G. 1999. Common Past, Divided Truth. *TRC: Commissioning the Past.* University of Witwatersrand, South Africa, June 11–13, 1999.

United Nations. 2004. *The Rule of Law and Transitional Justice in Conflict and Post-Conflict Societies: Report of the Secretary-General.* New York: United Nations.

van der Merwe, H. 1999. *The Truth and Reconciliation Commission and Community Reconciliation: An Analysis of Competing Strategies and Conceptualizations*, Ph.D. dissertation, Institute for Conflict Analysis and Resolution, George Mason University.

Vinjamuri, L. and Snyder, J.L. 2004. Advocacy and Scholarship in the Study of International War Crime Tribunals and Transitional Justice. *Annual Review of Political Science* 7(1), 345–62.

Weissbrodt, D. and Fraser, P.W. 1992. Report of the Chilean National Commission on Truth and Reconciliation. *Human Rights Quarterly* 14 (4), 601–22.

PART II
Current Issues in International Human Rights

Chapter 8
Documenting Human Rights Abuses Among the Diaspora: Lessons Learned from the Liberian Truth and Reconciliation Commission

Patricia B. Minikon and Susan Shepler[1]

> The stories are there, in ordinary-looking immigrant neighborhoods like Park Hill on Staten Island. At 160 Park Hill Avenue, just north of the Verrazano-Narrows Bridge, lives Eva Yawo, who once watched as rebel soldiers locked her father in a toilet and burned him alive. Victoria Parker, who lives next door at 180 Park Hill Avenue, was caring for seven children when a bomb attack began. She managed to grab three of them, but four she lost in the crowd; she has never been able to find them, or to stop looking. Around the corner, at 30 Park Hill Circle is Isaac Sampson, who watched at a checkpoint as his father's belly was sliced open. Trying to tell the story one night this spring, he choked on his words, stood up and left the room. "From Staten Island Haven, Liberians Reveal War's Scars" *New York Times*, 18 September 18 2007.

Introduction

For the first time in the short history of Truth and Reconciliation Commissions, the Liberian Truth and Reconciliation Commission (TRC) has reached outside the borders of the nation to take statements from ordinary Liberians living in the diaspora and hold public hearings for the diaspora. In this chapter we address the following questions about this innovation in transitional justice: What are the origins of the Liberian Truth and Reconciliation Commission Diaspora Project? What are its most innovative features? Why is it important for the Liberian TRC to have the testimony of Liberians living in the diaspora? What have been the main

1 We wish to thank the American University students who participated as volunteer statement takers. We also wish to thank American University for the funds to fly Commissioner Coleman out for a panel discussion on the Diaspora Project and for funds for Dr. Shepler's travel to Minnesota to attend the public hearings. Thanks to Phylicia Mortey for research assistance.

difficulties and challenges facing this project? We conclude with some practical "lessons learned" for future transitional justice projects, and with some theoretical implications from this project.

First a word about the authors is in order, since we write here as scholars but also as participants in the project. Patricia Minikon trained volunteers in Washington, D.C. on Liberian culture and was the only Liberian member of the local organizational committee for the D.C. area. In that capacity, she advised on cultural matters during the outreach phase of the project, formulated outreach strategies, planned outreach events, and engaged in grassroots outreach within the Liberian community. She traveled to Ghana to take statements from Liberian refugees as well. Susan Shepler is an Assistant Professor of International Peace and Conflict Resolution at American University in Washington, D.C. She coordinated the participation of a group of her graduate students as volunteer statement takers, and was a part of the Washington, D.C. organizational committee. She also organized a panel discussion to discuss the successes and challenges of the Diaspora Project that included one of the TRC Commissioners and various members of the D.C. organizing committee and volunteers.

Origins of the Diaspora Project

The Liberian civil war began on 24 December 1989, when Charles Taylor's National Patriotic Front of Liberia entered Nimba County, Liberia using the border with Cote D'Ivoire, and attacked government interests. Most Liberians, however, trace the beginning of the political dimension of the conflict to the riots of 12 April 1979 (commonly known as the "rice riots"), when University of Liberia and high school students demonstrated to protest an increase in the price of rice. Protestors were fired upon by government forces and rioting erupted. The civil war lasted until the signing of the Comprehensive Peace Agreement (CPA) on 18 August 2003. The CPA provided the authority to create The Truth and Reconciliation Commission of Liberian (TRC). On 12 May 2005, the Commission was established by an Act of the National Transitional Legislative Assembly (NTLA).[2] Its mandate is to investigate gross violations of human rights and violations of international humanitarian law, as well as other human rights abuses, and economic crimes committed during the period January 1979 to 14 October 2003. The principal parties to the CPA were the government of then President Charles Taylor, Liberians United for Reconciliation and Democracy (LURD), and the Movement for Democracy in Liberia (MODEL).

2 The NTLA was an interim unicameral legislative body established by the Comprehensive Peace Agreement of 2003. Liberia's legislative branch, historically and at present, are the House of Representatives and the Senate. These bodies became nonfunctional during the civil wars from 1989 to 2003.

The nine TRC Commissioners were sworn in on 21 February 2006, by newly elected Liberian President, Ellen Johnson-Sirleaf. Under the leadership of Chairman Jerome Verdier, each Commissioner was given responsibility for a segment of the Liberian population. Responsibility for the fifteen counties and the Liberian diaspora were assigned to various Commissioners. Commissioner Massa Washington, the only Commissioner living in the United States when she was selected for the position, was given responsibility for the diaspora.

According to Amnesty International (2008, 15), an estimated 25 per cent of the Liberian population fled the country due to the civil war. The number of displaced Liberians was estimated at 36,000 in Ghana, 26,000 in Guinea, 18,000 in Sierra Leone, and 13,000 in Nigeria, according to the TRC. Records from the Office of Immigration Statistics (2004) indicate that 17,833 Liberians immigrated to the US between 1995 and 2004, and 21,023 Liberian refugees arrived in the US during that time period as well.

With well over 132,000 Liberians displaced and the diaspora rumored to have played a role in funding the war, the TRC realized that in order to get a complete picture of the conflict and its context, it would have to engage Liberians no longer living in the country. According to Chairman Verdier (2008), in order for the TRC to sustain and build a lasting peace in Liberia, it had to engage with the diaspora because, if it was in their "hearts and minds that the conflict started," then it was time well spent reaching out to them in order to craft an enduring solution for the future. The Liberian diaspora has always been involved in affairs in Liberia, even when not specifically invited to do so. According to anthropologist Mary Moran (2005, 459),

> Since the military coup of 1980 and the outbreak of civil war in 1989, the United States has been host to over 100,000 Liberian citizens, including most of the country's educated elite and former political officials. Far from passively observing 'events' as they unfold in West Africa, these people have been actively organizing to influence outcomes at home as well as American foreign policy toward Liberia. They represent many diverse political and ideological positions as well as regional and ethnic groupings within Liberia. [We] must take into account these diaspora-based activists, their 'governance groups' and other organizations, and their interaction with and influence upon occurrences in West Africa.

The political influence of the Liberian diaspora, especially in the US, was a clear reason the TRC decided to extend its reach outside the borders of Liberia. Commissioner Washington (2007) stated that the TRC considered the "pivotal role of Liberians in the diaspora...in the body politic of Liberia and their strategic position as a major constituency and stakeholders in the future of [the] nation. In light of that influence, the Commission was "determined that [the diaspora be] given a voice in this all-important national process, less [it] fall short of achieving [its] full mandate." The Commission also saw a need for Liberians living in the diaspora to be involved in the reconciliation process. When Chairman Verdier (2008) addressed the Public Hearings in Minnesota, he said, "We realized there were Liberians who were out of the country [who] needed to understand as well."

Partnering

In order to implement the Diaspora Project, the TRC turned to The Advocates for Human Rights, formerly Minnesota Advocates for Human Rights (henceforth "The Advocates"). The choice of The Advocates was not surprising. The nonprofit has a well-established relationship with the Liberian diaspora in Minnesota. The organization provides asylum seekers with *pro bono* attorneys, and in this manner, had assisted many Liberians in Minnesota in obtaining legal representation in their quest for refuge from the horrors of the civil war and for legal immigration status. In addition, famed Liberian human rights attorney, Kofi Woods, sits on the Board of Directors of The Advocates.

The aspect of the Diaspora Project handled by The Advocates involved statement taking in the United States, the United Kingdom, the Budumburam Refugee Camp in Ghana, and public hearings in the United States.[3] After the Memorandum of Understanding, termed the "Robertsport Accord,"[4] was signed, the Project was launched on 22 June 2006. Starting in September 2006, the TRC and The Advocates did outreach via Zonal Workshops in Minnesota, the District of Columbia, and New York because these cities had the highest number of Liberian residents in the US. Later, there were town hall meetings in those locations, as well as in other cities that would host Project sites. Using a team of *pro bono* legal partners consisting of law firms and law schools, The Advocates organized the Diaspora Project statement taking in US cities with sizeable Liberian populations. These cities were Atlanta, Chicago, Minneapolis/St. Paul, New York, Philadelphia, Providence, and metropolitan Washington, D.C.[5] Statement taking for the US region began in Minneapolis in January 2007.

The Diaspora Project as an Innovative 21st Century Transitional Justice Response

During the Cold War, human rights took a back seat to the pursuit of ideological goals like the spread of democracy and communism. When it ended in the early nineties, the geopolitical reality for African states was that they were no longer

3 The TRC directly handled statement-taking in Nigeria.

4 Robertsport is the capital of Cape Mount County, Liberia.

5 The Advocates hosted a statement-taking weekend in North Carolina as well, in response to a request from the Liberian Organization of the Piedmont, although the state was not a Project site.

proxies in that war, and as such, their human rights records came under increased scrutiny by the international community. A series of United Nations resolutions passed in the late eighties and early nineties urged the establishment of national human rights institutions.[6] In order to deal with this increased scrutiny, many African states adopted measures, including truth commissions,[7] to address past human rights issues. In the West African region, for example, Ghana established the Commission on Human Rights and Administrative Justice in 1993, and Nigeria established the National Human Rights Commission of Nigeria in 1995. In later years, Nigeria (1999), Ghana (2002), and Sierra Leone (2000) established commissions to investigate mass human rights violations, although the most famous African investigatory commission remains the Truth and Reconciliation Commission of South Africa, which was established in 1995. When the Truth and Reconciliation Commission of Liberia was established in 2005, it had the benefit of the experiences of previously established commissions in Latin America and Africa. While the Liberian Commission has a lot in common with previous commissions, its statement collection methodology differs significantly from those of prior commissions. The decision to establish a Diaspora Project marked a major departure from prior commissions for the reasons outlined later in this chapter. The Project was an innovative methodological response to the problem of investigating a national conflict with significant international dimensions.

The first way in which the Diaspora Project deviates from prior data collection is the partnership between The Advocates and the TRC. The truth commissions established in Argentina and Chile collected statements from citizens abroad using embassies, not a third-party entity. The choice to have statement collection performed by an international nongovernmental organization (INGO) like the Advocates, diverges from past practices of receiving technical assistance only from INGOs like the International Center for Transitional Justice. Historically, human rights INGOs have not participated in statement collection on behalf of truth commissions, although the Guatemalan commission utilized data collected in the course of investigations by two human rights organizations operating locally and non-nationals on the staff of truth commissions have participated in collecting statements (Hayner 2002, 47). The TRC's break from past practices was a unique response to the unique challenge of mounting a transnational investigation and reflected the close ties between Liberians in the diaspora and The Advocates. The decision also was possible because of technological advances like the Internet, electronic mail, and small data storage devices like flash drives that allow the transfer of vast amounts of information that can be accessed later without regard

6 For example, UN General Assembly Resolution A/RES/48/134 and Commission on Human Rights resolutions 1987/40, 1988/72, 1989/52, 1990/73, 991/27, 1992/54, and 1993/55.

7 The term truth commission, as used within this chapter, is defined as a state-sponsored body established to investigate past mass atrocities and violations of human rights or humanitarian law. It is used interchangeably with the term investigatory commission.

for the slow bandwidth speeds that plague one's Internet experience in Liberia. Additionally, the availability and frequency of reasonably priced transatlantic airline flights made in-person consultations possible when needed and cellular telephones enabled live conversation in a country without the infrastructure for landline phones due to the civil war. The Advocates, on the other hand, was able to mount such a large-scale data collection process because it already had an established network of *pro bono* partners. Without such a network, the collection of statements from eight states, the United Kingdom, and Ghana, could have proven to be an insurmountable task. Partner law firms had offices in different US cities and in the United Kingdom and were able to leverage resources and personnel in multiple locations to make statement collection possible.

In order to gather statements from the Budumburum Refugee Camp in Ghana, The Advocates once again called on its network of *pro bono* partners who sent volunteers overseas. The collection of statements from encamped refugees was another distinguishing feature of the TRC's methodology. Collection of statements in the refugee camp allowed the TRC to capture the lived experience of displacement under the harshest conditions and allowed it to hear from nationals who experienced the war in its initial stages, as it moved from rural Liberia to the outskirts of the capital city of Monrovia. Many in the camp were long-term residents, so their stories provided the TRC with information on long-term displacement as well.[8] It is information of this nature that could assist the TRC in painting a complete picture of the conflict and in assessing how the armed conflict and the abuses changed in character from year to year during the fourteen-year period of active fighting. The data could also facilitate the TRC's assessment of how the conflict affected rural versus urban residents, and could prove important in the determination of what kinds of reparation programs are needed to make members of the two demographic groups whole again.

According to Chairman Verdier (2008), "There is a very long held belief that all the wars started in the diaspora;" hence, the collection of statements from Liberians in the diaspora was in essence a return to the source of the conflict. Inquiry into the role of diaspora community associations in the financing of the civil conflict, the fostering of ethnic tensions, and the grooming of ethnic identity was not undertaken by prior commissions; the TRC, by its inquiry into those aspects of the conflict, has expanded on prior truth commissions' investigatory purview. Likewise, the TRC's investigation into the lived experience of the US-based diaspora, the impact of the conflict on life in the diaspora, and the experience of displacement evidences a focus different from that of previous commissions. Past commissions in Latin America and Africa had focused on nationals' experience in the home country alone or focused on experiences outside their borders in the context of

8 In February 2008, Liberian refugees in Budumburum staged a series of demonstrations, which led the government of Ghana to request their repatriation to Liberia and third countries. The repatriation is ongoing in 2008 and the refugee camp will be shut down when it is completed.

the relationship to organizations inside the borders. For example, South Africa's investigation into atrocities committed by the African National Congress (ANC) in its training camps in Southern Africa was part of its inquiry into the South African-based ANC's level of responsibility for apartheid-era abuses. The TRC's inquiry, however, was not to assign responsibility for abuses, but to assess the conditions under which displaced nationals in the US have to live. Sharing the indignities one faces after migration to a new country and one's experience occupying a lower rung of the social strata certainly provides the opportunity for validation and acknowledgment. Therefore, affording Liberians the opportunity to tell their stories of underemployment, living in overcrowded housing conditions, and life in crime-infested neighborhoods may have been the TRC's way of achieving its goals "to share and hear from Liberians in the diaspora as a way of affording all Liberians the opportunity to be heard, to be listened to, to be acknowledged, and to be validated" (Verdier 2008). The ultimate use of the information collected remains to be seen in the final report.

The most notable feature of the Liberian TRC was the staging of public hearings outside its borders. Given the number of atrocities committed in the ANC-run training camp in Namibia, the Truth and Reconciliation Commission of South African had tried to hold public hearings there, but that government refused, citing interference with its own reconciliation efforts (South African Press Association 1997). The Minnesota-based public hearings were possible because the hearings posed no similar national security threat and the US has a longstanding tradition of allowing groups comprising of citizens or noncitizens to associate freely, in accordance with the Bill of Rights to the US Constitution.[9] In addition, the staging of the hearings was against the backdrop of the historic ties between the US and Liberia. Those ties go back to the establishment of the Republic in 1822 by freed US slaves, a point made during expert testimony at the public hearings and during testimony by former Assistant Secretary of State for African Affairs, Herman J. Cohen, who personally apologized for the US's inaction early in the crisis (2008). Further, the US has been an early supporter of Liberia's reconstruction; at present, the United States Agency for International Development operates multiple projects and the Peace Corps returned in 2008.

Public Hearings in Minnesota

After holding hearings in most of the counties of Liberia, the entire commission traveled to St. Paul, Minnesota, for a public hearing with Liberians in the diaspora. The hearings were held from 10–14 June 2008, at Hamline University in St. Paul. As Chairman Verdier said in his opening statement, "We consider that The

9 This assumption of freedom of association has been challenged in the wake of the Bush administration's designation of several US-based Muslim groups as terrorist organizations in the waging of the war on terror.

Diaspora, Minnesota here, is one of the counties as well."[10] The President of the Organization of Liberians in Minnesota, Mr. Kerper Dwanyan (2008) stated:

> We look forward to the experiences of sharing our experiences here. I personally look forward to doing that and also look forward to speaking on behalf of our community, speaking of the roles of the diaspora community in both agitating the conflict and resolving the conflict and what role the diaspora community can continue to play in this process.

In many ways, the public hearings in Minnesota were the culmination of the diaspora statement taking process. The performance of the hearings symbolized the seriousness in which the commission held the diaspora testimony. In addition, since the diaspora statement taking process had been so disjointed in space (that is, hundreds of volunteers took statements individually and then entered them into a password protected database) the staging of the hearings made the whole process seem more coherent to those who attended. Seeing the commissioners all lined up on the stage, with the US and Liberian flags behind them, and the singing of both countries' national anthems and the taking of oaths, gave the occasion the aura of a legal proceeding.

Of course, the hearings were not meant to allow all Liberians in the diaspora to tell their stories publicly. Indeed, over the five days, only a handful of carefully selected Liberians were allowed to testify. The hearings would, rather, showcase the variety of stories gathered throughout the diaspora statement taking process and review Liberia's political history and its relationship to the conflict. Dr. Augustine Konneh, a Liberian historian and professor now living and working in the US was an expert witness. Also, the hearings allowed the commissioners to hear from important former officials now residing in the US who disclosed facts not otherwise available. For example, Bishop Benny Warner testified about his time as William R. Tolbert's Vice President and his recollections of the rice riots. As stated above, the commission was also interested in collecting stories of displacement, and the problems that Liberians faced when they found themselves living in the US.

Each day, there were at least a hundred people in attendance at the hearings, mainly white women—presumably employees of various human rights organizations or students—and Liberian men. Some Liberians not in attendance told us that they were unable to take time off work to attend the sessions. For those not able to attend in person, the hearings were streamed live online and are now archived online at The TRC website.[11] During the hearings, there was lively

10 Because of the importance of remittances, El Salvador has a similar view of its diaspora population. Salvadorans living in the US are known as "the fifteenth department." See Coutin 2007.

11 https://www.trcofliberia.org/memorials/video-galleries/video-gallery/public-hearings/view-public-hearings/browse-by-location-of-hearing/saint-paul-minnesota-usa.

online debate in various diaspora forums about the events as they transpired.[12] In addition, small groups of Liberians gathered outside the hall in vigorous debate. In general, the reaction to the testimony of officials was disgust and outrage, and the reaction to testimony of victims was sympathy and shared grief. The question and answer periods at the end of each day's testimony were particularly heated. One woman in the audience got up and expressed her outrage that the Liberian diaspora associations were not sufficiently admitting their role in fomenting violence. There was a great deal of emotion in the room at points during the testimony. During one harrowing testimony of rape, one could hear quiet tears around the room. In this sense, the hearings for the diaspora really did provide a community emotional experience, both online and for those present at the hearings.

Kelsall (2005) discusses how in the Sierra Leone case, in one hearing he observed, observers were angry at the nature of the testimony yet on the last day of the hearings the atmosphere changed. This was not, he claims, because the perpetrators eventually told the truth. "Rather, the change was due to the addition of a carefully staged reconciliation ceremony to the proceedings, a ritual that created an emotionally charged atmosphere that succeeded in moving many of the participants and spectators ..., and which arguably opened an avenue for reconciliation" (363). He goes on to conclude that ritual may be more important to reconciliation than truth. In the case of the public hearings in St. Paul, there was no "ritual" performed, but the stories of victims were certainly made more powerful by the formal setting of the commission. There was a palpable feeling in the room of sympathy, a public and emotional acknowledgement of the suffering experienced during the war.

Challenges Faced by the Diaspora Project

Since the Diaspora Project was the first time something like this was attempted, there were certain to be challenges in carrying it out. The biggest, and most unanticipated challenge, at least by the American volunteers, was the difficulty in getting people to volunteer to give statements. There are many reasons for this. First are the reasons that mirror the situation in Liberia. Liberians in the diaspora are usually closely monitoring news from back home, and were certainly aware of the concerns within Liberia regarding the commission. Moreover, the diaspora-based press featured numerous articles articulating concerns of the diaspora: Was the commission politically neutral? Would they be able to go after the biggest offenders? Would the commission be able to dispense retributive justice or provide amnesty?[13] At the beginning of the outreach process, there was certainly a reticence

12 For example, the online forums of the Coalition of Concerned Liberians and the Yahoo Group, "On Liberian Medium."

13 See for example, Sieh, R. 2008. Liberia's war without plotters: Will key actors finally face TRC? *Front Page Africa* [Online, 10 March]. Available at: www.frontpageafrica.

by potential statement givers due to a "let's wait and see how this thing turns out" attitude and simply out of lack of information.[14] These issues were similar for Liberians living in Liberia, and were dealt with there through an outreach and "sensitization" campaign, although there has been criticism of that as well (see Gberie 2008). Similar levels of outreach were not possible in the US, and when the Diaspora Project began, Liberians in the diaspora learned about the Commission through their local community organizations or via Liberian community listservs, if at all.[15]

Also present among Liberians in general was the feeling that it was not worth revisiting old traumas, and a doubt that public truth telling would lead to justice.[16] Shaw details this phenomenon in Sierra Leone by focusing on "social forgetting… a different process from individual forgetting, in that people still have personal memories of the violence. But speaking of the violence—especially in public—was (and is) viewed as encouraging its return, calling it forth when it is still very close and might at any moment erupt again" (2005, 9). Kelsall (2005, 363) notes that, "public truth-telling—in the absence of strong ritual inducement—lacks deep roots in the local cultures of Sierra Leone."

However, there were challenges unique to the US-based diaspora population, having to do with their unique situation. Because most have been able to make new successful lives in the US, there was perhaps even less motivation to reopen old wounds. Some did not see the relevance of the project to their new lives in the US. From a distance, it may be easier to put atrocities suffered firmly in the past. Others felt their statement was not worthy of inclusion in the collection of stories because their experiences paled in comparison to those who had suffered more trauma. In some cases, hesitation to testify may have come from an unspoken and unacknowledged fear of retraumatization. Others were afraid about what giving a statement might mean for their immigration status. Many potential statement givers were resettled lawful permanent residents, refugees, or asylees who had to meet certain qualifications in order to receive a grant of that status. The immigration law specifically bars persons who have committed human rights abuses from acquiring

com [accessed: 5 December 2008]; (discussing "war letters" implicating various Liberians in the diaspora in soliciting funds to support Charles Taylor's war efforts); Nubo, G. 2006. The human rights farce and the UNMIL conspiracy. *The Perspective* [Online, 14 November]. Available at: www.perspective.org [accessed: 5 December 2008]; Dukulé, A. 2006. Can the TRC bring true reconciliation? *The Perspective* [Online, 30 June]. Available at: www.perspective.org.

14 Although the diaspora-based press produced numerous articles on the TRC, those articles are online only and as such, accessible by a limited audience—Liberians who are computer literate. Moreover, the press articles were not written with an outreach goal in mind and did not provide in-depth information about the TRC.

15 For example, in the D.C. area, outreach materials were distributed via email and in-person at local community organization events and meetings.

16 Findings based on the results of an online survey sent to the D.C. area electronic distribution list and informal conversations with Liberians at outreach events.

permanent immigration status and because statements given could potentially be subpoenaed by the US government, there were risks involved. Because most of the volunteer statement takers were Americans, and American lawyers at that, there may have been some mistrust. Liberian women may have been less willing to tell Americans their accounts of sexual violence.

Another challenge was the ethnic fractionalization in the diaspora community. There are multiple Liberian groups in the diaspora and most are organized around ethnic groupings or counties of origin. This ethnic polarization made it difficult to organize people around a Liberian national project. This is not surprising, since it is long acknowledged in the scholarly literature on refugees that ethnic and other sub-national identities may harden in diaspora (see Malkki 1995).

Naturally, there were different challenges for different cities as the Liberian diaspora has a different character in different cities in the US. In Washington, D.C., there are more former government officials and other elites. In New York, most of the Liberian diaspora are more recent arrivals, and they are clustered in low-income housing on Staten Island. The challenge for the organizers was to develop an outreach strategy for each city that met the needs of the diaspora community living there. In D.C. (the case with which we are most familiar), the challenge of customization was made more difficult by the fact that the volunteers working on the Project were not necessarily familiar with the nuances of the local Liberian community and the Project did not use the grassroots model wherein all statement takers would have been conducting outreach, simultaneously getting to know members of the Liberian community, and later taking statements of those persons who signed up during the outreach event worked. Prior acquaintance with statement givers would have allowed volunteers to recall the shared experience of the outreach event when initially trying to set up a statement taking appointment. That familiarity would have made the statement giver feel a little more comfortable about recounting the traumatic past. Recounting a traumatic event to a stranger is not as inviting a situation as recounting events to someone seen at least once before.

Lessons Learned

The choice of format for the Diaspora Project had important implications, created challenges, and imposed constraints. The use of the *pro bono* model meant that grassroots organizing and outreach, which in hindsight would have been the most effective means of encouraging participation in the Project, was not easily accomplished. The *pro bono* model entails assigning an attorney to a client motivated by the opportunity to obtain expensive legal representation at no cost. The attorney takes on the case with the reasonable assumption that the client is prepared to participate in the undertaking. On the other hand, many Liberian nationals who had experienced atrocities or witnessed unmentionable violence during the civil conflict were loathed to revisit that experience again because they had resettled in a new country, had put the past behind them, and had resumed what they considered to be a normal life. To complicate matters, in Washington, D.C., outreach and sign-ups were not necessarily conducted by the same persons who would take the statement. An attorney or non-attorney they had never met later contacted those who signed up to schedule an appointment. Under this arrangement, matching a *pro bono* attorney or volunteer to such a client leads to unfulfilled expectations and disappointing results.[17] First, the attorney, instead of engaging with a client who is eager to participate in the relationship, has to engage with one who is reluctant to revisit the past, the very topic about which the attorney must now conduct the interview. Frequently, nationals assigned to attorneys or non-attorneys would refuse to commit to giving a statement after signing up or would signal reluctance to participate by an inability to commit to a scheduled date and time to have the interview. Naturally, this led to frustrated volunteer statement takers. Had we been using the grassroots model, we could have arranged it so that canvassers doing outreach before a particular group or in a particular residential area would have been the same persons to take the statement, either immediately after conducting outreach or no more than 48 hours later, with the benefit of prior acquaintance. Streamlining outreach and statement taking in this manner was not easily adaptable to a structure where most attorneys and volunteers who took statements did not do outreach and were not assigned to a statement giver for at least a few days or more after the person had signed up.

The lessons learned from participation in the Diaspora Project in the Washington, D.C. metropolitan area can be divided into two groups: practical and theoretical. On the practical level, we realized that in addition to the traditional mediums of print and radio, we should have engaged in more grassroots outreach. We got more results when outreach was done via live conversations that allowed potential statement givers to ask questions, and address concerns, distrust, and uncertainties about the process. We should have used traditional Liberian media outlets more by running culturally relevant streaming video advertisements on their web pages and by writing articles and opinion pieces to counter negative press about the TRC process. Articles and opinion pieces by Project participants explaining the process and the purpose of the TRC would have helped to counter the barrage of articles in diaspora based newspapers questioning whether leaders of the various factions that fought the civil war would ever face the commission and questioning the focus on the victims and low-ranking alleged perpetrators. Liberia had never before established a truth and reconciliation commission and nationals did not understand what the process and the institution were supposed to accomplish, or the link between the commission's mandate and peacebuilding.

---

17 This is not to say that statement takers in Liberia were all personally known by statement givers. However, the circumstances in Liberia were different because statement takers were from the statement givers' local community and the TRC was a known national entity. In contrast, in the US, volunteers did not necessarily reside in the same local communities as statement givers and most of the partner law firms and law schools were not known entities to the Liberian communities of interest.

The nexus between the TRC's mandate, the data collection process, and the goal of establishing a foundation for future peace could have been better explained in outreach materials and should have been the focus of more live conversations. We should have pushed for more opportunities to conduct live outreach or hosted a series of outreach events that followed scheduled community events, but we did not have anyone working full-time on the tracking of Liberian community-based activities due to an all volunteer staff. Explaining to nationals early in the process why the TRC was initially focused on victims and survivors would have allayed fears that the statement taking process was a witch hunt for less powerful alleged perpetrators and could have encouraged more residents in the Washington, D.C. area to give their statements.

The timing of the Project played a role in outreach efforts. There is a huge celebration of Liberia's independence in July of each year. The event is well-attended and would have been an excellent opportunity to conduct outreach, except that the project started in the fall, after most community events were over because the summer season is when most events that draw large crowds are planned. Upon reflection, it becomes apparent that outreach needed to be conducted in casual and small gatherings organized for that very purpose, or incorporated into community events that drew large crowds. Statement taking should have been ongoing during such events or should have been done immediately after to take advantage of the energy generated for participation once a potential statement giver understood the nexus between the TRC's mandate, peacebuilding, and giving a statement and had all questions and concerns addressed.

Support from civil society organizations and the religious community influenced Liberians' willingness to participate. An invitation to speak about the project accompanied by a strong endorsement from the leadership of the organization resulted in nationals present signing up to give a statement once their concerns were addressed. Such invitations usually meant that there would be the opportunity to present information about the TRC process and time allotted for the audience to ask questions, sparking a productive dialogue that usually ended with those present expressing interest in participating. On the other hand, where there was no strong endorsement by the organization's leadership, participation was lackluster. On one occasion, we organized a roundtable discussion with clergy. No one showed up from one preacher's church and his congregation's absence was surprising until he opined that he did not feel Liberians were safe to freely discuss their war-time experiences. It is highly unlikely, given how the preacher felt, that he would have strongly urged his members to participate in the TRC process and in our roundtable event. Without his endorsement to participate, the likelihood of his congregation doing so was low.

The existence of a well-functioning Liberian community organization in the local diaspora community also played an important role in the ability to reach nationals. The existence of community association offices allowed the Project to establish a presence and even conduct outreach and statement taking using those offices. In Ghana, the Project took statements in the offices of several community organizations based in the refugee camp. This allowed the team to get to work quickly in an environment that was already familiar to the witnesses. The work was made easier by the fact that the refugees, for the most part, lacked the reticence seen in US residents. Statement givers queued in long lines and waited for hours in the sweltering heat to give a statement. Later, volunteers realized that this eagerness to participate may have been fueled by a rumor that the team would be able to facilitate resettlement to a third country.

The locale of statement taking affects the level of services nationals potentially have access to. The collection of statements in the US and in Ghana presented different opportunities for statement givers and different challenges for volunteers. Volunteers were unable to refer statement givers in the refugee camp for psycho-social counseling, whereas that referral, if needed, was possible in the US. Additionally, Liberians who desired legal consultation in relation to giving a statement could obtain one in the US, but that was not an option in Ghana. Although access to counseling, legal and mental, was available to US residents, the use of those services by Liberians was not tracked during the statement taking phase, so no conclusions can be drawn regarding the extent of retraumatization or the prevalence of legal concerns during statement taking among the diaspora.

Theoretical Implications of the Diaspora Project

We have written above about what is new about the Liberia TRC Diaspora Project, but what do the innovations we have described imply for the theory of transitional justice in particular and human rights practice in general?

The first thing that comes to mind is that this project implies a new and broader definition of the nation in the project of national reconciliation. The statements from the diaspora were in part to feed information into the report writing process, but they were also meant to include the Liberians living abroad in the reconciliation process, as part of the Liberian nation. In some ways this was necessary due to the extreme levels of participation by diaspora populations in the politics of Liberia before, during, and after the war. To include the diaspora in the truth and reconciliation process is an acknowledgement that displacement does not preclude political involvement.

The second theme to note is that the inclusion of foreign actors is a new and paradigm-shifting development. Nagy, in her critique of the "global project" of transitional justice notes that, "Foreign involvement in violence—through indifference, funding, training, cross-border raids, or conflict economies in arms, diamonds or oil—is largely absent from or negligible in official transitional justice records" (284). In the Liberia case, the inclusion of the diaspora allowed for inclusion of the importance of transnational flows: of funds, of goods, and of people. It was vitally important to Liberians in attendance at the public hearings that Herman J. Cohen, former US Assistant Secretary of State for African Affairs, testified and personally apologized for the US inaction in Liberia. Note too that

Chairman Verdier spoke to the power differential between the West and the Third World when he spoke of the important role of the diaspora community in agitating for change in the US, since they are closer to the center of power and have more resources.

Finally, the inclusion of the diaspora is, in our view, an acknowledgement of the shifting nature of sovereignty. It is certainly the case that most of the funding and expertise for the Liberia TRC came from outside the country, from various international actors. This is true for the vast majority of transitional justice initiatives around the world, and is therefore hardly a new observation about implications for national sovereignty of internationally constituted transitional justice mechanisms. It is not new surprising to note that the reconciliation project was not necessarily one exclusively between the Liberian state and its citizens. The more important point is that in this case those considered "citizens" of the nation include those who have lost their Liberian citizenship and who are no longer living within its territorial boundaries. Moran describes a meeting of Liberian intellectuals in the US, discussing governance in a post-Charles Taylor world, in a way that would have been impossible in Liberia at the time. She concludes, "It was the displacement of the participants from the site of the 'events' that made their intervention possible" (2005, 460). Add in the importance of the Internet and other telecommunications, and the growing debate in Liberia about the possibility of dual citizenship, and it is clear that the innovation in the TRC grew directly out of innovations in sovereignty. A broadened conception of the nation led naturally to a broadened conception of national reconciliation.

Nagy (2008) notes in her critique of the "global project" of transitional justice that, "In the determination of *who* is accountable for *what* and *when*, transitional justice is a discourse and practice imbued with power. …Artificial time frames and zones of impunity produce restricted accounts of violence and remedy" (287). The Liberian TRC is notable, therefore, for pushing back at some of these artificial boundaries and introducing an expanded notion of who should be held responsible and who should be reconciled.

Conclusions

In this chapter we have sought to answer several questions about the Diaspora Project of the Liberian TRC. We discussed the origins of the Project, the special importance of the diaspora to Liberian politics, the innovative partnership between the Commission and The Advocates, and the challenges of implementing the *pro bono* model during statement taking. We reviewed the public hearings in Minnesota and detailed lessons learned from our own experiences as participants in the project. Finally, we presented some thoughts on sovereignty and the implications of this project for shifting configurations of power in the realm of international relations.

As we write this, The Advocates has yet to submit its final report on the Diaspora Project to the Commission and the Commission has yet to conclude its research, let alone complete its final report. Therefore, obviously, we cannot comment on how the inclusion of diaspora voices will affect the eventual outcome of the process. We all wait anxiously and hopefully for real reconciliation and a peaceful future for all Liberians, wherever they may reside.

References

Amnesty International. 2008. *Liberia: Towards the Final Phase of the Truth and Reconciliation Commission.* 29 July 2008. Amnesty International Report no. AFR 34/002/2008.

Barry, E. 2007. From Staten Island Haven, Liberians Reveal War's Scars *New York Times*, 18 September [Online] Available at: http://www.nytimes.com/2007/09/18/nyregion/18liberians.html?_r=2&hp&oref=slogin [accessed: 15 December 2008].

Cohen, H. 2008. *Testimony Before the Truth and Reconciliation Commission of Liberia.* Diaspora Project Public Hearings 10–14 June 2008. St. Paul, Minnesota [Online] Available at: https://www.trcofliberia.org/memorials/video-galleries/video-gallery/pubilc-hearings/view-public-hearings/browse-by-location-of-hearing/diaspora/united-states/day-3-part-1-1-2/view [accessed: 15 December 2008].

Coutin, S. 2007. *Nations of Emigrants: Shifting Boundaries of Citizenship in El Salvador and the United States.* Ithaca: Cornell University Press.

Dwanyan, K. 2008. *Remarks of President, Union of Liberian Associations in the Americas, at the Opening Ceremonies of the TRC US Public Hearings 10 June 2008.* Diaspora Project Public Hearings 10–14 June 2008: St. Paul, Minnesota [Online] Available at: https://www.trcofliberia.org/memorials/video-galleries/video-gallery/pubilc-hearings/view-public-hearings/browse-by-location-of-hearing/diaspora/united-states/day-1-part-1-1-4/view [accessed: 18 November 2008].

Gberie, L. 2008. "Briefing: Truth and Justice on Trial in Liberia." *African Affairs* 107(428), 455–65.

Hayner, P. 2002. *Unspeakable Truths: Facing the Challenge of Truth Commissions.* New York: Routledge.

Kelsall, T. 2005. Truth, Lies, Ritual: Preliminary Reflections on the Truth and Reconciliation Commission in Sierra Leone. *Human Rights Quarterly* 27 (2), 361–91.

Malkki, L. 1995. *Purity and Exile: Violence, Memory, and National Cosmology among Hutu Refugees in Tanzania.* Chicago, University of Chicago Press.

Moran, M. H. 2005. Time and Place in the Anthropology of Events: A Diaspora Perspective on the Liberian Transition. *Anthropological Quarterly* 78(2): 457–64.

Nagy, R. 2008. Transitional Justice as Global Project: Critical Reflections. *Third World Quarterly* 29(2), 275–89.

Office of Immigration Statistics of the Department of Homeland Security. 2004. *Yearbook of Immigration Statistics* [Online]. Available at: http://www.dhs.gov/xlibrary/assets/statistics/yearbook/2004/Yearbook2004.pdf [accessed: 3 December 2008].

Pillay, S. and Scanlon, H. 2007. *Peace Versus Justice? Truth and Reconciliation Commissions and War Crimes Tribunals in Africa*. Policy Advisory Group Seminar. Cape Town, South Africa, Centre for Conflict Resolution.

Shaw, R. 2005. *Rethinking Truth and Reconciliation Commissions: Lessons from Sierra Leone. Special Report*. Washington, D.C.: United States Institute of Peace Press.

South African Press Association (SAPA) 1997. *Namibia: Government Not to Allow Truth Commission Hearings*. 17 May 1997 [Online]. Available from World News Connection database by subscription. [accessed: 22 October 2008].

Verdier, J. 2008. *Opening Statement by the Chairman of the Truth and Reconciliation Commission of Liberia*. Diaspora Project Public Hearings 10–14 June 2008. St. Paul, Minnesota [Online]. Available at: https://www.trcofliberia.org/memorials/video-galleries/video-gallery/pubilc-hearings/view-public-hearings/browse-by-location-of-hearing/diaspora/united-states/day-1-part-1-2-4/view [accessed: 18 November 2008].

Washington, M. 2007. *Remarks of the Chairperson of the TRC Committee on Diaspora Relations*. Official Launching of the TRC-US Diaspora Project Statement Taking Process on 24 February 2007 Minneapolis, Minnesota [Online]. Available at: https://www.trcofliberia.org/news-1/trc-happenings/remaks-at-the-official-launching-of-the-trc-us-diaspora-statement-taking-process/ [accessed: 23 October 2008].

Chapter 9

Viewing the Millennium Development Goals through Prisms of IR Theory: An Intersection of Human Rights and State Interests

Michaelene Cox

Experts point to an ongoing global financial crisis, one of epic scale, unfolding before us. Without doubt, the disaster will indiscriminately bleed across borders, class, ideologies, economies, and culture, and vividly demonstrate the growing anxieties and inadequacies of states in single-handedly tackling complex security issues in this, a spectacularly integrated world. Prospects for economic development, and all that rests upon such progress, are in jeopardy for both wealthy and poor countries. The crisis will most certainly have uneven impacts but it is fair to say that no corner of the globe will be fully immune to the social and political problems associated with the phenomenon. A crippled world economy is heady stuff to issues of peace and conflict at every level, since it is generally accepted that economic development is inextricably linked to political stability. If we define development from a public policy perspective as efforts to improve the well-being and quality of life, we see that the welfare and order of an international community is as intimately connected to the well-being of a state as the latter is to the well-being of its citizens. The exacerbation of structural violence, which refers to systemic barriers to achieving basic human needs, is highly interdependent with direct violence. It follows then that the persistence of extreme poverty, entrenched everywhere to varying degree, is a crisis as staggering as that of the current global financial predicament, and just as potently threatens the security that comes from successfully negotiating individual, state, and overall community welfare interests.

International strategies for the past decade or so to reduce levels of poverty and to address related issues have increasingly framed that mission in terms of human rights standards. This chapter highlights one dimension in the relations between state, global governance, and development by reflecting upon the Millennium Development Goals. The MDGs provide a contemporary case study to explore in context of international relations theory. Scholarly literature typically underscores a normative grounding to the MDGs, which suggests that some variant of critical theory or constructivist framework would lend itself well to explaining the social realities and policy-making issues surrounding the topic. However, to initiate here a dialogue about the value in applying diverse theoretical approaches to specific political problems, this chapter views the MDGs in context of two competing positivist traditions, structural realism and neoliberal institutionalism. It begins by first describing the Goals and their strategies, and updating readers on their status and prospects for achievement. A brief history of the MDGs and their relation to universal human rights initiatives will then be followed by a theoretical discussion tending to sovereignty issues.

A Perspective of Poverty

Eradicate, achieve, promote, reduce, improve, combat, ensure and develop—the eight broad objectives of the Millennium Development Goals each begin with these rather forceful verbs. They are commands, really, and resound with the language of military campaigns. The war against poverty fairly quickly spread from the rhetoric of US domestic policy in the latter century to an increasingly integrated international arena when UN member governments agreed upon a shared framework for development in 2000. The resulting MDGs are based on the conviction that a coherent and coordinated approach in mobilizing resources and support is required for implementing multiple and wide-ranging attacks on poverty and its correlates (UN General Assembly 2007). In short, international consensus now amplifies a state's responsibility towards its citizens and to the community-at-large in respect to developmental progress, and at the same time concludes that state capabilities in singly addressing that challenge are limited. Poverty then is one of a number of untraditional transnational issues placed on a contemporary global security agenda. Further deliberation of this link between extreme poverty and security will follow; in the meanwhile, let us consider the extent of poverty which now captivates world attention

It is no revelation that the most severe deprivation is concentrated in the developing regions, and in particular, Sub-Saharan Africa and South Asia. Although recent estimates of the scale and distribution of poverty show erratic progress is being made here and there, the data still paints a grim picture. The UN reports that more than one billion people worldwide struggle on an income of less than one dollar a day. More than three-fourths of those live in perpetual hunger and about 25,000 each day die of hunger-related causes. About a third of the world's population lives in slum conditions, and without adequate sanitation. Annually, childbirth or pregnancy accounts for the death of half a million women in developing countries, while child mortality figures hover around 10 million. Air pollution kills three million and HIV/AIDS infects about 30 million each year (UNDP 2008a). Illiteracy rates, lack of gender parity in education and employment, and other indicators of social deprivation are equally staggering. All of this and more points to a wide-ranging definition of poverty and to the vicious cycle perpetuating poverty as a global human security dilemma. Thus, developmental programs such as the MDGs address more than financial destitution; they speak to a wide-range of features comprising structural violence.

Most simply, the Millennium Development Goals with its new initiatives such as the Millennium Promise represent a road map for reducing poverty and other obstacles to human development by 2015 through international commitment and collaboration. And, like most international policy initiatives, there is considerable contention swirling about that plan. To start, development focusing on modernization and structural adjustment has shifted in recent decades to poverty reduction. Disagreement is not principally about the merits *per se* of addressing wide-scale poverty. After all, six of the eight Goals directly target the plight of children and one would be hard-pressed to detect even a murmur of objection for tending to the welfare of the young. The aspirations themselves conjure ideals of human empathy for they reside in a "cloud of soft words and good intentions and moral comfort; they are gentle…they are kind, they offer only good things to the deprived" as one writer so eloquently describes (Saith 2006, 1167). To be frank, mitigating deprivation is universally regarded as a good thing, most of the time. One of the most persistent disputes centers instead on the methods of defining, quantifying, and monitoring progress.

The MDG inclusion of 20 targets and 60 indicators to track progress on the eight goals attempts to synthesize measures for monitoring and implementing poverty reduction strategies, and is no more immune to suspicion and criticism from politicians, economists, scholars, civil society groups, and even patrons than the developmental programs that preceded it. Methodological concerns, such as conceptualizing poverty by choosing to focus on some issues while ignoring others, exasperate critics. Some also point to significant correlations among the goals and other unconsidered economic factors (Bourguignon et al. 2008, 21–2). Further, aside from the trouble of securing adequate funds to do so, the challenge to cohesively and practically implement and supervise developmental policies through multiple UN channels and state agencies is knotty (Harcourt 2005, 2). Yet architects of the MDGs argue that even this imperfect attempt to establish priorities and devise numerical targets and indicators for development provides the best hope for monitoring and reporting country and global efforts over a multi-year span, as well as generally cultivating clear communication and consistent alliance among a broad community (UN General Assembly 2001). Indeed, the annual Millennium Development Goals Report provides us with a fairly detailed progress report, replete with statistics and sympathetic photographs of smiling children and industrious women (UN 2008b). This year's report reminds us that we have passed the midpoint between adoption of the Goals and their projected realization, and that there is still a long-term collective effort required for attaining these ambitious global development aspirations. If the report isn't enough to convey a sense of urgency, then the MDG Monitor likely will. The on-line tracking system includes interactive maps and country-specific profiles of development, and a clock ticking down each second before 2015. Watching the countdown is mesmerizing; time does not dawdle. But when the clock stops, what then?

Goal 1: Eradicate extreme poverty and hunger.
Halve, between 1990 and 2015, the proportion of people whose income is less than one dollar a day. Achieve full and productive employment and decent work for all, including women and young people. Halve, between 1990 and 2015, the proportion of people who suffer from hunger.

Goal 2: Achieve universal primary education.
Ensure that, by 2015, children everywhere, boys and girls alike, will be able to complete a full course of primary schooling.

Goal 3: Promote gender equality and empower women.
Eliminate gender disparity in primary and secondary education, preferably by 2005, and in all levels of education no later than 2015.

Goal 4: Reduce child mortality.
Reduce by two-thirds, between 1990 and 2015, the under-five mortality rate.

Goal 5: Improve maternal health.
Reduce by three quarters, between 1990 and 2015, the maternal mortality ratio.

Goal 6: Combat HIV/AIDS, malaria and other diseases.
Have halted by 2015 and begun to reverse the spread of HIV/AIDS. Achieve, by 2010, universal access to treatment for HIV/AIDS for all those who need it. Have halted by 2015 and begun to reverse the incidence of malaria and other major diseases.

Goal 7: Ensure environmental sustainability.
Integrate the principles of sustainable development into country policies and programmes and reverse the loss of environmental resources. Reduce biodiversity loss, achieving, by 2010, a significant reduction in the rate of loss. Halve, by 2015, the proportion of people without sustainable access to safe drinking water and basic sanitation. By 2020, to have achieved a significant improvement in the lives of at least 100 million slum dwellers.

Goal 8: Develop a global partnership for development.
Develop further an open, rule-based, predictable, non-discriminatory trading and financial system; address the special needs of the least developed countries. Address the special needs of landlocked developing countries and small island developing states. Deal comprehensively with the debt problems of developing countries through national and international measures in order to make debt sustainable in the long term. In cooperation with pharmaceutical companies, provide access to affordable essential drugs in developing countries. In cooperation with the private sector, make available the benefits of new technologies, especially information and communications.

Figure 9.1 The Millennium Development Goals and Summary Targets

Source: Adapted from Report of the Secretary-General (UN General Assembly 2001)

Relentless review and debate about the Millennium Development Goals and the approaching target date is heard in nearly every academic discipline and public arena, and so makes it scarcely necessary to describe each of the Goals here in detail. Still, a list of the MDGs and their targets, and a summary of their status, will better inform a subsequent discussion of poverty relief, human rights, and state interests. Figure 9.1 catalogues the eight Goals and their quantifiable targets.

With advances in development uneven, some progress on some goals in some countries might lead an optimist to say the glass is half-full. One must consider the source and context of that assessment. Although not directly linked to the MDGs, Human Development Indices released by the United Nations Development Programme (UNDP) reveal that 80 developing countries show improvement in education, and that a few countries in Africa such as Botswana and Zambia show some recovery in regards to HIV/AIDS statistics (UNDP 2008b). Also in praise, and in his first annual report to the UN General Assembly after assuming the post of Secretary-General, Ban-Ki Moon notes being especially impressed with dramatic advancements thus far in African states (UN General Assembly 2007). He further declares that the MDGs are his central priority while in office. The Secretary-General warns that the very credibility of the UN will be judged by the results it produces in human rights and humanitarian missions—not by its aspirations—and so calls the international community to "narrow the gap between aspiration and achievement" (UN General Assembly 2007, 1–2). His strategy to do so includes focusing on UN organizational reform, building consensus and commitment among member states to deliver the promise of the MDGs, and maintaining strong government leadership. Despite there being serious hurdles, he states that if member states fulfill their commitments by implementing national and international development strategies, that the Goals will be realized in most countries.

However, forecasts from others in the international community are less bright. The European Union expresses "strong concern" that absolute numbers of poor are increasing and that their lives will not be appreciably improved by the target year (*Eurostep Weekly* 2008). In a report to the European Commission, researchers find that income growth in Asian countries is primarily responsible for global progress on poverty rates, and that the only other Goal on track by developing countries is gender parity in education (Bourguignon et al. 2008, 8). The UN provides a helpful on-line visual of the status of 18 MDGs targets, with four shades of colored cells corresponding to degrees of compliance for each region of the developing world (UN 2008a). A far starker picture emerges, however, when we collapse those shaded categories of progress into black and white in Figure 9.2 below. Now two measures indicate the positive and negative outlooks by region. It is fruitful to concentrate on targets being met, rather than broader goals, since there are many dimensions and measures of the latter. White cells show targets met or near being met, and where progress is sufficient to be met by 2015. Shaded cells reflect targets where progress is insufficient and unlikely to be met by the target date, and where there is no progress or even deterioration in those regions. The predominance of dark cells now leaves little room to hope that the outlook for most of the world is promising. This visual aid illustrates the half empty glass.

	Africa		Asia				Oceania	Latin	CIS	
	N	SubS	E	SE	S	W			Eur	Asia
GOAL 1:	**Eradicate extreme poverty and hunger**									
Poverty										
Employ										
Hunger										
GOAL 2:	**Achieve universal primary education**									
School										
GOAL 3:	**Promote gender equality and empower women**									
Enrollment										
Employment										
Representation										
GOAL 4:	**Reduce child mortality**									
Mortality										
Measles										
GOAL 5:	**Improve maternal health**									
Mortality										
Health										
GOAL 6:	**Combat HIV/AIDS, malaria and other diseases**									
HIV/AIDS										
T.B.										
GOAL 7:	**Ensure environmental sustainability**									
Forests										
Drinking Water										
Sanitation										
Slums										
GOAL 8:	**Develop a global partnership for development**									
Internet										

Figure 9.2 Regional Prospects for Meeting the Millennium Development Goals by 2015

Shading indicates no progress or deterioration, or progress insufficient to reach targets
Source: Adapted from the Millennium Development Goals Progress Chart (UN 2008a)

In fact, saying the glass is only half empty is still too optimistic. The checkerboard progress chart suggests that only one third of the targets will probably be met as scheduled. Much of the improvement will be seen in East Asia where 12 of the 18 are likely to be realized, and in North Africa and Latin America/the Caribbean where 10 targets are promising. Conversely, prospects for two-thirds of the targets are disappointing. The fate for Sub-Saharan Africa and Oceania is most dismal with not a single target expected to be reached. West Asia fares only a bit better having four of the 18 possibly being met. Targets that have least potential across the board for being achieved by 2015 include obtaining greater representation of women in government, combating tuberculosis, and improving maternal health. Reducing mortality in children and pregnant women, and protecting forest lands are also least successful targets. We must keep in mind that the aforementioned progress or lack of progress on the Goals and targets is predicated on the continuation of trends up through last year. There is much to suggest, though, that the recent global economic climate will likely upset those trends.

Redoubled efforts in terms of domestic reform, international commitment, and aid may conceivably offer a more encouraging view into the future of the developing world. Of course, the current slide in international financial markets and the global economy does portend a less favorable economic environment for the remaining countdown. Outlooks for poverty relief are mixed. The World Bank imparts a message of both optimism and despair. While there are 20 per cent more people living in developing countries since 1990, the proportion of those living in extreme poverty has dropped from 28 per cent to about 19 per cent. The absolute numbers of those living in such devastating circumstances, however, is still confounding. By 2015, more than 600 million will remain ensnared by the structural violence of poverty (World Bank 2008). Further, although there are both important advances and set-backs reported on progress of the MDGs, current patterns predict that most countries will fail meeting most of their goals (MDG Monitor 2008).

Finger pointing suggests an ambiguity in placing blame for limitations of the program. For example, although foreign aid levels have generally increased, planners had calculated only necessary costs for successfully implementing the Goals and not what might be sufficient to meet them. Failures may likely be attributed to aid (Clemens, Kenny and Moss 2007). Yet in weighing hopes for any realistic progress in African countries, one writer appreciates the role of aid but says that change must come from within the state and society. The argument is made that what is at stake is economic development as well as true democracy, and that Africans must assume responsibility for their own destiny and "change from their 'business as usual' approach and attitude" (Okonofua 2005, 9). Then again, another observer writing in the same year argues that significant progress on developmental progress was doomed from the start. The technocratic and top-down approach undertaken by the MDG group is inadequate in addressing the political complexities of poverty. "It seems to be leaving the negotiating of politics to others or at best to the UN corridors while relying on 'campaigns' and 'experts' to calculate the figures and then sell the strategies to governments and civil society," she says (Harcourt 2005, 2). And then, there is the economy. UN General-Secretary Ban Ki-Moon prefaces the Goals' most recent status report with a warning that success in reaching targets is threatened. He attributes previous advancements to the earlier decade's "largely benign development environment" and acknowledges that current global economic troubles may "unravel" efforts now to reduce poverty (UN 2008b, 3). So what is it—aid, domestic politics, the development framework itself, or the international economy that largely foretells the fate of the MDGs? The roles of all these and a multiplicity of other factors deserve serious scrutiny; this chapter merely intimates the complexity in systematically assessing the successes and failures of the Goals. It calls to mind that the political relevancy of the MDGs is at the heart of most critiques.

Re-viewing MDGs as Rights

Tracing the political roots of the Millennium Development Goals moves us toward a discussion of its links to human rights, human security, and impact on state sovereignty.

Establishment of the MDGs followed from a spate of major international summits, conferences, and UN General Assembly declarations and resolutions in the early 1990s. Those activities produced a number of ambitious goals and promises by government leaders and civil society to tend to various human welfare issues, but many generally fizzled after hoopla of the moment faded. Two of the earliest events in this wave were the UN General Assembly of the Convention on the Rights of the Child, and the World Summit for Children in New York. The latter declared an international commitment to the survival, protection and development of children and formulated a half dozen or so objectives to reach by the twenty-first century (UNICEF 1990). A few years later, the well-publicized UN International Conference on Population and Development met in Cairo. There, more than 20,000 government and non-government delegates gathered to discuss matters such as immigration, infant mortality, education of women, and other population issues. A consensus among 179 countries was reached to adopt a 20-year program to achieve four quantitative goals on universal education, reduction of infant and child mortality, reduction of maternal mortality, and access to reproductive and sexual health services (UNFPA 1994). Then, in the following year, the historic Fourth World Conference on Women in Beijing gathered and constructed twelve priorities to address gender equality and development issues for women worldwide called the Platform for Action which was to be carried out over the following five years (UN Division for the Advancement of Women 1995). The Platform for Action articulated a clear connection with the mission of preceding international conferences, and in particular to the principles adopted by the World Conference on Human Rights, which had met two years earlier in Austria. The Vienna Declaration and Programme of Action served to remind the broader community of its responsibilities to promote universal respect for and protection of human rights as set forth in the Universal Declaration of Human Rights (UDHR) in 1948. On its agenda was discussion about the links between development, democracy and economic, social, cultural, civil and political rights, as well as an assessment of UN capabilities to further a plan of action in those matters (UN Office of the High Commissioner for Human Rights 1993). Thus, time-bound and measurable goal-setting related to poverty reduction in many of these early projects cleared a path for the direction and the substance that the MDGs would take.

But it was only with the publication of a heavily-marketed report in 2000 called "A Better Future for All: Progress towards the International Development Goal" that formulation of the Millennium Development Goals was given definitive shape and impetus. The controversial 25-page report was jointly produced by the UN Secretariat, the International Monetary Fund (IMF), the World Bank (WB), and the Organization for Economic Cooperation and Development (OECD). During the Copenhagen Plus Five summit, critics charged that recommendations in the report to developing countries reflected ideologies and self-interests of those four institutions and perverted efforts to assist the Global South. They pointed to a series of proposals that urged developing countries to open their markets to imports, exports and finance (UN 2000). The proposals were heavily borrowed from a preceding 1996 OECD Development Assistance committee publication that included seven time-bound goals to address economic, social and environmental ideals, most notably the slashing of extreme poverty in developing countries by 2015. We find that a notable shift occurs around this time from broad human rights-based approaches to approaches more narrowly incorporating quantifiable dimensions of poverty (Saith 2006, 1170).

The transformative character of the decade's political climate therefore clearly manifested itself in the adoption by 189 governments of the United Nations Millennium Declaration in 2000. Among other things, the General Assembly articulates a strong position on poverty eradication, social rights and environmental sustainability. Industrialized countries are called upon to partner with least developed countries to open trade flows, enhance debt relief, and implement other developmental assistance. Often overlooked in some reviews of the Declaration is that it does not seek to replace or subvert other goals adopted during the 1990s by various global conferences. The justification and basic framework of the MDGs, and even its measurable goals, is found in this Declaration, but details required considerable follow-up. Hence, two years later the UN Secretary-General commissioned the Millennium Project, an independent advisory board, to propose specific strategies for meeting the Goals. He brought on board noted economist Jeffrey Sachs to lead a task force of more than 250 experts from around the world to proffer recommendations for steering the MDGs, researchers who represent virtually every sort of public and private enterprise. Other partners in the Project include UN agencies, government officials, and international financial institutions.

Efforts quickly concentrated on methodological matters, though the heart of the Millennium Project still reflects abstract humanitarian ideals imbedded in the UDHR. Most significantly, the UDHR provides a legal foundation for asserting economic rights. Thus, the 1948 proclamation establishes a ready link between international poverty relief movements such as the MDGs and human rights. The first article of the UDHR begins with, "All human beings are born free and equal in dignity and rights," after which the document unveils a bevy of universal principles that include rights from specific forms of want or need (UDHR 1948). Nearly sixty years later, the Millennium Declaration states its purpose is to "free all men, women, and children from the abject and dehumanizing conditions of extreme poverty" (UN General Assembly 2000). The concept of dignity is echoed in both, a sentiment also showcased in most development programs in the 1990s. Those programs use the language of rights profusely, too. At least one scholar fails to notice this legacy found in the MDGs, arguing that the Goals do not reference rights, and are "framed to avoid the obligations associated with economic and social rights" (Nelson 2007, 26). But, if there is any doubt as to whether the MDGs are a rights-based program, one need only reread the opening paragraph in Section III of the Millennium Declaration which states, "We are committed to making the right to development a reality for everyone" (UN General Assembly 2000). With this assertion, and by association with the UNDHR and the standards of universal rights set forth in that document, claims for poverty relief today are commonly recognized by the international community as subsistence rights.

For this chapter to argue whether the Goals articulate a set of human rights or not, is moot and not even an interesting proposition. Signed onto by 147 heads of state and government and adopted by 189 countries, it certainly appears that a right to economic development is universally acknowledged now. The fact that implementation of the Goals and their targets is endangered, and that we may not see those rights adequately protected by domestic and international policies, institutions and actors by 2015, does not diminish their legitimacy—or so one would think. The plethora of literature churned out over the last decade or so continues to revisit the notion of "freedom from poverty as a human right." This, in fact, is the title of a recent and already oft-cited UNESCO volume that collects instructive essays on related topics, such as moral obligations toward the poor and poverty as a human rights violation (Pogge 2007). Critical contributions of the various authors do not generally address the normative assumption at the bedrock of the MDGs; that is to say, they do not challenge the notion that extreme deprivation is bad and that people indeed have a right not to suffer, but they take on instead the mechanics and politics of providing poverty relief. For example, the target-focused MDGs are seen as marginalizing the rights-based substance of the project (Salord 2005, 115). The purpose of poverty relief, writes another, "should be understood as more than a 'goal' and the aim should be its eradication, not its administration" (Alegre 2007, 237). Alternatively, some political theorists appreciate significant deliberation directed on goals. Human rights struggles, they say, are necessarily represented by the process instead of the end-point (Koshy 1999, 27). For a discussion about the antecedents of modern human rights claims in general, and what those claims usually mean, we can turn to a corpus of theoretical studies. Among those studies, one notable observation about the nature of an international regime of human rights since the mid-twentieth century detects two distinct features. One is the internationalization of rights, a growing number of state-to-state diplomatic efforts, supranational institutions, and international law; and the second is universalization, a growing adoption of human rights principles by governments and peoples (Koshy 1999, 3). This duality in the international regime of rights spawns considerable challenges to actors and institutions, not the least of which is passionate debate in public and private forums. Social and economic rights cannot be discussed without reference to past and present relations between the rich and poor, and the histories of exploitation and dependency entrenched at every unit level of analysis.

Aside from any moral justification appended to struggles against extreme poverty, an association with universal standards of human rights lends a sense of political legitimacy and urgency that can support mobilization and reform for relief. Legitimacy accorded to a growing body of international norms is therefore most visibly manifested by assent and custom. The UN approach to human rights rests on this legal positivist tradition. States agree upon how rights are defined. Within this framework, social and economic rights are therefore socially-constructed. As expected, the exercise of power by governing elites and the presumption of privilege to adopt or reject legal rights provoke charges of bias. Protests have been registered that "the poor and dispossessed do not have a voice in the formation of the international legal rights that are often proclaimed in their name" (Felice 1999, 565). Most assuredly then there are political implications for integrating claims for poverty relief with human rights rhetoric. Observers, proponents and critics alike, attribute the popularity of the rights argument to the predominantly neoliberal climate of the early 1990s and the growing internationalization of human rights regimes. Social justice groups in the United States, for example, benefited from generous funding by private institutions such as the Ford Foundation. In the wake of post-Cold War debates about globalization and growing economic inequality, the rhetoric of rights—even when the discourse was applied inconsistently—effectively mobilized and reconciled grassroots activists with policymakers. By couching subsistence rights in the language and morality of human rights, worries about socialism and governmental reach were effectively diffused (Chong 2006, 25). At the international level, agreement on the principles of the UNDR and its offshoots was no doubt possible simply because it was not technically binding on member states and not overtly challenging to state sovereignty under the UN Charter's principle of non-interference. It was in this fashion that the struggle against extreme poverty became legitimized, internationalized, and universalized, and propelled to the forefront of domestic and global agendas at the millennium.

"Security" Through Which Lens?

Emergence of the concept of human security in the early 1990s, as an alternative paradigm to the post-Cold War traditional concept of national security, further fueled discussions of universal rights issues. Although debate between scholars and practitioners remains unabated in the twenty-first century as to the nature of this relationship, there is general agreement that ideas of natural law and natural rights are fundamental to both concepts of human rights and human security. The two frameworks find common ground in that attention is given to the individual and to issues fundamental to the protection of human dignity. These issues are diverse and plentiful, and include now a body of political, social, and economic norms. The human rights approach commonly rests on a legalistic interpretation, with multilateral agreements steadily accumulating, while the concept of human security is mainly unsettled. There is still a loose international dimension to the latter since states retain considerable discretion in how they manage human security when defining the matter as national interest. Echoing disagreements about the appropriate extent and methods of the Millennium Development Goals in protecting subsistence rights, mounting critical interest also surrounds the institutionalization and guarding of human security goals, defined by the UN as freedom from fear and freedom from want (UNDP 1994). For proponents of the MDGs to argue that it is an established universal rights-based program, suggests that this facet of economic development transcends traditional sovereignty. Critics claim that as a result, state interests are impaired because the Goals further the ideology and economic well-being of a select few actors.

However, the extent to which international regimes affect the state is open to question. In theory and in practice the principles of sovereignty, of course, have long been noted as never being absolute. For example, there is near-consensus now that states have certain obligations to their citizens and to the wider community, and that the "architecture of global governance" requires further adjustment in acclimating states to their new responsibilities (Council on Foreign Relations 2008). Year after year, the UN General Assembly continues to revisit questions of national sovereignty; a recent plenary session agenda was dominated by discussions of state sovereignty in light of issues such as the MDGs, terrorism, disarmament, and global warming (UN General Assembly 2008). Indeed, pressures imposed upon the state by changing international norms hark way back, and if there are new challenges now to the Westphalian order they are examples of protracted and incremental transformations to sovereignty.

What is novel within the past several decades is the ubiquitous presence of international government organizations, transnational non-state organizations, and other "activists beyond borders" as civil society advocates are commonly referred. These actors are observed to increasingly command specific state policies by exacting accountability or by discrediting government leaders (Krasner 2001, 246). The impact to states in a modern and diverse political system is two-fold. Impositions upon a national government to accommodate global expectations in respect to human welfare, for example under the rubric of Responsibility to Protect principles, might be said to undermine state autonomy in the manner and degree to which they govern (Toope 2008, 17). But response to appeals from within for a state to exercise its power to properly address social grievances in domestic policy or practice, or through traditional bilateral diplomacy, arguably bolsters its legitimacy. Domestic and international actors all the while, galvanized around issue networks, epistemic communities, and instrumental goals, weigh in on the reconceptualization of sovereignty (Sikkink 1993, 440–41). Consequently, the human rights regime is described as having a Janus face in its connection to the state (Berkovitch and Gordon 2008, 898–9). All in all, however, the state continues to serve as a pivotal force in human rights matters. Advocates for subsistence rights necessarily must be sensitive to a political environment in which traditional and contemporary views of state rights and responsibilities may clash. It may appear patronizing to do so, but in the face of state resistance, human rights proponents can supplement appeals to morality with a more pragmatic approach to winning compliance. National interests, it is argued, are inexorably tied to the welfare of a state's citizens.

For instance, wording that attempts to negotiate this tension between state autonomy and international demands for poverty reduction is found in a voluminous report issued by a UN advisory board led by Sachs. Entitled *Investing in Development*, the report advises a collaborative and coherent approach be taken in implementing strategies to attain the Millennium Development Goals:

> The host country should lead and own the effort to design the MDG strategy, drawing in civil society organizations; bilateral donors; the UN specialized agencies, programs, and funds; and the international financial institutions, including the IMF, the World Bank, and the appropriate regional development bank (UN Millennium Development Program 2005, 232–5).

The language of the report reassures states that they are in control, that ownership and leadership of managing the MDGs rests with national governments, and that other actors will assume a partnership role to facilitate change. The title of the report itself presents poverty reduction strategies as an investment, and so as a developmental tool for furthering state interests. Articulating a clear link between poverty and national security is perhaps the most effective line of attack for proponents of subsistence rights and human welfare.

One of the earliest discussions before the global community that defined human security and introduced it as a matter of state interest appeared in a 1994 UNDP Report. The Report noted that world peace will not be secured by arms but by socio-economic development, and that a sense of individual well-being is necessary for nations to obtain pacific goals:

> For too long, the concept of security has been shaped by the potential for conflict between states. For too long, security has been equated with threats to a country's borders. For too long, nations have sought arms to protect their security. For most people today, a feeling of insecurity arises more from worries about daily life than from the dread of a cataclysmic world event. Job security, income security, health security, environmental security, security from crime, these are the emerging concerns of human security all over the world (UNDP 1994, 3).

The Report argues from a practical, as well as humanitarian, perspective. "When the security of people is attacked in any corner of the world, all nations are likely to get involved…It is less costly and more humane to meet these threats upstream rather than downstream, early rather than late" (UNDP 1994, 3). This merging of traditional security interests with development or human security is picked up soon thereafter by others. For instance, the connection between national security and poverty, and in particular, the structures of inequity that perpetuate the latter is subsequently elucidated by one scholar:

> When a privileged elite defends its too large share of too few resources, the link is created between poverty, inequality and the abuse of human rights. The denial of basic freedoms…forces people to choose between accepting gross injustice and securing a fairer share by violent means. As conflict unfolds, the political leaders that emerge often find that the easiest way of mobilizing support is on an ethnic basis. Thus do the various causes of conflict weave in and out (Smith 1997, 15).

Much academic literature reflects upon this development—poverty reduction as a national security interest—as constituting an essential component of the neoliberal vision at the cusp of the new century (Thomas 2001; Weber 2004; Woodward 2004; Chong 2006; Saith 2006). Argued for here is a visible and indispensible role of government in the market economy to prevent conflict and tend effectively to structural violence. In addition to state policies fostering free trade and foreign direct investment to facilitate economic growth, for example, the neoliberal framework turns its eye to military spending as an impediment to economic development and even peace itself. Thus, both human security and military security are intertwined in reform efforts (Woodward 2004, 5). When seen in this light, the rationale of Millennium Development Goals appears to serve both individual and state interests. Contemporary liberal democracies trace their roots to political philosophers of centuries past, when Hobbes and Locke, for example, suggest that the primary function of the state is one of protecting lives and property. Human rights issues are predicated on this protectionist duty of government, and have extended that notion of duty to protect to the collective body of states as well. Beginning in the early 1980s and fairly concurrent with this popular view towards expansion of responsibility, neoliberal theory builds upon the intellectual tradition of structural realism and offers alternative theoretical frameworks for the study of international relations. A variety of liberal approaches can be found in international relations theory, but it is neoliberal institutionalism under scrutiny here which sees collaboration and the creation of international institutions in the self-interest of states. The arrangement assumes the character of a social contract. Unilateral state action presents obstacles, costs, and sobering consequences in contemporary world politics and so states create organizations and rules to help deal with those problems collectively (Putnam 1988; Moravcsik 1997; Buchanan and Keohane 2006). The agreements are voluntary and self-enforcing, and so what follows is the construction of additional informal or formal regimes to enforce rules and resolve disputes. Importantly, the neoliberal framework rests upon a key assumption inherited from realists. States, who remain crucial actors, are rational and so state preferences lead governments to make policies based on cost-benefit calculations. For the neoliberal, preferences and the weight placed upon those preferences may vary from state to state. If articulated to include the pursuit of social justice and the reduction of poverty, for instance, such courses of action may be evaluated in terms of economic development and/or traditional security concerns.

Rationalism thus serves as an intersection point between neoliberal and neorealist approaches to viewing the Millennium Development Goals in context of state sovereignty and international and domestic pressures to reform. To what degree are governments motivated to comply with the principles of the MDGs? Or, as restated more generally by one scholar, where do human rights add value? Rights-based development approaches, as one scholar notes, can offer:

- enhanced accountability;
- higher levels of citizens' empowerment, ownership, and free, meaningful, and active participation;
- greater normative clarity and detail;
- easier consensus and increased transparency in national development processes;
- integrated safeguards against unintentional harm by development projects;
- more effective and complete analysis; and
- a more authoritative basis for advocacy (Robinson 2005, 38).

In short, they offer political and moral legitimacy. It remains for governments to gauge this benefit within the milieu of domestic and global politics, and particularly in respect to signing binding treaty ratifications and consenting to various manifestations of soft law. Rationalists argue that national leaders will more likely commit to the principles of the MDGs, therefore, if the cost of compliance is avoided or minimized. Fewer costs will occur if state policies and practices are already consistent with the expectations of the MDGs, or if the Goals are not strictly monitored or enforced. States do not surrender sovereignty to international institutions, for they are likely to engage in pacts "only when compliance is a foregone conclusion and hence costless" (Cole 2005, 475).

Prospects for effective cooperation and collective action strategies, however, hinge on the outcomes of prolonged negotiation struggles between states. The view that states are ultimately self-interested explains the desire of the powerful to influence those outcomes. The degree to which compliance with MDGs is voluntary is debatable, as is the perceived value credited to policies fostering subsistence rights. Even soft power in the hands of some can be sufficient to influence others to adopt the principles of the Goals without objective and full information to make rational choices. Detractors of the development program suggest that there is much evidence of "co-optive power" wielded by some states and the international regimes that in large part they have constructed. This muscles some to want what others want them to do (Nye 1990). And so, the neoliberal institutional strategy draws considerable criticism on a number of fronts. Another related denunciation of the MDGs focuses on its heavy reliance of neoliberal market mechanisms to address global inequities, since capital accumulation inherent in market forces arguably contributes to human insecurity. This generally constitutes a "critique from the South" of capitalism and existing power hierarchies (Soederberg 2004; Amin 2006). Aside from debates about market economies and structural components of the MDGs, such as the measurement of progress, contention includes the ideological foundation of the project itself—and, the role of the state in regards to human rights.

Very much in line with rationalist thought, structural realists still deviate considerably from liberal institutionalists. They are provoked with the sanguine view that international institutions offer national governments a means to solve major challenges in an anarchical system, such as reducing extreme poverty, through cooperation and collective action. Structural realists may quarrel among themselves on a number of points, such as how much power states should seek to control, but they agree that human nature is not an explanation for why states want power. Nor do they consider cultural differences, government regime type, or who the particular leaders in government are as being significant. It is the architecture of the international system itself that provides the incentives to compete and produces the self-help environment for which states struggle for survival. Among various assumptions supporting this structural perspective, is the belief that states cannot fully comprehend the intentions of other actors and so cannot trust them. As rational actors, then, they devise strategies and form alliances to enhance their relative standing in the world so as to curb threats of attack. Their own interests are paramount to those of the community. International institutions are a tool to realize those interests, and are useful only in so far as the rules and processes do not subvert state preferences. There are limitations to the allure of these international institutions. There are deficiencies in the operating of the institutions themselves (Mearsheimer 1994; Barnett and Finnemore 1999). In addition to this, power politics as described above, limits bargaining processes to enable great powers to structure rules for obtaining their own preferred outcomes. This scheme of coercive cooperation creates "clubs of agglomeration" where different incentives and benefits are offered to new, and less powerful, participants (Rosecrance and Stein 2001, 225–6). If we recall, it was the initiation and leadership of rich nations that through the IMF, World Bank, and OECD coordinated the early framework of the MDGs which was later enjoined by developing countries. Another theoretical shortcoming levied against neoliberal institutionalism and related policy prescriptions, is that states are not primarily focused on their own potential benefits, but obsessed with their relative standing and gains among the community. Institutions provide differential payoffs and so compliance with international human rights norms dealing with subsistence rights, will not be standard among states.

It is illuminating to view how both neoliberal and neorealist theories frame the strategic role of the US in implementing the MDGs process. Washington consensus in the early 1990s was that economic stability and poverty reduction in the developing world would result from market-friendly reforms without heavy state intervention. Adoption of neoliberal principles included "working under the assumption that states should relinquish all power, except for guaranteeing and enforcing the rule of law…to the rational forces of the marketplace" (Soederberg 2004, 281). It was necessary, naturally, to coordinate the effort through various financial institutions, including the largest bilateral aid agency, the US. Agency for International Development. While the global development agenda included a litany of issues, such as debt relief, humanitarian aid, emerging markets, quality of governance, and so forth, the Millennium Development Goals focused on reducing extreme poverty through narrowing down those parts of the whole. Formal US support for the Goals was announced in 2002 by President George Bush, shortly before the International Conference on Financing of Development convened in Monterrey, Mexico. The conference was the first hosted by the UN to address important financial and development matters. The Bush administration quickly generated the "Monterrey Consensus" which articulated a neoliberal approach for realizing the MDGs. Now, the development program would emphasize "the responsibility of the poor countries themselves in addressing their development agendas, making external assistance contingent on such efforts" and in addition, "while paying lip service to the MDGs" allow the US to manipulate the agenda and policy processes of global institutions such as the UN (Saith 2006, 1170–71). It was, in the view of many, an imperialistic flaunting of power that under the auspices of a neoliberal institutional approach to addressing subsistence rights was in truth a case study of structural realism.

A popular image of the realist-oriented framework is that of a cold eye cast upon matters of morality and ethics. Extreme deprivation and human suffering springing from the structural violence of poverty apparently holds no stock for what seems a nihilistic and fatalistic viewpoint. The prospects of progress, defined as human development and social justice, is utopian. Yet found even in classical realist scholarship, such as that of Morgenthau, is reference to moral responsibility. Although there is a rejection of universal moral values and the liberal argument to realize those values through institutions, realists see the struggle for power also as a struggle for ethical leadership (Cozette 2008, 671–2). Here, rights-based initiatives have room to negotiate a place on state agenda. Realists do oscillate, however, between arguing that states concentrate efforts on feasible goals and that states ignore seemingly impossible objectives. Observers suggest that it is not a matter of deciding what is realistic, but producing the necessary political will (de Vita 2007, 119). It is the strength of that political will that perceived state interests determine.

The Millennium Development Goals pose an opportunity for states to reexamine, and reconstruct, their preferences in an international system that increasingly finds the language and substance of human security tied with traditional security interests. Rights-based approaches to human security, such as poverty reduction measures, require that we look at alternative theoretical frameworks to place their purposes and structures, histories and futures, in context of world politics and state sovereignty. Compassion is not within the exclusion domain of any one approach, nor is pragmatism. For better or worse, the Millennium Development Goals purport to embrace both. The chapter ends here with the MDGs target date a great deal closer. More than a year transpired from conception of this volume to its publication. When the clock stops at 2015, the world will stop too, to herald momentarily the successes and failures of yet another massive undertaking to define and safeguard human rights.

References

Alegre, M. 2007. Extreme Poverty in a Wealthy World: What Justice Demands Today, in *Freedom from Poverty as a Human Right: Who Owes What to the Very Poor?* edited by T. Pogge. Oxford: Oxford University Press, 237–54.

Amin, S. 2006. The Millennium Development Goals: A Critique from the South, *Monthly Review* 57(10). Available at: http://monthlyreview.org/0306amin.htm [accessed: 18 December 2008].

Barnett, M. and Finnemore, M. 1999. The Politics, Power, and Pathologies of International Organizations. *International Organization* 53(4), 699–732.

Berkovitch, N. and Gordon, N. 2008. The Political Economy of Transnational Regimes: The Case of Human Rights. *International Studies Quarterly* 52(4), 881–904.

Bourguignon, F., Benassy-Quere, A., Dercon, S., Estache, A., Gunning, W., Kanbur J., Klasen, R., Maxwell, S., Platteau, J. and Amedeo, S. 2008. *European Report on Development*, European Commission. Available at: http://ec.europa.eu/development/icenter/repository/mdg_paper_final_20080916_en.pdf [accessed: 15 December 2008].

Buchanan, A. and Keohane, R. 2006. The Legitimacy of Global Governance Institutions. *Ethics & International Affairs* 20(4), 405–37.

Chong, D. 2006. *The Right to Subsistence: Strategic Implications of the US Social Justice Movement's Adoption of Human Rights*. The Annual Conference of the American Political Science Association, Philadelphia, PA, 31 August–3 September 2006.

Clemens, M., Kenny, C. and Moss, T. 2007. The Trouble with the MDGs: Confronting Expectations of Aid and Development Success. *World Development* 35(5), 735–51.

Cole, W. 2005. Sovereignty Relinquished? Explaining Commitment to the International Human Rights Covenants, 1966-1999. *American Sociological Review* 70(3), 472–95.

Council on Foreign Relations. 2008. *Program on International Institutions and Global Governance. World Order in the 21st Century: A New Initiative*. Available at: http://www.cfr.org/project/1369/international_institutions_and_global_governance.html [accessed: 30 August 2008].

Cozette, M. 2008. What Lies Ahead: Classical Realism on the Future of International Relations. *International Studies Review* 10(4), 667–79.

de Paladella Salord, M. 2005. MDGs as Friends or Foes for Human and Child Rights. *Development* 48(1), 115–21.

de Vita, A. 2007. Inequality and Poverty in Global Perspective, in *Freedom from Poverty as a Human Right: Who Owes What to the Very Poor?* edited by T. Pogge. Oxford: Oxford University Press, 103–32.

Eurostep Weekly (7 April 2008). Strong Concerns over Progress Towards Millennium Development Goals. Available at: http://www.eurostep.org/wcm/dmdocuments/ES-Weekly/2008/ESW_502.pdf [accessed: 28 November 2008].

Felice, W. 1999. Viability of the United Nations Approach to Economic and Social Human Rights in a Globalized Economy. *International Affairs* (75)3, 563–98.

Harcourt, W. 2005. The Millennium Development Goals: A Missed Opportunity? *Development* (48)1, 1–4.

Koshy, S. 1999. From Cold War to Trade War: Neocolonialism and Human Rights. *Social Text* (58)1, 1–32.

Krasner, S. 2001. Abiding Sovereignty. *International Political Science Review* 22(3), 229–51.

MDG Monitor 2008. Tracking the Millennium Development Goals. An Initiative of the United Nations. Available at: http://www.mdgmonitor.org/index.cfm [accessed: 22 December 2008].

Mearsheimer, J. 1994. The False Promise of International Institutions. *International Security* 19(3): 5–49.

Moravcsik, A. 1997. Taking Preferences Seriously: A Liberal Theory of International Politics. *International Organization* 51(4), 513–53.

Nelson, P. 2007. *Human Rights, the Millennium Development Goals, and the Future of Development Cooperation*, The Annual Meeting of the International Studies Association, Chicago, IL, 28 February–3 March 2007.

Nye, J. 1990. *Bound to Lead: The Changing Nature of American Power*. New York: Basic Books.

Okonofua, F. 2005. Achieving the Millennium Development Goals in Africa: How Realistic? *African Journal of Reproductive Health* (9)3, 7–14.

Pogge, T. (ed.) 2007. *Freedom from Poverty as a Human Right: Who Owes What to the Very Poor?* Oxford: Oxford University Press.

Putnam, R. 1988. Diplomacy and Domestic Politics: The Logic of Two-Level Games. *International Organization* 42(3), 427–60.

Robinson, M. 2006. What Rights Can Add to Good Development Practice, in *Human Rights and Development: Towards Mutual Reinforcement*, edited by P. Alston and M. Robinson. New York: Oxford University Press, 25–41.

Rosecrance, R. and Stein, A. 2001. The Theory of Overlapping Clubs, in *The New Great Power Coalition: Toward a World Concert of Nations*, edited by R. Rosecrance. Landham, MD: Rowman and Littlefield, 221–34.

Saith, A. 2006. From Universal Values to Millennium Development Goals: Lost in Translation. *Development and Change* 37(6), 1167–99.

Sikkink, K. 1993. Human Rights, Principled Issue-Networks, and Sovereignty in Latin America. *International Organization* 47(3), 411–41.

Smith, D. (ed.) 1997. *The State of War and Peace Atlas*. London: Penguin Books Ltd.

Soederberg, S. 2004. American Empire and 'Excluded States': The Millennium Challenge Account and the Shift to Pre-Emptive Development. *Third World Quarterly* 25(2), 279–302.

Thomas, C. 2001. Global Governance, Development and Human Security: Exploring the Links. *Third World Quarterly* 22(2), 159–75.

Toope, S. 2008. Lecture at the University of British Columbia, Canada, 2 October 2008. Available at: http://www.president.ubc.ca/speeches/SplaneLecture_Right_to_Escape_Poverty.pdf [accessed: 15 December 2008].

UN. 1948. *The Universal Declaration of Human Rights*. Available at: http://www.un.org/Overview/rights.html [accessed: 10 October 2008].

UN. 2000. *A Better Future for All: Progress towards the International Development Goal*. Available at: http://www.paris21.org/betterworld/home.htm [accessed: 9 December 2008].

UN. 2008a. *Millennium Development Goals Progress Chart*. Available at: http://mdgs.un.org/unsd/mdg/Resources/Static/Products/Progress2008/MDG_Report_2008_Progress_Chart_En.pdf [accessed: 5 January 2009].

UN. 2008b. *Millennium Development Goals Report*. Available at: http://www.un.org/millenniumgoals/2008highlevel/pdf/newsroom/mdg%20reports/MDG_Report_2008_ENGLISH.pdf [accessed: 5 January 2009].

UN Division for the Advancement of Women. 1995. *Fourth World Conference on Women*. Available at: http://www.un.org/womenwatch/daw/beijing/ [accessed: 7 October 2008].

UN General Assembly. 2000. *United Nations Millennium Declaration* (A/res/55/2). Available at: http://www.un.org/millennium/declaration/ares552e.htm [accessed: 7 October 2008].

UN General Assembly. 2001. *Report of the Secretary-General on the Road Map towards the Implementation of the United Nations Millennium Declaration* (A/56/326). Available at: http://www.un.kz/img/docs/en/402.pdf [accessed: 10 October 2008].

UN General Assembly. 2007. *Report of the Secretary-General on the Work of the Organization*. Supplement No. 1 (A/62/1). Available at: http://mdgs.un.org/unsd/mdg/Resources/Static/Products/SGReports/62_1/a-62-1_e.pdf[accessed: 10 November 2008].

UN General Assembly. 2008. *63rd General Assembly Plenary on State Sovereignty, Disarmament Matters, World Leaders Urge Solidarity* (GA/10757). Available at: http://un.org/News/Press/docs/2008/ga10757.doc.htm [accessed: 18 December 2008].

UN Millennium Development Program. 2005. *Report to the UN Secretary-General. Investing in Development: A Practical Plan to Achieve the Millennium Development Goals*. Available at: http://www.unmillenniumproject.org/documents/MainReportComplete-lowres.pdf [accessed: 10 January 2009].

UN Office of the High Commissioner for Human Rights. 1993. *World Conference on Human Rights*. Available at: http://www.unhchr.ch/html/menu5/wchr.htm [accessed: 7 October 2008].

UNDP. 2004. *New Dimensions of Human Security*. Available at: http://hdr.undp.org/en/media/hdr_1994_en_overview.pdf [accessed: 15 October 2008].

UNDP. 2008a. *Annual Report Poverty Reduction*. Available at: http://www.undp.org/publications/annualreport2008/pdf/ENG_IARforweb_Ch3a_Poverty%20Reduction0608.pdf [accessed: 18 January 2009].

UNDP. 2008b. *Human Development Reports*. Available at: http://hdr.undp.org/en/statistics/ [accessed: 30 December 2008].

UNFPA. 1994. *Master Plans for Development: Summary of the ICPD Programme of Action*. Available at: http://www.unfpa.org/icpd/summary.cfm [accessed: 7 October 2008].

UNICEF. 1990. *Information Publication: World Declaration on the Survival, Protection and Development of Children*. Available at: http://www.unicef.org/wsc/declare.htm [accessed: 7 October 2008].

Weber, H. 2004. Reconstituting the 'Third World'? Poverty Reduction and Territoriality in the Global Politics of Development. *Third World Quarterly* 25(1), 187–206.

Woodward, S. 2004. The State Failure Agenda: from Sovereignty to Development. LaCaixa Foundation and Ford Foundation Conference on Peace and Development, Madrid, Spain, 21 October 2004. Available at: http://www.statesandsecurity.org/_pdfs/lacaixapaper.pdf [accessed: 11 November 2008].

World Bank. 2008. *Global Monitoring Report*. Progress on the MDGs. Available at: http://web.worldbank.org/WBSITE/EXTERNAL/EXTDEC/EXTGLOBALMONITOR/EXTGLOMONREP2008/0,contentMDK:21901842~isCURL:Y~menuPK:4860348~pagePK:64168445~piPK:64168309~theSitePK:4738057,00.html [accessed: 26 December 2008].

Chapter 10
Human Rights, Glocal Ecopolitics, and Contested Landscapes of Sovereignty

Peter J. Stoett

Introduction

We witnessed a harsh reminder of the limits imposed by the institution of state sovereignty when the Cyclone Nargis hit Burma (Myanmar) in May of 2008, killing over 100,000 people. It quickly became painfully evident that the Burmese government was not only unwilling to devote the necessary resources towards aiding those so tragically affected, but would deny the entry of assistance offered by the international community.[1] Surely here was a clear case when a habitually abusive regime and natural disaster collided in terms that justified external intervention, yet little was done to enforce the provision suggested by the Responsibility to Protect document described elsewhere in this volume. If prediction linking extreme weather events with global warming hold true, this will not be an uncommon dilemma.

This chapter will suggest that environmental issues are not new to the human rights discourse, but are relatively embryonic at the international level, and are infused with a new sense of urgency. As climate change continues to dominate the ecopolitical discourse, related diplomatic activity will further challenge conventional understandings of sovereignty, and may even lead to a re-evaluation of international relations based on an emerging ethic of global environmental justice. Indeed scholars such as Karen Litfin (1997) and Robin Eckersley (2004) have argued that sovereignty has been refashioned by what are, inherently, transnational common ecological problems. However, it would be not only premature but misguided to assume that sovereignty will fall as the dominant institution defining global interactions amongst legally recognized states. Rather, growing concern over inter-related environmental issues with serious human rights implications, ranging from hazardous waste disposal to alien invasive species to global warming, will contribute to the construction of yet another contested landscape of sovereignty, one where "glocal" issues are most visible, and contradictory visions of the future—one inspired by a new international ethic based on environmental

1 Indeed, the military government was sufficiently audacious as to hold a planned "referendum" on constitutional changes designed to ensure its own power just weeks after the disaster.

justice, the other by the exacerbation of division between and within states—can be seen on the horizon.

The core of ecopolitics is the nexus between environmental security and human rights. This concerns not only present rights (including entitlements and obligations), but must reflect past justice issues and possible future scenarios, which raises untidy questions about the applicability of reparations and intergenerational justice recently explored by international environmental ethicists such as Steve Vanderheiden (2008). Indeed, spurred by the climate change debate—here an international dialogue is unavoidable—many authors are treating climate change ecopolitics as an aspect of environmental justice, at the local to global levels (Boyle and Anderson 1998; Athanasiou and Baer 2002; Hossay 2006; Roberts and Parks 2007). Meanwhile, it is the question of *adaptation* to climate change that is emerging as the dominant human rights issue, since there is ample opportunity to ensure some measure of fairness exists as people strive to adapt to changes over which they have little or no control.

This chapter will introduce a basic conception of environmental justice with a strong human rights orientation; discuss its implications at the international and regional levels; stress the importance of climate change adaptation strategies as key tools to achieve global environmental justice; and suggest what has been termed the "glocal" level of analysis (Robertson 1995; Courchene 1995; Jasanoff and Martello 2004; Gore and Stoett 2009) is the most relevant if we are to attain a useful understanding of ecopolitics and human rights today. In this context, when transnational issues permeate local concerns and *vice versa*, sovereignty is not a rigid fixed concept, but one that will retain legal and practical significance even as its application assumes greater flexibility. I will also stress the idea that, though the adaptive costs of climate change have emerged as dominant human rights concerns, other biosecurity issues with serious impact on human health, often related to climate change, such as invasive alien species, water purity, overfishing, toxic pollutants, and many other challenges to sustainability, are certainly worthy of discussion. The tendency to subsume all human rights concerns under the global warming debate may in fact be counterproductive, a theme to which I return in my conclusion. However, the newfound urgency the debate over climate change adaptation has generated is both undeniable and, in the long run, may prove to be a most positive development.

Global Environmental Justice[2]

The right to a clean environment and the right to avoid suffering because of the actions of others is a core element of sustainability. Though some deep ecologists and animal welfare advocates remain critical of the anthropocentricism of

2 Parts of this section appeared in a paper presented to the International Studies Association Annual Meeting of 2007 in Chicago; and in Stoett 2008.

international human rights law (see Redgwell 1998), it is fairly widely accepted that the right to a safe environment is a fundamental human right. As Dinah Shelton suggests, a human rights approach to environmental protection seeks "to ensure that the natural world does not deteriorate to the point where international guaranteed rights such as the rights to life, health, property, a family, a private life, culture, and safe drinking water are seriously impaired. Environmental protection is thus instrumental, not an end in itself" (2003, 1). However, one can position this in opposite terms, suggesting the "legal protection of human rights is an effective means to achieving the ends of conservation and environmental protection" (Anderson 1998, 3).

Access to natural resources necessary for survival, and conducive habitat; this theme is commonly employed in studies on the injustice of colonization/assimilation/displacement of indigenous peoples (Pallemaerts 1986; Hitchcock 1994), but can also apply to the links between multinational corporations and repressive governments for the purpose of resource extraction, most notably perhaps, oil (Obiora 1999), to unemployed resource workers who have lost their livelihood due to over-exploitation driven by global markets, indigenous peoples cheated of their genetic plant material, or children poisoned by pesticides sprayed on export-based banana plantations. In September of 2008 the Maldives convened a Chatham House debate during the Ninth Session of the UN Human Rights Council on the motion that "climate change violates the rights of all peoples to live in a safe and sustainable environment," citing the eventuality of displacement due to rising sea-levels that have little to do with Maldivian tourism or fisheries (the motion passed—narrowly—but has no binding significance).

Human rights and environmental security intersect in numerous ways, and indeed it is easily argued that one is impossible without the other in a world where anthropogenic activity is the defining feature. Some geologists argue that we have moved into a new era since humankind has had such a profound impact on the natural ecosystems which sustain us. Simon Dalby urges the recognition that:

> ...it is not only the atmosphere hat we have changed but also other important natural systems, not least the nitrogen and phosphorous cycles in the biosphere. The cumulative impact of these parallel disruptions of other material and energy cycles and maritime systems and terrestrial land uses suggests...that the geological period known as the Holocene, the past 10,000 years since the most recent ice age, is now effectively over. The apt term 'Anthropocene' [denotes] a new geological period when a dramatic new series of forces has been unleashed on the planetary biosphere, changing the atmosphere as well as geomorphic processes and most natural cycles that involve a biomass of any substantial size (Dalby 2006, 21; see also Crutzen 2002).

Any serious thought about what it means to be human, and to have corresponding rights and obligations, cannot escape the basic fact that we have also redefined what it means to be natural, and the inequity of ecological harm is a self-evident travesty.

The latter indicates that environmental justice has become a major normative force today; but we are equally concerned with environmental rights (including animal welfare) as factors proscribing certain types of human behaviour, and prescribing obligations towards those most affected. "These claims may be based either upon the specific attribution of responsibility to the countries of the North for the carbon emissions which are responsible for global warming, or upon a human rights-based claim that the wealthy must assist those who are at risk of large-scale rights deprivation and are effectively unable to help themselves" (Steiner et al. 2007, 1454) such as tropical islanders displaced by rising sea levels. The failure to pursue environmental justice at an international level can only lead us further on the path towards a world defined by *bioapartheid*; a systemic physical separation of people who have suffered the deleterious impacts of the health threats related to climate change, infectious diseases, and even the malnourishment resultant from absolute poverty, from those with the means to escape these threats to human security, who are free to roam wherever their transnational capital can take them. This may or may not involve the application of military power to maintain such separation; it may or may not overlap with religious war; it may or may not assume a visibly racial character.

This is to some extent nothing new, and similar arguments have been made about ecological crises throughout the past half-century. Previously, the advent of nuclear weapons was considered by many to be the technological change that would lead invariably to major alterations of the international system.[3] The ecological crises, it has been argued by various political theorists, may lead to a similar deconstruction of the rigidities of the state-based system, leading toward neofunctionalist or even world federalist creations.[4] While these were no doubt cases of grandly designed carts put before reluctant horses, the idea that large-scale changes in natural and technological realities can change social realities is as old as the study of history itself. However, the institution of sovereignty as a legal device to ensure the survival of the nation-state proved much too strong to be disassembled over fluctuating levels of concern about environmental problems. State managers have, however, been willing to make concessions to the imperatives of global environmental governance, signing hundreds of multilateral conventions that demand certain behavioural prohibitions on the part of their citizens (see Esty and Ivanova 2002).

I would suggest that a variety of factors make the consideration of *global environmental justice* the new ethical frontier, the nexus between ecological thought and international relations theory we need to further develop and promote in order to avoid the complete dissolution of global society today. Significantly, global environmental justice is not merely related to the mitigation of the anthropomorphic

3 See, most auspiciously, Herz 1957.

4 For a summary of the conceptual nexus between ecological thought and international relations theory, as well as a call for greater integration between the two, see Laferrière and Stoett 1999 and 2006.

causes of global warming; it also demands that adaptation measures undertaken by states and other actors do not further marginalize already vulnerable groups. Can global warming provide the empirical backdrop for a dramatic and widely shared (if necessarily not universal) shift in perspective? Can it bring us closer to the normalized pursuit of Amartya Sen's "goal rights system" (1988)?

We can begin with the scientific observation, easily verified, that it is "the poor and marginalized of the world who often bear the brunt of pollution and resource degradation" (Pulido 1996, xv). This would seem to be self-evident, because those most affected by extreme weather events, such as cyclones, droughts, and forest fires, so often have little if any access to public self-defence mechanisms. The administrative state and the protection of private property privilege those with structural power and enable them to either escape or avoid the negative impact of undesirable environmental change. This does not, of course, negate the fact that some extreme weather events, infectious diseases, and other manifestations of climate change will ultimately affect both rich and poor; but they most certainly will not be similarly or equally affected so long as the former have adequate resources and the latter have little but communal ties to assist them. Surely the lesson of Hurricane Katrina, which after all affected one of the most prosperous and powerful states in the international system today, is that poverty kills. J. Timmons Roberts and Bradley Parks (2007) offer widespread evidence that this is the case on the global level as well. Beyond the more likely exposure to environmental harms that they endure, the capacity to adapt, either by physically leaving geographic areas or by seeking adequate health care, is a cause of mortality for the world's poor.

Lest I am accused at this stage of simply collapsing climate change into the category of extreme weather, I would note that the longer term concerns expressed by the Intergovernmental Panel on Climate Change and other expert documents about the impact of climate change do not evoke just the fear of more frequent and less predictable events, but the impact of increased greenhouse gases on the very ability of nature to sustain human life. Increased water scarcity will serve to further harm and alienate those for whom accessible, clean potable water is but an occasional exception already. Food security will be severely compromised without adaptation measures as increased droughts become even more common in areas where much land has been devoted to cash cropping instead of subsistence farming. Coastal areas, where hundreds of millions of lower income people live (not just on small island states, or on the islands of Indonesia, but in major urban areas), will face unprecedented challenges if sea levels rise to the extent predicted by most models. Millions of workers in the fishing industry will lose income if more fisheries collapse not only due to overfishing but coral bleaching and warmer marine temperatures.

Price-Smith (2002) demonstrates that climate change-induced health threats are indeed capable of further reducing both national security and development prospects for many southern states. In the long run, short of space flight (itself of questionable sustainability) there will be no escaping the consequences of such large-scale changes, regardless of income, because a bioapartheid system will invariably have too many pressure points to avoid increased militarization, and it will lack legitimacy amongst the vast majority of humankind. But in the short run, the distribution of suffering and death will be inextricably linked to the distribution of wealth, and it is only in a market-based fantasy world that this discrepancy will be overcome by the rising tide of economic growth through globalization. The fact that those who will suffer the most have benefited the least from the industrial processes that have caused that suffering suffices to make this an issue of not just needs, but of justice, and what has been popularly termed *environmental justice* in particular.[5]

While it would be problematic to speak categorically of an environmental justice *movement*, the last several decades have seen the rise of increased concern over the fairness implications of pollution in particular, and in both the northern and southern hemispheres, and in both the east and west, before and especially after the advent of what Ulrich Beck has famously referred to as the "risk society" where risk producers suffer less than risk victims (1992). The pursuit of environmental justice is associated with achieving intergenerational justice (Almond 1995; Haughton 1999) and interspecies justice (Hayward 1994; Low and Gleeson 1998), but it is mostly associated with "debates about distributional inequalities and the actions needed to address them" (Illsley 2002, 70). Definitions vary: it is considered "the fair treatment and meaningful involvement of all people regardless of race, colour, national origin or income, with respect to the development, implementation and enforcement of environmental laws, regulations and policies" (Bullard 1999, 7); more succinctly, the "just distribution of environmental goods and bads among human populations" (Dobson 1998, 20; see also Dobson 2003; Fletcher 2003; Wenz 1988; Westra and Wenz 1995).[6] It is, ultimately, concerned with norms, which in turn can be viewed as standards of behaviour "defined in terms of rights and obligations" (Kratochwil 1989, 59). Much of the literature links racism with differentiated environmental policy, while some borrows from feminist literature and some is more driven by concerns with income and class. When taken as the critical examination of norms, it is fair to say that applying the concept to an international perspective that is enhanced by various critical theories of global politics is an obvious step, one already taken by many analysts concerned about

5 The inequality here is startling. According to Roberts and Parks, "the average US citizen dumps as much greenhouse gas into the atmosphere as nine Chinese…eighty Bangladeshis…[and] and over five hundred citizens of Ethiopia, Chad, Zaire, Afghanistan, Mail, Cambodia, and Burundi" (2007, 146). Note that if we take inter-generational arguments seriously then it is obvious that those who will inherent the problems related to climate change did nothing to create them. This raises some thorny issues, however (see Vanderheiden's discussion, 2008), so I will stick largely to arguments related to contemporary justice as described below.

6 Of course social ecologists would reject any human hierarchy as part of the problem; justice could only be truly found under anarchic conditions (see Bookchin 1982). Most proponents of environmental justice, however, are not anarchists but would use the state an agent in the realization of environmental justice claims and any resultantly necessary redistribution of wealth.

the long-term impact of colonialism and imperialism, the cultural impact of market economies, the effects of various forms of discrimination on life opportunities, the environmental impact of globalization, and a plethora of other questions.

Arguably, the normative position that environmental justice should apply as universally as possible has yet to be taken seriously at the global level by the majority of state politicians and international policymakers. It has not escaped the usual rhetorical diplomacy that is associated with North-South issues, of course. We have had an endless stream of declarations, varying in terms of their expressed enthusiasm, to the effect that environmental protection and economic development are entwined. Indeed the multilateral ecopolitical stage was set, and is still dominated by the image, of the 1972 Stockholm United Nations Conference on the Human Environment; and the Rio Declaration that emerged from the UN Conference on Environment and Development in 1992 acknowledges the right to "develop," though we have often reverted to little more than a vague notion of increased GNP to base the measurement of progress on this front, the UN Human Development Index aside. The 2002 Delhi Ministerial Declaration on Climate Change and Sustainable Development mirrors the UNCHE's assumption that environmental protection will not override the "priorities" of "economic and social development and poverty eradication." International environmental law offers some direction here, since it certainly promulgates the cardinal principle that states should not take actions which cause ecological damage to other states, though this is more applicable, it seems, in cases of cross-border pollution than in terms of global obligations (Taylor 1998; Okowa 2000). Further, while "the prevention of significant environmental harm to non-national parties is well-established as a regulative norm in international governance…the direct participation of affected parties in realizing the relevant rules is at best embryonic" (Mason 2006, 299).[7]

H. von Seht offers a useful typology of primary and secondary effects of climate protection measures. Primary measures "comprise those avoided effects that could have resulted directly from an increased raising of the mean temperature of the plant's surface" (2002, 24). For example, fewer negative impacts of sea level rise, such as loss of land and the destruction of habitation close to coastlines, would be positive effects; on the negative side, reduced chances to cultivate new agricultural land in areas currently too cold for agriculture would represent an opportunity cost. Secondary effects are "all those effects that do not result from or depend on a reduction in the increase of the mean temperature of the planet's surface" (2002, 25). For example, in the case of a biomass power station replacing a coal-fired power plant, new sales potential for the producers of biomass (local farmers) and increased turnover in the construction sector (demolition of old and construction

7 The Stockholm Declaration on the Human Environment, Principle 21, gives states "the responsibility to ensure that activities within their jurisdiction or control do not cause damage to the environment of other States or of areas beyond the limits of national jurisdiction"; as myth, see Knox 2002. This dictum is slightly amended as Principle 2 of the Rio Declaration.

of the new power station) would be positive secondary effects; reduced turnover in the mining sector due to the missing demand for coal would be a negative secondary effect.

The United Nations, meanwhile, refers to several types of adaptation, broadly defined as "adjustment in natural or human systems in response to actual or expected climatic stimuli or their effects, which moderates harm or exploits beneficial opportunities": anticipatory, autonomous, planned, private, public, and reactive adaptation. That anticipatory, or proactive adaptation, and reactive adaptation, which "takes place after impacts of climate change have been observed," will be costly is beyond doubt at this late stage.[8] The question we face, on a global level, is whether the poor will have to pay a disproportionate price for the negative secondary effects of both anticipatory and reactive adaptation measures. If they do, or are not assured otherwise, why would we assume they will participate in global governance plans to achieve either, or for that matter further mitigation efforts?

Climate change adaptation measures will inevitably further expose the fundamental inequalities inherent in the global economy and the international state system. There are most certainly many others, but some of the major points of contention that will not only become more audible as climate change affects more human lives, but will become unbearable sources of social tension if we cannot overcome the divisions weather-related stresses will exacerbate, may be listed here. The most obvious separates North and South (see Anand 2004). This permeates whatever constructive dialogue exists: the measured injustice of the colonial legacy, the suffering related to debt reduction and structural adjustment programs, the link between poverty and race; all of these factors will bear additional scrutiny and become unavoidable issues in the post-2012 Kyoto debate. The Kyoto Adaptation Fund deserves special commentary here.[9] This mechanism should

8 Working Group on Climate Change and Disaster Risk Reduction of the Inter-Agency Task Force on Disaster Reduction of the United Nations, *On Better Terms: A Glance at Key Climate Change and Disaster Risk Reduction Concepts*, Consultation Version 2006, 19. Autonomous adaptation, also referred to as spontaneous adaptation, "does not constitute a conscious response to climatic stimuli but is triggered by ecological changes in natural systems and by market or welfare changes in human systems"; planned adaptation "is the result of deliberate policy decision, based on awareness that conditions have changes or are about to change and that action is required to return to, maintain, or achieve a desired state"; private adaptation "is initiated and implemented by individuals, households or private companies"; and public adaptation is "initiated and implemented by governments at all levels." These are obviously not mutually exclusive categorizations.

9 See Müller 2007 for a discussion of the democratic deficits inherent in the GEF, and how these might be overcome in a one-state, one-vote COP/MOP for the Kyoto Adaptation Fund and the related Nairobi Declaration of late 2006. The Marrakesh Accords to the United Nations Framework Convention on Climate Change established three new funds at its Seventh Conference of the Parties (COP-7) in November 2001 (cf. Barnett and Dessai 2002): a Least Developed Country (LDC) fund and a Special Climate Change (SCC) fund were established under the Convention, and an Adaptation fund was established

undergo three transformative events, immediately: the name should be changed, so as to relinquish the stranglehold on the imagination Kyoto has proven to hold; it should be divorced from its reliance on the Clean Development Mechanism; and the Fund's paltry resources should be expanded to reflect the true nature of the challenge before us. Indeed, a Climate Change Adaptation Fund should be financed with the enthusiasm that guided the Marshall Plan in post-war Europe, or the infrastructure investment taking place in the United States and China.[10] The money committed to Agenda 21, much of which never materialized, would be but a small measure of what is needed to cope with adaptation for many states in the tropical regions, and for many people in the Arctic regions as well.

Another fissure that will receive increased attention is the debate in environmental policy circles over whether we need a drastic reduction in human consumption in order to sustain life on earth. While it is unlikely this would be imposed from any centralized source (both resource consumption and population policies are surely seen as highly guarded sovereignty issues) it remains of primary importance to many that the true problem is seen not as overpopulation of the poor but overconsumption by the rich. Global warming issues highlight this debate but also indicate what a false dichotomy this really is: clearly, both overpopulation and overconsumption are global problems today. If climate change adaptation is handled properly, so that the price is not paid by those most affected but least responsible, the moral outrage and resentment associated with victimhood can perhaps be avoided. At the same time it is clear that heavily populated states will have to make sacrifices as well, though at this time one of the most heavily populated states, the United States, has been reluctant to cooperate in this regard at the national level (regional and local initiatives are much more promising, however).

It is obvious that we need to strengthen multilateral efforts at disaster relief and prevention, disease surveillance and epidemiology, conflict prevention, poverty alleviation, and many other humanitarian demands; and none of these important issues should be sidelined by the current fears over global warming. Rather, they should be taken as part of a broader effort towards the limited redistribution of wealth and power to reflect a democratic world polity, and to live up to the demands enlightened self-interest makes on the privileged. "Global Governance" will remain little more than a quickly tiring codeword for imperial management (Soederberg 2007) if it does not involve a serious resource commitment from the

---

under the Convention's Kyoto Protocol. The UNFCC (United Nations Framework on Climate Change), which preceded the Kyoto Protocol, contains two Articles (4.8 and 4.9), and Kyoto contains Article 3.14, all of which call on developed states to limit the harms imposed by mitigation measures, though they are less open about adaptation measures. See Barnett and Dessai 2002.

10 I realize that it is still considered defeatist in some environmentalist circles to openly discuss adaptation, rather than insisting on the preventive cure of mitigation efforts. This stark position makes less sense every day; and does little to address the issues related to global environmental justice discussed in this chapter.

wealthier states, and from wealthier individuals and corporations within states, in the pursuit of environmental justice.[11] Again, this need not entail the diminishment of the institution of sovereignty, but rather a realignment of sovereign priorities.

The codification of such an ethic will remain elusive, however. There have been small measures of success in this regard. For example, the legal campaign by the Alliance of Small Island States has at least drawn public attention to their potentially disastrous plight. Articles 4.8 and 4.9 of the UNFCC have led to the creation of the Special Climate Fund. Articles 8(1) and 8(2) of the Rome Statute give the International Criminal Court jurisdiction for intentional "widespread, long-term and severe damage to the natural environment" in war that exceeds military objectives. The 1991 Espoo Convention on Environmental Impact Assessment in a Transboundary Context; negotiated under the auspices of the UN Economic Commission for Europe (UNECE); and the Espoo Kiev Protocol on Strategic Environmental Assessment; and the 1998 Aarhus Convention on Access to Justice in Environmental Matters (also a UNECE creation; see Lee and Abbot, 2003) explicate the need for environmental justice and planned adaptation measures, as does the Lugano Convention on Civil Liability for Damage Resulting from Activities Dangerous to the Environment, and the 1998 Strasbourg Convention on the Protection of the Environment Through Criminal Law. None of these measures amounts to a firm legal context, but they may be seen an embryonic by future legal historians.

The fact remains that global warming is being caused not by globalization per se, but the type of globalization rich states and transnational elites have decided to pursue. Rather than succumb to what Hirst and Thompson refer to as "potentially destructive arguments about the emergence of a global economy dominated by ungovernable market forces, which is at variance with the evidence" (2000, 58), we can simply observe the absurdity of billions of public dollars being funnelled into what are, essentially, subsidized large final emitter industries, such as the coal and oil industries, and the military industries which are perhaps the most carbon intense producers/consumers on the planet. While the practice of subsidizing carbon intensity has received widespread condemnation in Europe and elsewhere, it is still seen as a modernization project in much of the southern hemisphere, with or without authoritative state structures to maintain its hegemonic appeal. As Lester Brown suggests,

> At a time of mounting public concern about climate change driven by the burning of fossil fuels, the world fossil fuel industry is still being subsidized by taxpayers at more than $210 billion per year. Fossil fuel subsidies belong to another age, a time when development of the oil and coal industries was seen as a key to

11 Iris Marion Young writes of a political responsibility model which avoids fault or liability based arguments: "whereas blame or liability seeks remedy for a deviation from an acceptable norm, usually by an event that has reached a terminus, with political responsibility we are concerned with structural causes of injustice that are normal and ongoing" (2004, 388).

> economic progress—not as a threat to our twenty-first century civilization. Once in place, subsidies lead to special interest lobbies that fight tooth and nail against eliminating them, even those that were not appropriate in the first place.[12]

If a large fraction of this subsidization was redirected toward a Climate Change Adaptation Fund, we would be on the right track towards making an historical, constructive contribution to increasing North-South trust and confidence, though this would simultaneously raise all the usual questions about how, and to whom, such resources can be directed without encouraging corruption and dependence. Faced by the enormity and potential severity of the climate change challenge, these would seem to be procedural barriers that could be broken with intelligent and diligent implementation. It would be fatalistic to assume the challenges posed by global warming simply cannot be overcome: we have certainly stared down nuclear Armageddon in the past. The bipolar era was defined by the threat of mutually assured destruction, the long-term prognosis of radioactive wastelands defining our vision of a post World War world. There is no doubt that such a war would have spelt the end of global society as we know it, and that such a war is still possible serves to not only remind us of the folly of ideologically-driven arms races, but of the hard reality of geopolitical concerns. This realization, coupled with the survival of the humanitarian impulse amongst civilized societies, is what drives the cautious optimism found on these pages, along with the desire to further the cause of international justice, defined succinctly by Paul Harris as "*a fair and just sharing (or distribution) among countries of benefits, burdens and decision making authority associated with international relations*, in this case within the context of international environmental issues" (1999; italics in original; see also Brown 1992; Caney 2005; Paterson 2001).

This should impart upon states the obligation to not only seek mitigation and adaptation norms that embrace global environmental justice, but for us as individuals to take a similar approach. Indeed, as Michael Mason suggests, it is the "intersection of individual rights and responsibilities with (inter)state obligations that offers concrete possibilities for citizen participation in global decisionmaking" (2006, 285). The empowerment of individuals, be they wealthy or of limited means, is certainly a relevant factor here. The state can only provide so much guidance, provocation and punishment should it wish to maintain relevance and legitimacy.

The *Glocal* as the New Normal

Despite economic crises and the maintenance of the state as the central organizing political institution of humanity, globalization continues to define the current era.

12 Adapted from Chapters 4 and 12 in Lester R. Brown, *Plan B 2.0: Rescuing a Planet Under Stress and a Civilization in Trouble* (New York: W.W. Norton & Company, 2006), available for free downloading at www.earthpolicy.org/Books/PB2/index.htm.

Along with many others, I would argue that we have reached the point where most human rights and environmental issues must be treated as *glocal* phenomena.[13] This hardly precludes the legality of sovereignty in international relations; indeed, there are armies of soldiers, diplomats, lawyers, and myth-makers to ensure its dominance. However, the evolving status of human rights discourse, which must encompass the consequences of ecopolitical developments, accentuates the link between global concerns and local needs.

The glocal political space is not an easily defined one, but is rather evident whenever we discuss concrete policy proposals to ensure sustainability and human dignity. This does not imply that the unending relativist/universalist debate will ever end, but that judicious decisions to act to protect human rights and the environment must take both local conditions and global imperatives into account. The proliferation and causal significance of non-state actors, in both the international private and transnational non-governmental sectors, is empirical evidence of this phenomenon. A landscape of sovereignty emerges wherein concrete barriers to interstate cooperation are seen as constraints on positive action, as impediments to much-needed change in conventional energy production, waste disposal, toxic agriculture, and other fixtures of the modern industrial age.

The links between global and local concerns and levels of activity are growing stronger as environmental justice becomes an operative feature of human rights discourse. Regional organizations have dealt with what appear to local cases of environmental rights. For example, "…in *Lopez Ostra vs. Spain*, the European Court of Human rights held that Spain's failure to prevent a waste treatment plant from polluting nearby homes violated the petitioner's 'right to respect for her home and her private and family life', and held the state liable for damages" (quoted from a petition to the Inter-American Commission on Human Rights of March 2007, in Steiner et al. 2007, 1459). Municipal efforts to curb greenhouse gas emissions are inspired by international networks concerned with the impact of global warming on Arctic and tropical people. Efforts to conserve endangered species are often provoked by international organizations but it is widely accepted that they must involve local populations and respect their rights and resource entitlements to be effective (see Stoett 2002).

It is commonly assumed that procedural/participatory rights promise "environmental protection essentially by way of democracy and informed debate. The enthymeme in this argument is that democratic decision-making will lead to environmentally friendly policies" (Anderson 1998, 9). However, such decision-making must be suffused with the recognition of its international, regional, and municipal implications if it is to be effective today. We can no longer clearly distinguish between municipal, regional and international approaches to protect human rights and the environment (see for example Goimley 1976); ecopolitics takes place in the glocal. As Emery Roe wrote in 1994, we "need not search

13 See R. Robertson (1995) for a brief history of the term; and Gore and Stoett (2009) for applied Canadian case studies.

far to see that the global warming scenario, like the controversy itself, operates within a wider discourse about global change, global economy, global politics, global conflict, global resources, and global environment, to name but a few.... the crisis scenario is grist not only for a specific science controversy, but also for a broader analytic increasingly taken to dominate public discourse about putatively supranational policy problems" (Roe 1994, 27). Human rights are at the core of this inherently glocal discourse.

Conclusion

There is little doubt that climate change will result in massive population movements, increased spread of disease and alien invasive species, and the further diminution of precious resources such as fisheries. That this is a human rights issue of the tallest order is also beyond question, and the human rights community is slowly awakening to this fact. To those concerned with environmental justice in the past four decades, this is not news, but to those accustomed to conceiving of sovereignty in a simplistic fashion, it will be a startling development. Nonetheless, there is no evidence that states are willing to unfold the rigid canopy of sovereign rule as a consequence, despite the breathtaking pace of developments since the United Nations Conference on Environment and Development of 1992 (which, incidentally, did as much to reconfirm the prioritization of sovereignty as it did to advance global environmental governance). What is more likely, indeed extant, is the reconfiguration of sovereignty, wherein new understandings of its meanings will compete with older ones; wherein new ethics will reshape our ideas of what it entails to exercise and protect sovereignty.

Climate change has emerged as the dominant issue that evokes concerns of global environmental justice, but it is hardly the only issue that should do so; indeed, international trade, resource consumption, and exploitative investment patterns have associated ecological footprints that often infringe on basic human rights, and it would be a mistake to focus all of our attention on global warming. Nonetheless it is easily argued that all of these issues are inter-related, and they will continue to fashion yet another contested landscape of sovereignty in the future. If we are indeed facing a threat to our social survival, the alternative to the pursuit of global environmental justice will be the fortification of global bioapartheid, wherein those who can afford to do so revert to Garett Hardin's infamous "lifeboat ethics" (Hardin 1974). This is a recipe not for sustainability, but for dystopia.

References

Almond, B. 1995. Rights and Justice in the Environment Debate, in *Just Environments*, edited by D. Cooper and J. Palmer. London: Routledge, 3–20.

Anand, R. 2004. *International Environmental Justice: A North-South Dimension.* Aldershot: Ashgate.
Anderson, M. 1998. Human Rights Approaches to Environmental Protection: An Overview, in *Human Rights Approaches to Environmental Protection*, edited by A. Boyle and M. Anderson. Oxford: Clarendon Press, 1–23.
Athanasiou, T. and Baer, P. 2002. *Dead Heat: Global Justice and Global Warming.* New York: Seven Stories Press.
Barkham, J. P. 1995. Environmental Needs and Social Justice. *Biodiversity and Conservation* 4(8), 857–86.
Barnett, J. and Dessai, S. (2002) Articles 4.8 and 4.9 of the UNFCCC: Adverse Effects and the Impacts of Response Measures. *Climate Policy* 2(3), 231–39.
Beck, U. 1992. *The Risk Society: Towards a New Modernity*. Trans. Mark Ritter. London: Sage Productions.
Bookchin, M. 1982. *The Ecology of Freedom: The Emergence and Dissolution of Hierarchy*. Palo Alto: Cheshire Books.
Boyle, A. and Anderson, M. (eds). 1998. *Human Rights Approaches to Environmental Protection.* Oxford: Clarendon Press.
Brown, C. 1992. *International Relations Theory: New Normative Approaches.* Hemel Mempstead: Harvester Wheatsheaf.
Bullard, R.D. 1999. Dismantling Environmental Racism in the USA. *Local Environment* 4(1), 5–19.
Caney, S. 2005. *Justice Beyond Borders: A Global Political Theory*. Oxford: Oxford University Press.
Courchene, T. 1995. Glocalization: the Regional/International Interface. *Canadian Journal of Regional Science* 18(1), 1–20.
Crutzen, P. J. 2002. Geology of Mankind. *Nature* 3 (January), 23.
Dalby, S. 2006. Environmental Security: Ecology or International Relations? in *International Ecopolitical Theory: Critical Approaches*, edited by E. Lafferiére and P. Stoett. Vancouver: UBC Press, 17–33.
Dobson, A. 1998. *Justice and the Environment: Conceptions of Environmental Sustainability and Theories of Distributive Justice*. Oxford University Press.
Dobson, A. 2003. *Citizenship and the Environment*. Oxford: Oxford University Press.
Eckersley, R. 2004. *The Green State: Rethinking Democracy and Sovereignty*. Cambridge. Massachusetts: MIT Press.
Esty, D. and Ivanova, M. 2002. *Global Environmental Governance: Options and Opportunities*. New Haven: Yale Center for Environmental Law and Policy.
Fletcher, T. 2003. *From Love Canal to Environmental Justice: The Politics of Hazardous Waste on the Canada-US Border*. Peterborough, Ontario; Broadview.
Goimley, P. 1976. *Human Rights and the Environment: The Needfor International Co-operation.* Leyden: A.W. Sijthoff.
Gore, C. and Stoett, P. 2009. *Environmental Challenges and Opportunities: Local-Global Perspectives on Canadian Issues*. Toronto: Emond Montgomery.

Hardin, G. 1974. Living on a Lifeboat. *Bioscience* 24(10), 561–8.

Harris, P. 1999. *What's Fair? International Justice from an Environmental Perspective.* Paper to the International Studies Association Annual Meeting, Washington, D.C., 16–20 February 1999.

Haughton, G. 1999. Environmental Justice and the Sustainable City. *Journal of Planning Education and Research* 18(3), 233–43.

Hayward, T. 1994. *Ecological Thought: An Introduction.* Cambridge: Polity Press.

Herz, J. 1957. The Rise and Demise of the Territorial State, *World Politics* 9(4), 473–93.

Hirst, P. and Thompson, G. 2000. Global Myths and National Policies, in *Global Democracy: Key Debates*, edited by B. Holden. London: Routledge, 47–59.

Hitchcock, R. 1994. International Human Rights, the Environment, and Indigenous Peoples. *Colorado Journal of International Environmental Law and Policy* 5(1), 15–18.

Hossay, P. 2006. *Unsustainable: A Primer for Global Environmental and Social Justice.* London: Zed.

Illsley, B. 2002. Good Neighbour Agreements: The First Step to Environmental Justice? *Local Environment* 7(1), 69–79.

Jasanoff, S. and Martello, M. L. (eds). 2004. *Earthly Politics: Local and Global in Environmental Governance*. Cambridge: MIT Press.

Knox, J. 2002. The Myth and Reality of Transboundary Environmental Impact Assessment. *American Journal of International Law* 96(2), 291–6.

Kratochwil, F. 1989. *Rules, Norms, Decisions: On the Conditions of Practical Reasoning in International Relations*. Cambridge: Cambridge University Press.

Laferrière, E. and Stoett, P. (eds). 1999. *International Relations Theory and Ecological Thought: Towards a Synthesis*. London: Routledge.

Laferrière, E. and Stoett, P. (eds). 2006. *International Ecopolitical Theory: Critical Approaches*. Vancouver: University of British Columbia Press.

Lee, M. and Carolyn, A. 2003. The Usual Suspects? Public Participation Under the Aarhus Convention. *Modern Law Review* 66(1): 80–108.

Litfin, K. 1997. Sovereignty in World Ecopolitics. *Mershon International Studies Review* 41(2), 167–204.

Low, N. and Gleeson, B. 1998. Situating Justice in the Environment: The Case of BHP and OK Tedi Copper Mine. *Antipode* 30(3), 201–26.

Mason, M. 2006. Citizenship Entitlements Beyond Borders? Identifying Mechanisms of Access and Redress for Affected Publics in International Environmental Laws. *Global Governance* 12(3), 283–304.

Müller, B. 2007. Nairobi 2006: Trust and the Future of Adaptation Building. *Oxford Institute for Energy Studies* [Adobe Acrobat file], EV 38. Available at: www.oxfordenergy.org/pdfs/EV38.pdf [accessed: 8 February 2009].

Obiora, A. 1999. Symbolic Episodes in the Quest for Environmental Justice. *Human Rights Quarterly* 21(2), 464–512.

Okowa, P. 2000. *State Responsibility for Transboundary Air Pollution in International Law.* Oxford: Oxford University Press.

Pallemaerts, M. 1986. Development, Conservation, and Indigenous Rights in Brazil. *Human Rights Quarterly* 8(3), 374–400.

Paterson, M. 2000. *Understanding Global Environmental Politics: Domination, Accumulation, Resistance*. Basingstoke: Macmillan.

Paterson, M. 2001. International Justice and Global Warming, in *The Ethical Dimensions of Global Change*, edited by B. Holden. New York: St. Martin's Press, 181–201.

Price-Smith, A. 2002. *The Health of Nations*. Cambridge, Massachusetts: MIT Press.

Pulido, L. 1996. *Environmentalism and Economic Justice*. Tucson: University of Arizona Press.

Redgwell, C. 1998. Life, the Universe and Everything: A Critique of Anthropocentric Rights, in *Human Rights Approaches to Environmental Protection*, edited by A. Boyle and M. Anderson. Oxford: Clarendon Press, 71–87.

Roberts, J. T. and Parks, B. 2007. *A Climate of Injustice: Global Inequality, North-South Politics, and Climate Policy.* Cambridge: MIT Press.

Robertson, R. 1995. Glocalization: Time-space and Homogeneity-Heterogeneity, in *Global Modernities*, edited by M. Featherstone, S. Lash, and R. Robertson. London: Sage, 25–44.

Roe, E. 1994. Global Warming as Analytic Tip, in *Global Climate Change and Public Policy*, edited by D. Feldman. Chicago: Nelson-Hall, 19–38.

Sen, A. 1988. Rights and Agency, in *Consequentialism and its Critics*, edited by S. Scheffler. Oxford: Oxford University Press, 187–223.

Shelton, D. 2003. The Environmental Implications of International Human rights Tribunals, in *Linking Human Rights and the Environment*, edited by R. Picolotto and J. Taillant. Tucson: University of Arizona Press, 1–30.

Soederberg, S. 2007. *Global Governance in Question: Empire, Class, and the New Common Sense in Managing North-South Relations*. Toronto: Arbeiter Ring Publishing.

Steiner, H., Aston, P. and Goodman, R. 2007. *International Human Rights in Context: Law, Politics, Morals*. 3rd edition. Oxford University Press.

Stoett, P. 2002. The International Regulation of Trade and Wildlife: Institutional and Normative Considerations. *International Environmental Agreements: Politics, Law and Economics* 2(1), 195–210.

Stoett, P. 2008. "A Climatic Normative Catalyst: Climate Change and Global Environmental Justice", *The ICFAI Journal of International Relations* 2(3), 56–72.

Taylor, P. 1998. *An Ecological Approach to International Law*. London: Routledge.

Vanderheiden, S. 2008. *Atmospheric Justice: A Political Theory of Climate Change.* Oxford: Oxford University Press.

Von Seht, H. 2002. Socio-economic Impacts of Local Environmental Policies: An Analysis for the Field of Climate Protection. *Local Environment* 7(1), 23–34.

Westra, L, and Wenz, P. 1995. *Faces of Environmental Racism: Confronting Issues of Global Justice*. London: Rowman and Littlefield.

Wenz, Peter. 1988. *Environmental Justice*. Albany: State University of New York Press.

Young, I. M. 2004. Responsibility and Global Labor Justice. *Journal of Political Philosophy*, 12(4), 365–388.

Chapter 11
The Transnational Effort for Disability Rights: The Marriage of Disability Rights to Human Rights

Kenneth R. Rutherford

Introduction: The Case of the Disability Rights Movement

The post Cold War era has been characterized by increasing involvement of non-governmental organizations (NGOs) engaged in transnational political activity. It has received considerable attention in the past decade due to the successful transnational NGO advocacy efforts in achieving the Mine Ban Treaty (MBT) and the ratification of the International Criminal Court (ICC). The downfall of the Soviet Union and the end of the Cold War also ushered in an era signaled by greater attention and concern toward the rights and dignity of people with disabilities (PWDs) that resulted in the UN Convention on the Rights of Persons with Disabilities (CRPD), which entered in to force on 3 May 2008. This movement was spearheaded by NGOs that were supported by governments freed from the political restraints during the Cold War in order to negotiate the fastest human rights treaty in history.

During the Cold War, the global human rights agenda lacked space for persons with disabilities and the human rights challenges they face. In a few countries, notably the United States, domestic disability rights laws were developed during the Cold War, but failed to gravitate to the global political agenda. Burdened by the rituals, prejudices and agendas that constitute their checkered history, states were unable and unwilling to translate disability rights statements and declarations toward international legal codification based on human rights principles.

In most other countries, however, disability rights progress was slow and unimpressive. With the end of the Cold War, NGOs moved to fill this gap in world politics. This movement has been remarkably fast and pervasive. The post-Cold War era allows a greater role for NGOs to try to focus government attention on disability rights. It took more than a decade after the Cold War ended, but domestic leaders, such as President Vicente Fox of Mexico coupled with a newly empowered and experienced group of NGOs, including those from the Nobel Peace Prize award winning International Campaign to Ban Landmines, created broad transnational avenues for communication and collaboration to join together in a novel way to help governments draft and negotiate an international law for the rights and dignity for persons with disabilities. Their partnership during the initial stages of the negotiations created an unanticipated acceleration of the development of a convention on the rights of people with disabilities.

Six hundred million people—almost ten percent of the world's population—are disabled. Eighty percent live in the developing world. They are among the poorest of the poor and too often live as social and economic outcasts. There are few effective laws that guarantee inclusion and full participation in society for persons with disabilities. At the beginning of the CRPD negotiation process in the summer of 2002, only an estimated 40 of 190 UN member states had anti-discrimination laws (Disability Rights Bulletin 2002). In the developing world, persons with disabilities have few advocacy resources or legal tools to effect a change in their status, much less secure their full participation in society.

The CRPD's achievement illustrates and strengthens arguments that the world is going through a significant phase of philosophical political modification, and that the sovereign state, as modernity has tended to define it, is more accepting and welcoming of NGOs. In the past fifteen years one case of transnational politics stands out for achieving a demanding goal—the human rights of persons with disabilities—with extraordinary tempo: the Convention on the Rights and Dignity of People with Disabilities.

This chapter will address the political space created by the end of the Cold War to allow governments and NGOs use the human rights framework for addressing the rights of disabled people.

Disability and Human Rights: Divided Agenda or Walking Together?

The genesis for the CRPD was that failure of the United Nations Universal Declaration of Human Rights (UNDHR) adopted in 1948 by the UN General Assembly (UNGA) was in articulating and anticipating universal application. The UNDHR claims that all human beings "are born free and equal in dignity" and that everyone is entitled to all the rights and freedoms without distinction of any kind. Persons with disabilities were theoretically and legally entitled to the same human rights as all people. But in reality, the situation of people with disabilities across all societies is an affront to the core principles guaranteed by the UNDHR and remained outside the framework of international law and national human rights norms around the world.

In the international human rights legal framework, persons with disabilities are, for all practical purposes, invisible, despite the fact that all human beings are entitled to the full range of human rights protections. Disability is persistently marginalized as a human rights issue within the United Nations system and in the work of international non-governmental organizations, including human rights organizations.

With the wide variety of human rights treaties and conventions, some may ask why the CRPD is necessary. The CRPD is critical for the human rights of persons with disabilities because, unfortunately, they constitute one of the most vulnerable population groups due to the lifelong and severe nature of disability-based discrimination, and the systemic nature of the obstacles people with disabilities face in integrating into their communities on an equal basis with others. Persons with disabilities around the world face many forms of discrimination and abuse—some subtle and some blatant. Thus, sadly, despite the various international documents that provide for the right of all human beings to enjoy full coverage and protection of human rights, there has been a persistent marginalization of the disability issue as a human rights issue. Thus, even though disability rights has been specifically addressed in some existing human rights frameworks, and while these documents do add content to the human rights field, most such provisions are for the most part not housed in a treaty, nor are they widely regarded as having attained the status of binding law. The continued discrimination against persons with disabilities necessitated the adoption of a legally binding instrument to establish clear legal oglibations on states to protect their rights and dignity.

The issue of human rights and persons with disabilities is not new. In 1971, the UNGA adopted the "Declaration on the Rights of Mentally Retarded Persons" and in 1975 the "Declaration on the Rights of Disabled Persons." In 1981, the UNGA proclaimed the International Year of Disabled Persons. The following year, it adopted the "World Program of Action concerning Disabled Persons in Resolution." In 1983, the International Labor Organization (ILO) agreed to the Convention on Vocational Rehabilitation and Employment for Disabled Persons. In the meantime, the UN launched the UN Decade (1983–1992) for Disabled Persons and in 1987 hosted the Global Meeting of experts reviews the Implementation of the World Program of Action concerning Disabled Persons. At this meeting, the experts recommended that the UNGA convene a special conference to draft an international convention on the rights of disabled persons. That same year, Italy prepared a draft disability rights treaty that is submitted to the UNGA, but there was no formal agreement to proceed.

The next major event at the UN regarding the human rights of people with disabilities occurred on 20 December 1993, when the UNGA adopted the UN Standard Rules on the Equalization of Opportunities for people with disabilities. The rules emphasized that people with disabilities are limited not by their disabilities but by society's mental and physical obstacles that reinforced a disempowering attitudes toward persons with disabilities. The Standard Rules for the "Social Model," which states that society has barriers that preclude persons with disabilities to full and equal participation from a "Charity Model"—providing direct assistance with limited follow-up and the "Medical Model, which doctors know best and treat disability as a disease was a huge paradigm shift.

The medical model defines disability as a health condition or disease to be addressed by doctors and rehabilitation specialists who pursue treatments and cures for disabling conditions. The focus is on changing disabled people so they can perform more efficiently in a society that has been constructed by and according to non-disabled people. The approach means, for example, that just having the correct surgery or the right application of medication will alleviate and solve the disability and thus would not be an issue. The medical model's goal is to change persons with disabilities so they can be more "normal." Many countries in the Middle East and Islamic world still use medical model.

While some governments and societies have adopted a social inclusion and a rights-based approach to disability issues, many more still rely on charity models of assistance, or a narrow medical model that focuses on finding medical "solutions" to limitations caused by a disability. The latter models ignore the need to address the vast array of limitations created and imposed by of discrimination, exclusion, and ignorance.

The latest model is based on human rights, whose guiding principle is that disability rights are equal to human rights and are not special rights. The Human Rights Model grew out of civil rights movement in late 1960s, which helped to launch the process for the achievement of the Americans with Disabilities Act (ADA), and using the UNDHR and the Standard Rules. The human rights model focused on the role of society in gaining equality for all its citizens, including persons with disabilities. The model shifts from fixing individuals to eliminating socially constructed barriers that prevent PWDs from participating fully in their countries. People are not something to be fixed but embraced. This model is used in the United States.

An Empowering Process

The human rights model view was not actualized at the UN until Mexican President Vincente Fox issued a call to action in 2001 at the UNGA for a wide-ranging disability rights convention that included protections for the rights and dignity of persons with disabilities. On 19 December 2001 the UNGA adopted the Mexican sponsored resolution 56/168, calling for the establishment of an ad hoc Committee to consider proposals for an international human rights treaty for people with disabilities. The resolution specifically urged "that further efforts are made to ensure the active participation of non-governmental organizations in the ad hoc Committee" and "encourages member states to involve persons with disabilities, representatives of disability organizations and/or experts from developing countries in their delegations to the meetings of ad hoc Committee."[1] Thereafter, an ad hoc Committee was created which is open to the participation of all UN Member States as well as observers to the UN.

The ad hoc Committee's mandate was to consider proposals for a comprehensive and integral international convention to protect and promote the rights and dignity of persons with disabilities. Before the first meeting of the ad hoc Committee took place, the Mexican Government in cooperation with the UN hosted an inter-

1 *Comprehensive and Integral Convention to Promote and Protect the Rights and Dignity of Persons with Disabilities,* adopted by the United Nations General Assembly on the report of the Third Committee (A/56/583/Add.2), 88th Plenary Meeting, 19 December 2001.

regional expert meeting to discuss the treaty's development and goals in Mexico from 11-14 June 2002. The first meeting of the ad hoc Committee took place from 29 July 29 through 9 August 2002 at the UN headquarters in New York City. The meetings initiated the start of a new phase for people with disabilities.

At this first session, disability rights NGOs were granted entry and participated in the public meetings of the ad hoc Committee, which was attended by more than fifty governments.[2] As a further sign of appreciation and respect, the UN granted meeting space at the UN headquarters, just across from the conference hall, for the NGOs to meet daily to meet and discuss and serve as a resource center. In addition, a computer with accessible software was available for NGO delegates.

Just as important, NGOs secured a meaningful participation roll in the convention drafting, and helped Mexico and other supporters achieve the CRPD. For example, near the end of the first session of the ad hoc Committee, Mexico asked the NGO community to generate pressure on governments to save the process because the United States and a small number of Asian countries were blocking the call for a convention. In support of Mexico's request and the convention's development, NGOs sent emails to governments requesting governments to press for a resolution by the ad hoc Committee to acknowledge the urgent need to draft a convention.[3] For example, Jerry White, Executive Director of the Landmine Survivors Network, wrote the US Ambassador to the UN, John Negroponte and other State Department with the following message that expressed his

> deep concern about recent repots that the United States Government may be undermining efforts and momentum to generate a call for an international convention on the human rights of people with disability. I strongly urge you to help garner support in the US government and among our allies to press for a resolution by the ad hoc Committee acknowledging the urgent need to take steps toward a new convention…The United States can lead the way, sowing seeds of goodwill among nations and disabled populations alike (Jerry White 2002).[4]

During the meetings, NGOs wrote a an open letter to the Committee's delegates stating that the convening "marked a new phase in human history for people with disabilities [and that] [t]his historical occasion provides an opportunity for those who reject the systemic global discrimination against people with disabilities, and the marginalization of disability as a human rights issue" (Disability Rights Bulletin 2002). NGOs also called on delegates to recommend that a new convention for the disability rights should be recommended by the ad hoc Committee to the UNGA.

---

2 The impetus for this research project occurred while I was working with the international disability rights movement at the first ad hoc committee meeting at UN Headquarters in New York.

3 During the First ad hoc Committee meeting, NGOs awarded Mexico its Disability Awareness Badge of Honor, *Disability Rights Bulletin* (1), 29 July 2002.

4 Jerry White, e-mail to United States State Department, 8 August 2002.

A prominent NGO leader, Adnan Al Aboudy, who is a bi-lateral leg amputee and Director of the Landmine Survivors Network's Jordan office stated that

> It is important to show the world that people with disabilities are entitled not to charity but to the means necessary to enjoy their human rights. A convention will oblige governments to allocate resources in their budgets so that opportunities are available to people with disabilities on an equal basis as everyone else. It will also facilitate participation by people with disabilities in decisions affecting their status.[5]

The ad hoc Committee's recommendation created an unexpected momentum of the process to develop a convention on the rights and dignity of people with disabilities. For example, the convention recommendation received a boost when the UN Secretary-General Kofi Annan stated that he supported the process for a new convention for the human rights of people with disabilities.[6]

NGOs themselves scrambled to develop a transnational coalition structure that would be a campaign with clear leadership and messaging. For example, campaign updates, distributed via email or in hard copy, where email was not readily accessible, proved especially valuable in guiding NGOs to educate governments regarding the convention and the approach in which NGOs could participate in support for and activities related with the convention process and to attend relevant meetings. The process's primary consideration—the procedures through which the convention should developed embodied the principle of "nothing about us without us." The reasons for this are knowledge and experience. Persons with disabilities have a unique perspective on what it is like to live with disability.[7] This perspective was referenced in order for the convention to create legal protections that address in concrete terms the social, political, and cultural circumstances that impact the human rights condition of persons with disabilities. For example the involvement of landmine survivors in the MBT and Convention on Cluster Munitions (CCM) negotiating processes expressly incorporates the need for assistance to the landmine disabled and their human rights.[8]

---

5 As quoted in *Disability Negotiations Rights Bulletin* 1(1) 29 July 2002. Subsequently, Adnan would become an official member of the Jordanian delegation to the CRPD negotiations.

6 Address given at the UN headquarters, 19 June 2003.

7 In addition, the draft resolution adopted in the Report of the ad hoc Committee and submitted to the UNGA expressly acknowledges the need to involve PWDs as active contributors to the work of the ad hoc Committee. Also the Standard Rules Implementation Measures also highlights the role of persons with disabilities. UN Standard Rule 4(2) states that "States should involve organizations of persons with disabilities in all decision-making relating to plans and programs concerning persons with disabilities or affecting their economic and social status."

8 Officially known as the *Convention on the Prohibition of the Use, Stockpiling, Production and Transfer of Anti-Personnel Mines and on their Destruction.*

Jordan provides a unique case of working with NGOs and people with disabilities throughout the negotiations. It participated in all the meetings related to the CRPD, and was at the forefront of pushing "throughout the process and has fully supported the substantiation of the Convention."[9] It participated in almost all the negotiating sessions headed by the general secretary of the Ministry of Social Development.[10] Jordan was one of the first Arab countries to include persons with disabilities on their official delegations. One of the reasons for Jordan's inclusion of Adnan and Alia was its "firm belief in the active participation of people with disabilities and their representative organizations in the drafting of this convention, and in its monitoring and implementation. There is no excuse for leaving people with disabilities outside the room as their treaty is being negotiated."[11] During the negotiations, Adnan remarked that disability and human rights are linked:

> It is important to show the world that people with disabilities are entitled not to charity but to the means necessary to enjoy their human rights. A convention will oblige governments to allocate resources in their budgets so that opportunities are available to people with disabilities on an equal basis as everyone else. It will also facilitate participation by people with disabilities in decisions affecting their status (*Disability Rights Bulletin* 2002).

Another important issue was to achieve cross-disability representation as it was essential that the ad hoc Committee be exposed to the cross-disability perspective, and this should include the voice of the most marginalized groups of persons with disabilities. For example, I am a double amputee and the father of a disabled child, but we do not have common needs and thus those needs must be reflected by diverse representation of people with disabilities. For example, while I am disabled as a bi-lateral amputee my son is also disabled but our disabilities are not similar and hence we need to achieve that cross-disability representation at the ad hoc Committee.

9 HRH Prince Ra'ed bin Zaid, speech presented to the Rehabilitation International Paralympic Committee Symposium, Athens, Greece (undated).

10 Author Interview with Mona Abdeljawad, MENA Regional Coordinator, Landmine Survivors Network, through e-mail, Amman, Jordan, 12 April 2005.

11 Prince Ra'ed bin Zaid, speech presented to the Rehabilitation International Paralympic Committee Symposium, Athens, Greece. (undated). Despite Jordan's location in one of the most volatile and insecure parts of the world, it plays a leading international and regional role in alleviating suffering and protecting the rights of persons with disabilities. Jordan's leadership on disability rights was recognized in 2005 when it received the Franklin Delano Roosevelt International Disability Award, named for the US president who suffered with polio and lived many years in a wheelchair. The award was presented at a UN headquarters ceremony to Jordan's King Abdullah II by the president's granddaughter, Anna Eleanor Roosevelt, who commended Jordan for putting the disabled "in the forefront of its national agenda" and for providing inspiration by example in eliminating obstacles that "all too often prevent those with disabilities from joining the mainstream of civil society" "Jordan's King Accepts Disability Award," New York Times, 23 March 2005.

A key issue during the ad hoc committee negotiations was accessibility within UN. The ad hoc Committee Report acknowledged there is much to be done to improve accessibility for persons with disabilities to UN facilities and documentation—the draft resolution calls for improved accessibility. Persons with disabilities worked with UN to achieve this goal, and correct perceptions of those in UN who may have believed that the necessary accommodations will be prohibitively expensive or cumbersome. For example, in 1995, the UN facilities in Vienna were not accessible when I participated in a landmine conference in 1995. At the time, I was wheelchair bound and thus had to be carried up the stage to present and also enter and exit through the back door of the parking lot as the front entrance was not wheelchair accessible.

The partnerships and sharing of expertise between governments and disability advocates from every part of the world was crucial to ensure that the treaty would be reflective of the issues faced by persons with disabilities. This first ad hoc committee meeting also marked a transitional point in the history of the disability movement. For the first time the disability issue assumed a position as one of the human rights issues mostly in part due to the intensive efforts exerted by non-governmental organizations and people with disabilities to promote awareness of human rights violations pertaining to all disability categories around the world; even within the UN buildings and conference venues which are not fully accessible for persons with disabilities. These efforts maintained the steady progress of support for this agreement in spite of difficulties, obstacles, and procrastination caused by some participant countries. However, the final recommendations stressed the need to consolidate and protect the full human rights and basic freedoms of people with disability on an equal footing and in an effective manner.

When negotiating the treaty, one of the major priorities was filling a need in the content of the core human rights treaties, which does not adequately address the specific circumstances of persons with disabilities and the practices frequently leading to the violation of their human rights. A second priority was to develop a convention that unequivocally protects the fundamental human rights and freedoms of PWDs and fully acknowledges their legitimate membership and participation in the international human rights system. The main issue to address on this point was that the current international human rights framework is rarely used to protect the human rights of persons with disabilities.

Convention on the Rights and Dignity of People with Disabilities

The CRPD entered in to force on 3 May 2008 as the most comprehensive human rights treaty ever negotiated. It is also the first comprehensive human rights treaty of the twenty-first century and marks a major milestone in the effort to promote, protect and ensure the full and equal enjoyment of all human rights and fundamental freedoms of persons with disabilities, and to promote respect for their inherent dignity. The CRPD was opened for signature and ratification on 30 March 2007, at United Nations Headquarters and was signed by a record 81 countries and the European Community. In addition, 44 countries signed the Convention's Optional Protocol, a mechanism to address individual violations and make country visits.

The new CRPD and its Optional Protocol promotes, protects and guarantees that *everyone* can enjoy equality, dignity and rights. It is also significant for the negotiating process of including PWDs and NGOs as full partners during eight sessions of an ad hoc Committee of the General Assembly from 2002 to 2006, and helping to make it the fastest negotiated human rights treaty.

With the CRPD's entry into force the world is now closer to the principle that all people are born free and live with dignity and rights, regardless of the source of their disability.

The broad definition for PWDs and categories of disabilities affirms that human rights will be enjoyed by all PWDs with a wide range of disabilities. The CRPD identifies the rights persons with disabilities as well as the obligations on States parties to the Convention to promote, protect and ensure those rights. The CRPD also obligates states to clarify the steps that they must take to promote, protect and ensure the rights in the Convention. It also address enabling measures, such as identifying specific steps that states must take to ensure an enabling environment for the enjoyment of human rights, namely: awareness-raising, ensuring accessibility, ensuring protection and safety in situations of risk and humanitarian emergencies, promoting access to justice, ensuring personal mobility, enabling habilitation and rehabilitation, and collecting statistics and data.

The CRPD is intended as a human rights instrument with an explicit social development dimension. It adopts a broad categorization of persons with disabilities and reaffirms that all persons with all types of disabilities must enjoy all human rights and fundamental freedoms. It clarifies and qualifies how all categories of rights apply to persons with disabilities and identifies areas where adaptations have to be made for persons with disabilities to effectively exercise their rights and areas where their rights have been violated, and where protection of rights must be reinforced.

The CRPD also articulates the human rights of persons with disabilities and provides mechanisms for monitoring states' compliance with convention obligations. The process itself also generated a host of additional benefits: raising public awareness, highlighting human rights abuses, developing the knowledge-base of governmental and non-governmental participants, and offering capacity-building opportunities for disability groups as a result of increased global focus on their issues. The CRPD also defines the equality, inclusion and full participation of persons with disabilities in society, and respect for their dignity and autonomy, as universal human rights. It will serve as a beacon for persons with disabilities everywhere, giving them the tools they need to successfully advocate for their human rights.

In sum, the CRPD marks a "paradigm shift" in attitudes and approaches to persons with disabilities. It takes to a new height the movement from viewing persons with disabilities as "objects" of charity, medical treatment and social protection towards viewing persons with disabilities as "subjects" with rights, who are capable of claiming those rights and making decisions for their lives based on their free and informed consent as well as being active members of society.

Warfare and Disability: Discouraging Trends

This section addresses the relationship among disability, war, violence and disaster, and some of the reasons for the inadequate treatment often accorded to persons with disabilities. This combination is a particularly potent one, which contributes significantly to the incidence of disability. Nearly one hundred years ago, more than 90 per cent of victims of war were combatants, while today nearly 90 per cent of war victims are non-combatants. During periods of conflict or disaster, they are frequently the forgotten people; and in post-conflict or post-disaster regions, the real needs of victims—particularly persons with disabilities—are all too often ignored.

One can look to any situation of conflict or disaster and find increased incidence of disability. A few poignant examples include the use of weapons that are purposefully designed to main and not kill, such as landmines, and civil wars that are frequently fought with small arms and weapons such as machetes, which lead to countless casualties, many of whom must live with long-term physical and mental impairments.

Cluster munitions are another weapon that causes disability by it indiscriminate anti-personnel effects in two ways—its widespread (or footprint) impact on the ground and the malfunction rates that result in unexploded munitions littering the area.[12] During the 12 July–14 August 2006 Israeli-Hezbollah war in southern Lebanon, for example, Israeli forces used more than 1,800 surface-launched artillery projectiles to deliver more than four million cluster sub-munitions, which resulted in more than one million unexploded munitions.[13] In the post-strike time period, the "footprint" remains dangerous for decades since many of the sub munitions fail to explode and, therefore, lie dormant and remain a deadly threat until detonated by movement, typically by civilians reclaiming and using their

12 The failure rate of cluster munitions in actual battle is regularly higher than advertized by governments and manufacturers because pristine test by well-rested, trained and stress-free personnel during good weather and on hard ground differ significantly than actual use in the field. The variation can be partially explained by weather conditions, height at release, ground conditions, vegetation density, angle of drop and a range of human elements, such as a pilot failing to arm the cluster munitions. In addition, during the arming sequences, a lot can go wrong. At every stage three to five points of failure can be realized. These points include the carrier fuse functions, ejection charge fires, arming pin withdrawal process, an on and on. If the munitions fail to arm the self-destruct function also fails.

13 Handicap International, *Circle of Impact: The Fatal Footprint of Cluster Munitions on People and Communities*, May 2007, 120. The Israeli cluster strike figures do not include air delivered cluster munitions.

land.[14] According to the Landmine Action report, *Foreseeable Harm: The use and impact of cluster munitions in Lebanon: 2006*, an average of three to four civilians were being injured every day in Lebanon by cluster munitions more than two months after the August ceasefire (Nash 2006, 3). It also concluded that in the first years after the 2005 Israeli-Lebanese cease-fire, 97 per cent of all unexploded ordinance and landmine casualties in Lebanon were due to cluster munitions (Nash, 16).

During these times of conflict or disaster, persons with disabilities are often disregarded or ill-treated and therefore placed in increased jeopardy and vulnerability. For example, during first days of the Rwandan genocide in 1994, many states sent in troops to rescue their nationals. Although white doctors and nurses were evacuated from the psychiatric hospital in Kigali, none of the people institutionalized there were evacuated, or given the protection of UN peacekeepers. Later reports confirmed the mass slaughter of all residents at the institution.

Even once the immediate danger of conflict or disaster has subsided, persons with disabilities often still find themselves severely disadvantaged. For instance in post-conflict/disaster physical reconstruction areas the incorporation of principles of universal design would be prudent from a human rights perspective. Yet despite the fact that it is always more cost-effective to incorporate accessibility features at the beginning of a construction project, accessibility is often considered only as an afterthought—if it is considered at all.

The nature of conflict and disaster is such that there will always be a high human price to pay. Human rights law as represented by the CRPD will ensure that the price paid by persons with disabilities is not disproportionately high. By effectively mainstreaming disability as an issue, we can better serve those who currently experience conflict or disaster, and ensure that during periods of reconstruction, the "victims" are empowered to make the transition to "survivors."

Nearly ten years ago, I became a member of the world's disabled population, when I lost my legs to a landmine in Somalia. With some of the strongest disability rights laws in the world, such as the Americans with Disabilities Act (ADA), I benefited from legal protections in allowing me to fully participate in society and access opportunities that most persons with disabilities in the world do not have.

Since then I co-founded the Landmine Survivors Network (LSN), with another American landmine survivor, Jerry White, to become a positive voice for change by empowering individuals, families and communities affected by landmines and other remnants of war to recover from trauma and reclaim their lives. Since LSN's founding in 1997, we have established survivor networks in six mine-affected countries: Bosnia, El Salvador, Ethiopia, Jordan, Mozambique, and Vietnam. We have provided assistance to thousands of families affected by landmines, made nearly 40,000 home and hospital visits to survivors, and helped launch hundreds of survivor-owned businesses.

---

14 A cluster munitions footprint is the ground area covered by sub munitions.

We also helped the International Campaign to Ban Landmines (ICBL) promote victim assistance language in the negotiations for the Mine Ban Treaty (MBT), which was eventually signed in 1997. It became the first weapons control law to include obligatory assistance for victims of a weapon (Article 6.3 MBT). In only ten years, victim assistance evolved from a two-sentence sub-paragraph into a comprehensive framework for implementation and interpretation of victim assistance, which recognizes that it is a "human rights issue."[15]

While unprecedented, victim assistance provisions in the text of the MBT are vague and insufficient to effectively assist victims of landmines to enjoy their human rights. Ten years of implementation brought to light its flaws and shortcomings. States parties addressed these through developing a clear and comprehensive framework for implementation.[16] During the First Review Conference in Nairobi in 2004, state parties to the MBT articulated their understanding of victim assistance as a "human rights issue" as an issue of human rights of mine survivors as a sub-group of a larger community of persons with disabilities (Nairobi Action Plan).

These rights are also codified in the CRPD, which provides a human rights framework for implementation of victim assistance. It both complements and supplements victim assistance in the context of the MBT. The states have consistently recognized the symbiotic relationship between the CRPD and the victim assistance.

This innovative language for victims of the weapon being addressed by international law is especially important because arms treaties and human rights are inextricably connected. It is during armed conflicts that some of the worst human rights violations occur. We had seen landmine survivors, who had lost their limbs and sight also become economically and socially marginalized and ostracized. Survivors of war and violence often sustain severe injuries and disability. Few have access to quality health care, rehabilitation therapy or prosthetics. In many cultures, persons with disabilities are treated as social garbage.

Considered a burden on society, persons with disabilities are frequently denied access to health care, education and employment, and shunned by family and community. Helping people with disabilities to claim their rights and become active citizens is one of the most powerful ways human rights law can improve the lives of landmine and other conflict survivors around the world.

This connection between human rights for persons with disabilities and armed violence, however, was not recognized by the international community until the Convention on Cluster Munitions (CCM), which prohibits the use of cluster munitions and provides broad obligations for victim assistance, including at the "highest applicable human rights standards," including highlighting the CRPD. When it was adopted in May 2008 and signed in Oslo, Norway on 3 December

15 Nairobi Action Plan, Report of the 2004 Nairobi Summit on a Mine-Free World, which is officially known as the First Review Conference of the 1997 Mine Ban Treaty.

16 Nairobi Action Plan, Victim Assistance Questionnaire, Form J, etc.

2008 by 94 countries, the CCM became the first international arms control treaty to mention human rights (CCM Preamble and Article 5).

The CCM is also the first international legal instrument that bridges that artificial divide. It creates a new international standard for victim assistance, codifying the obligations of the states to assist those victimized by the weapon they seek to ban. It is the latest in a line of treaties that informed the development of the framework for victim assistance in the context of arms treaties. It is fair to say that the dots connecting weapons treaties and human rights have been evolving fairly consistently, articulating the rights of those victimized by weapons.

Conclusion

With the CRPD's achievement, disability rights became the first major form of human rights addressed at the global level in the first decade of the twenty-first century. There are good reasons to applaud and encourage political attention of marrying human rights and the legal rights of people with disabilities. Many of those who have disabilities have a hard life. Those who have lost limbs or faculties in those countries—be it from war or other causes—have the hardest life of all. People with disabilities must deal with the trauma, the physical pain, and with an environment in which there are often few to no laws protecting their rights and serving their medical or rehabilitative requirements. Their disabilities usually result in the loss of jobs, inability to go to school, and the impoverishment of their entire families. This is not just because of physical barriers.

There are profound social barriers as well.

Do the disability rights advancements at the global level buttress the notion that the NGO role in the post-Cold War world indicates the changing character of world politics? Will there be more victories arising through NGO participation in critical issue areas, such as alleviating poverty, controlling small arms or rescuing the environment?

The inclusiveness of Cold War politics has given way to a more cosmopolitan and patchwork framework, which allows NGOs to participate significantly. As evidenced by the disability rights and other NGO led movements, such as the ban on anti-personnel landmines and cluster munitions as highlighted above, there is a growing accommodation for wider community interests in global politics for NGOs. More specifically, the NGO role in helping to realize the CRPD highlights this suggestion. During the Cold War, NGOs and governments inherited a political system that separated the global community through competing ideologies based on security and marginalized humanitarian principles. Today, people with common interests are not immobilized by the enduring legacy of contrasting Cold War ideologies that confined political actors to particular positions and issues.

The CRPD negotiations at the UN were distinguished by participants from a variety of faiths and cultures to focus on a key humanitarian issue regardless of political ideologies. For example, Serbian, Bosnian and Croatian strategized with Latin American disability rights advocates, and Arab peace-builders worked closely with African and European advocates to communicate strong disability rights message government representatives. In other words, the post-Cold War world allowed transnational politics, such as the disability rights developments resulting in the CRPD, brings people together to pursue praiseworthy goals, goals that states ignore, belittle or simply cannot mobilize to attain, goals such as a disability rights world. This form of politics allows people not only to bypass or supplement states, but also to challenge them to expose globally their human rights violations of persons with disabilities.

A new, specialized international convention on the human rights of persons with disabilities should not be viewed as a panacea for the deplorable human rights violations experienced by persons with disabilities. Much work must be done at all levels—internationally, regionally, nationally and local for their rights to be guaranteed in a meaningful way.

The CRPD is a window of opportunity to ensure that persons with disabilities are no longer the invisible subjects of the international human rights system. It offers an essential legal tool to legally empower persons with disabilities to claim their rights and to challenge the attitudes and practices that prevent the enjoyment of these rights.

More broadly, the CRPD's achievement highlights the important NGO role in its development negotiating processes. Their dedication to the rights and dignity of PWDs contributes in a variety of significant ways to better understanding how sovereignty and human rights are considered since the end of the Cold War.

At the local and regional levels, where national legislation to protect the rights of persons with disabilities is particularly weak, or even non-existent, the CRPD articulates their human rights of and provides mechanisms for monitoring states' compliance with convention obligations. It also provides a host of additional benefits: raising public awareness; highlighting human rights abuses; developing the knowledge-base of governmental and non-governmental participants; and offering capacity-building opportunities for disability groups as a result of increased global focus on their issues.

It is also important for traditional human rights organizations to be engaged in the CRPD implementation as many have not traditionally addressed the human rights violations of persons with disabilities. They must work to raise the profile of disability as a human rights issue in the work of the CRPD.

In addition, much work needs to be done to educate the public about human rights generally and the need to protect the human rights of persons with disabilities specifically. Human rights organizations must act to foster support for the convention amongst members of the public generally if a completed convention is to be ratified by states. Even when governments sign, most citizens do not realize its contents or what it means. Regardless, the end of the Cold War provides NGOs and other actors political space to realize the CRPD and help support implementation of its goals.

References

The 1997 Convention on the Prohibition of the Use, Stockpiling, Production and Transfer or Anti-Personnel Mines and on their Destruction. Available at: http://www.un.org/Depts/mine/UNDocs/ban_trty.htm [accessed: 9 February 2009].

Abdeljawad, Mona (2005). MENA Regional Coordinator, Landmine Survivors Network, Amman, Jordan. e-mail communication, 12 April 2005.

Americans with Disabilities Act of 1990.

Comprehensive and Integral International Convention to Promote and Protect the Rights and Dignity of Persons with Disabilities, Adopted by the United Nations General Assembly on the Report of the Third Committee (A/56/583/Add.2), 88th Plenary Meeting, 19 December 2001.

Convention on Cluster Munitions. Available at: http://www.clusterconvention.org/pages/pages_ii/iia_textenglish.html [accessed: 9 February 2009].

The Convention on the Rights of Persons with Disabilities (CRPD) United Nations General Assembly Resolution 61/106. Available at: http://www2.ohchr.org/english/law/disabilities-convention.htm [accessed 9 February 2009].

Declaration of 1981 as the International Year of Disabled Persons. United Nations General Assembly, 8 December 1981 (Resolution 77).

Declaration on the Rights of Disabled Persons. 9 December 1975. United Nations General Assembly (Resolution 3447).

Declaration on the Rights of Mentally Retarded Persons. 20 December 1971. United Nations General Assembly (Resolution 2856).

Disability Rights Bulletin. 29 July 2002.

Ending the Suffering Caused by Anti-Personnel Mines: Nairobi Action Plan 2005–2009. 29 November–3 December 2004. Nairobi Summit on a Mine-Free World (Or First Review Conference of the 1997 Mine Ban Treaty).

Handicap International. 2007. *Circle of Impact: The Fatal Footprint of Cluster Munitions on People and Communities*. Available at: http://en.handicapinternational.be/download/0606_WEB_FINAL_REPORT_HI_BD.pdf [accessed: 9 February 2009].

HRH Prince Ra'ed bin Zaid. Speech presented to the Rehabilitation International Paralympic Committee Symposium, Athens, Greece (undated).

Nairobi Action Plan. *Victim Assistance Questionnaire*.

Nairobi Summit on a Mine-Free World. First Review Conference of the States Parties to the Convention on the Prohibition of the Use, Stockpiling, Production and Transfer of Anti-Personnel Mines and on their Destruction. 29 November-3 December 2004.

Nash, Thomas. 2006. Foreseeable Harm: The Use and Impact of Cluster Munitions in Lebanon. *Landmine Action Report*. October 2006.

Standard Rules on the Equalization of Opportunities for Persons with Disabilities, 20 December 1993, United Nations General Assembly Resolution 48/96.

United Nations Decade of Disabled Persons (1983-1992). United Nations General Assembly (Resolution 26). Available at: http://www.un.org/documents/ga/res/39/a39r026.htm [accessed 9 February 2009].

United Nations World Program of Action Concerning Disabled Persons. United Nations General Assembly (Resolution 51). Available at: http://www.un.org/disabilities/default.asp?id=23 [accessed 9 February 2009].

Vocational Rehabilitation and Employment (Disabled Persons) Convention. 1983. Governing Body of the International Labor (ILO) Office. Available at: http://www.ilo.org/ilolex/cgi-lex/convde.pl?C159 [accessed 9 February 2009].

White, Jerry (2002). E-mail communication to the United States Department of State, 8 August 2002.

Chapter 12
Small Arms, Sovereign States and Human Rights

Suzette R. Grillot[1]

Millions of people around the world live in arms-affected areas and are vulnerable to insecurity, instability, and fear. While it has been difficult to connect the unchecked spread of small arms and light weapons[2] to the security and insecurity of nations, states and regions, the proliferation of such weapons have clearly been connected to the security of humans (Hampson, Hay and Daudelin 2001, 98–124). Millions of human lives are at risk because of the global availability, circulation, and misuse of small arms.[3] From violent conflict in countries like the

1 The author thanks Brooke Hammer for her outstanding research assistance and insightful feedback, and Noha Shawki and Michaelene Cox for their editorial assistance and support for this project.

2 A United Nations 16-member Panel of Governmental Experts on Small Arms identified small arms and light weapons as the following: assault rifles, pistols, sub-machine guns, light machine guns, mortars, portable anti-aircraft guns, grenade launchers, portable anti-tank missile and rocket systems, mortars of less than 100 caliber, anti-personnel landmines and hand grenades. Small and light arms are those weapon systems that can be carried and operated by an individual or a small team of people. See the United Nations Report, A/52/298, at http://www.un.org/Depts/ddar/Firstcom/SGreport52/a52298.html.

The UN definition, however, remains somewhat controversial even though it is often cited in small arms studies. A universally accepted definition of small arms and light weapons remains elusive.

3 The term "misuse" of small arms has been used frequently and has only recently been detailed to mean the following: misuse "by state agents" involves "genocide, intentional killings, excessive force, torture, systematic rape, disappearance, arbitrary arrest, and displacement." Misuse "by individuals or groups when the state fails to exercise due diligence" involves "killings motivated by ethnic, religious or social intolerance, terrorist acts, systematic criminal homicide, systematic domestic violence, systematic post-conflict violence, criminal trafficking in persons." Misuse "by state agents in armed conflict" involves "genocide, grave breaches including executing or torturing non-combatants and prisoners of war, attacking peacekeepers or humanitarian workers, committing atrocities against civilian populations, excessive or indiscriminate force, use of weapons causing superfluous injury or unnecessary suffering, use of child soldiers." Misuse "by armed individuals and groups in armed conflict" involves "genocide, war crimes, crimes against humanity, attaching peacekeepers or humanitarian workers, use of child soldiers, hostage-taking, terrorism." See Frey, B.A. 2004. Small Arms and Light Weapons: The Tools Used

Democratic Republic of Congo, Uganda, Colombia and Afghanistan to armed violence in Chechnya, Mumbai, Rio de Janeiro and Baghdad, small arms and light weapons are readily available and regularly used and misused to perpetrate death and destruction and damage lives and societies.

This chapter provides an overview of the human consequences of small arms and light weapons, as well as the impact of human rights norms on the control of these weapons. Given that the large scale spread and misuse of small arms and light weapons increased at the end of the Cold War as patterns of globalization emerged more fully and constraints on state and non-state behavior shifted rather significantly, the small arms issue has become more salient and in need of attention (Stohl and Grillot 2009). The chapter outlines some of the specifics regarding the supply and demand of small arms and light weapons, and details many of the human consequences of the unchecked spread of these weapons. It also provides discussion of state and non-state actors and how the small arms issue affects state sovereignty. Finally, the chapter offers an overview of how and to what extent human rights norms are relevant in addressing the proliferation and misuse of small arms and light weapons. Ultimately, this is an issue of much concern and many solutions where yet more work must be done.

The Supply and Demand of Small Arms and Light Weapons

Perhaps the most significant feature of contemporary conflict is the almost exclusive presence and use of small arms and light weapons (Lumpe and Gabelnick 1999; Renner 1997; Lock 1997, 117–32). Unlike traditional concepts of war, where nation-states engage in interstate rivalry and violent conflict, the nature of warfare today is characterized largely by intrastate and ethnic conflict. These kinds of conflicts involve not only governments, but rebels, militias, tribes, clans, ethnic groups, religious groups, criminals, traffickers, and even mercenaries (Boutwell and Klare 1999, 1). Today's conflicts involving these kinds of actors have been found to have a close relationship with small arms flows. Some suggest that "internal arms races" emerge in those areas experiencing violent conflict and suffering from weak governments and divided societies. The arms races further increase the desire and necessity to acquire small arms (Klare 1999a, 13–20; Small Arms Survey 2005b, 267–301; Stohl, Schroeder and Smith 2007, 22–37).

Several characteristics distinguish small arms and light weapons from other, larger weapons systems and help us understand why small arms have proliferated as they have. First, small arms are inexpensive and widely available. They are manufactured by many around the world for military, police, and civilian purchase. On the arms market one may find weapons that are newly manufactured, that are flowing out of military stockpiles as excess weapons, or that are being recycled

to Violate Human Rights. *Disarmament Forum* [Online], 3, 40. Available at http://www.unidir.ch/pdf/articles/pdf-art2140.pdf [accessed: 26 January 2009].

from one conflict to another. The fact that many countries allow private ownership of weapons means that private individuals may introduce small arms into the flow of weapons as well (Boutwell and Klare 1999; Stohl, Schroeder, and Smith 2007, 12–17; Small Arms Survey 2002).

Second, small arms are becoming increasingly lethal as new technology is being incorporated so that weapons fire more quickly, more accurately, and more effectively. The lethality of small arms, therefore, means that factions and groups have access to significant firepower that often matches that of military and police forces. Third, small arms and light weapons are relatively easy to use, transport, and hide. These weapons require very little training to use and maintain, are rather durable over long periods of time, and are easy to smuggle. Because they are small, light and long-lasting, they provide numerous opportunities to flow into and out of conflict-ridden and war-prone areas (Boutwell and Klare 1999, 2; Klare 1999b, 4–5).

Situated at either end of the arms flow are the suppliers and the recipients. One cannot, in other words, fully comprehend the small arms and light weapons issue without examining the dynamics of both supply and demand. Many countries and private firms are capable of producing a spectrum of weaponry—from the most simple to the more complex. Many countries also have a surplus of armaments that they seek to liquidate from time to time. Moreover, individual suppliers or brokers, working either legally or illegally, also play a role in increasing the supply of small arms locally and globally (Small Arms Survey 2001, 95–139; Cattaneo 2004, 141–7; Stohl, Schroeder and Smith 2007, 17–21).

The supply, therefore, is plentiful—especially in certain regions of the world. The United States and Russia, for example, lead the world in weapons sales, producing and selling billions of dollars worth of small arms and other conventional weapons systems each year.[4] The former Soviet region as a whole serves as a significant source of small arms as many of these highly militarized countries have sold (and continue to sell) their military assets in pursuit of hard currency. Moreover, powerful criminal elements in this region engage in arms brokering and smuggling (Fatau Musah, 1998; Gonchar and Lock 1995, 116–26). Countries like Bulgaria, Ukraine, Romania, the Czech Republic, Russia, and others have sold huge quantities of small arms and light weapons to various actors throughout the world—including warring groups in Africa, Asia and the Balkans (Smith 1999, 85–90; Grillot 2003a; Grillot 2003b; Grillot 2003c).

Regarding demand, numerous governments, groups, factions, terrorists, and individuals seek to acquire small arms and light weapons. There are numerous areas and regions in the world where such conflict is prevalent and the demand for

4 For arms sales statistics, see SIPRI. *The SIPRI Yearbook*. Stockholm and Oxford: SIPRI and Oxford University Press, and on-line at http://www.sipri.org [accessed: 26 January 2009]. Also, *The Reports of the Federation of American Scientists' Arms Sales Monitoring Project from fas.org*. Available at http://www.fas.org/asmp/profiles/worldfms.html [accessed: 26 January 2009].

arms is significant. Sub-Saharan Africa, for example, is rife with violent conflict and disintegrating societies. Various parts of the Middle East, Africa, Asia, and Latin America also suffer from these realities. Addressing not only the supply of small arms, but the demand for them as well, is key in facing the challenging problems associated with the spread of light weapons (Small Arms Survey 2006, 141–63).

The Human Impact of Small Arms and Light Weapons

There are a number of specific effects on human lives resulting directly or indirectly from the war, conflict, and armed violence that involves the spread and use of small arms and light weapons. From death and destruction to poor health care and lack of educational opportunities, war and conflict significantly impact human lives. The presence and use of small arms before, during and after conflict cause considerable damage and prevent post-conflict rebuilding and healing. Although not an exhaustive list, a number of these effects are discussed below.

Deaths and Injuries

Nearly 750,000 people die each year as a result of armed violence of some sort—typically war or homicide (Geneva Declaration 2008, 1–30).[5] The majority of these deaths, about 500,000, are caused by murder in non-conflict settings (Geneva Declaration 2008, 67–88; Muggah and Berman 2001, 3). Although it is not entirely clear how many of these deaths are the result of small arms and light weapons, estimates suggest that at least on the battlefield, somewhere between 60 per cent and 90 per cent of all casualties are caused by small arms (Small Arms Survey 2005d, 230, 249). Small arms availability in a post-conflict setting also lead to a number of "excess" or "indirect" deaths due to crime, poor access to health care, widespread disease, malnutrition and other factors that are a result of violent conflict (Small Arms Survey 2005d, 251–6). For example, in particular areas of Darfur, Sudan in 2004, the overwhelming majority of conflict related deaths were "indirect" or "excess"—61.5 per cent in Niertiti, Darfur and 89.5 per cent in El Geneina, Darfur (Small Arms Survey 2005d, 253). Without a doubt, armed violence and the use of firearms—particularly small arms and light weapons—are largely responsible for numerous deaths every year. In fact, the Small Arms Survey

5 There are significant difficulties associated with generating specific data on conflict and non-conflict related deaths. For discussions of these difficulties, see the Geneva Declaration. 2008. *Global Burden of Armed Violence* [Online]. Available at: http://www.genevadeclaration.org/pdfs/Global-Burden-of-Armed-Violence.pdf [accessed: 26 January 2009]; and the Small Arms Survey. 2005. *Small Arms Survey 2005: Weapons at War*, 230–249 [Online]. Available at: http://www.smallarmssurvey.org/files/sas/publications/yearb2005.html [accessed: 26 January 2009].

suggests that "no other weapon category is as ubiquitous" when it comes to violent conflict around the world (Small Arms Survey 2005d, 248).

Forced Displacement

Violent conflict and arms infestations have regularly led to the displacement of millions of people. Statistics vary, but the United Nations High Commission on Refugees (UNHCR) reports that in 2007 there were approximately 16 million refugees worldwide, with an additional 26 million conflict-generated internally displaced peoples (IDPs) and 25 million non-conflict-induced IDPs (UNHCR 2007, 2). Approximately half of those who are displaced by armed conflict are children (Machel 2000), and about 45 per cent of displaced people are in Asia (Baron, Buus Jenson and de Jong 2003, 243–70). Ultimately, tens of millions of people over the past 20 years, since the end of the Cold War, have been forced from their homes due to armed violence and conflict (Small Arms Survey 2002, 167). Displacement often leads to additional side-effects including illness, malnutrition, crime, human rights violations, and refugee camps being used to traffic arms (Small Arms Survey 2002, 160, 168; Muggah and Berman 2001, 22; Baron, Buus Jenson, and de Jong 2003, 246–8).

Child Soldiers

Because small arms and light weapons are small and light, one of the significant effects they have had on human security is the increased use of children as soldiers. Children as young as nine or ten are capable of carrying and operating small arms that weigh relatively little (Muggah and Berman 2001, 29). Children that have been displaced or orphaned during conflict are particularly at risk of being recruited, either voluntarily or forcefully, into armed forces and gangs. In fact, approximately 300,000 children serve in an army or militia of some sort and regularly engage in violence—particularly in countries such as Afghanistan, Angola, Chad, Colombia, Democratic Republic of Congo, Liberia, Myanmar, Sierra Leone, Somalia, Sri Lanka Sudan, Uganda and Yemen (Machel 2000, 9–12; Coalition to Stop the Use of Child Soldiers 2008). In other cases, children use violence to earn money. In Colombia and Kenya, for example, poor children in need of cash are paid $100 to kill a policeman (Muggah and Berman 2001, 29). Moreover, children are further victimized by serving as slaves to their adult commanders—and as direct victims of armed violence as casualties of war (Muggah and Berman 2001, 15; Child Soldiers Global Report 2008).

Diminished Peacekeeping and Interference with Humanitarian Assistance

In arms affected, post-conflict areas where peacekeeping operations are working to prevent a return to violence, peace-keepers often come under attack and are regularly challenged by the presence and use of residual weaponry—

particularly small arms and light weapons. Since the beginning of United Nations peacekeeping operations in 1948, more than 2500 peace-keepers have been killed while performing their duties in more than 60 peacekeeping missions.[6] Moreover, weapons availability and use have significantly affected humanitarian workers in post-conflict environments. Between July 2003 and July 2004 alone, 100 humanitarian workers were killed while assisting the populations of war torn societies (Muggah and Buchanan 2005a). In a survey of 2,000 humanitarian aid personnel from 17 different international organizations working in 96 countries, more than 20 per cent of the respondents reported that armed threats have negatively affected about 25 per cent of their aid work. As a result, relief agencies are regularly employing armed guards in an effort to conduct relief missions. More than 30 per cent of the survey respondents suggested that they use guards in order to deliver humanitarian aid (Muggah and Buchanan 2005b). The most significant risks humanitarian workers face include criminal violence, such as armed robbery and assault, and even rape at gunpoint (Muggah and Buchanan 2005a).

Negative Social and Cultural Effects

Although there is some debate about the indirect effects of guns in society, many suggest that weapons availability facilitates armed criminal activity (Small Arms Survey 2003b, 136). In many countries, the availability of small arms has contributed to an increase in violence and the development of criminal gangs. A household survey in Cambodia, for example, suggested that 60 per cent of the residents of Phnom Penh have been victimized by violent crime at the hands of armed individuals and groups (Small Arms Survey 2003b, 138). From region to region and country to country, guns are used by criminals and corrupt officials alike to engage in illicit activities. Moreover, criminal activity and the use of small arms, particularly by officials and security forces, have contributed to a "militarized national psyche and culture of violence" in many societies (Ginifer and Ismail 2005, 10). Criminal elements within society are leaving the impression, by which others then live, that gun violence is an acceptable and legitimate, or at least necessary, means for resolving disputes, providing for security, and enhancing personal gain and well-being. Rather than order and force being the responsibility of state and government, they "flow from the barrel of a gun," which develops a culture of gun possession and use in less stable societies — further fueling armed violence, conflict, death and destruction (Ginifer and Ismail 2005, 10; Small Arms Survey 2005a, 205–27).

---

6 See the United Nations peacekeeping fatalities statistics at http://www.un.org/Depts/dpko/fatalities/StatsByYear%201.pdf. Also see the United Nations Peacekeeping background note at http://www.un.org/Depts/dpko/dpko/bnote.htm for fatalities related to each peacekeeping operation.

Human Rights Abuses

One of the more significant effects excess and widespread availability and misuse of small arms and light weapons has on human lives is the brutal treatment and abuse humans may suffer at the hands of authorities, officials and security forces (Frey 2004). Human rights organizations such as Amnesty International and Human Rights Watch have reported for years how and to what extent the unchecked spread and misuse of weapons lead to human rights abuses in countries around the world. A 2004 Amnesty International report on Liberia, for example, details how "government forces and armed opposition groups were responsible for widespread abuses against civilians including killings, torture, rape and other forms of sexual violence" (Amnesty International 2006, 23). Human rights abuses using small arms have also been recorded in Sudan, Nepal, Iraq and Colombia, just to name a few (Amnesty International 2006, 11–14, 18; Amnesty International 2007). Moreover, specific categories of weapons have been targeted as particularly inhumane in their use in combat. Cluster munitions and landmines have most recently been categorized as inhumane weapons that indiscriminately kill and maim thousands of people every year.[7]

Poor Economic Growth and Investment

War-torn and unstable societies struggle to facilitate economic growth and enhance economic well-being—particularly in areas where small arms remain widely available. Weapons affect economic growth in many ways. First, resources that could and should be used to aid economic growth are often diverted away from economic activities toward military spending and weapons purchases (Control Arms Campaign 2004). Second, damaged infrastructure, such as roads and bridges, makes trade and commerce more costly and less feasible (Small Arms Survey 2003b, 143). Third, armed gangs and bandits steal products and decrease the likelihood of trade transactions (Small Arms Survey 2003b). All of these factors have an ultimate impact on prices, consumption and economic livelihood. External actors are far less likely to direct investment to insecure and unstable areas, and tourists are not likely to travel to and spend their financial resources in localities plagued by excess weapons availability and misuse. A World Bank survey of corporations, for example, showed that violence and insecurity are the greatest risks investors consider when determining where to target their funds (Small Arms Survey 2003b, 144). Ultimately, economic development is connected to stability and security. Where small arms are widely available and lead to instability and insecurity, poor economic growth and investment are likely to follow.

7 For specifics on inhumane weapons, see the Human Rights Watch documents at http://www.hrw.org/en/category/topic/arms/inhumane-weapons.

Inadequate Health Care

In addition to the economic consequences of arms availability and misuse, and the resulting impact on human security, social services such as health care are diminished during times of conflict and in areas where the post-conflict environment is wrought with volatility and uncertainty. Large numbers of gunshot wound injuries overburden local hospitals and weaken their ability to effectively treat not only firearm victims, but other ill and injured patients as well (Small Arms Survey 2003b, 140–41). Gun violence in Brazil, for example, is considered to be one of the most critical health issues in the country with health facilities incapable of keeping up with the numbers of firearm injuries they see (Galeria and Phebo 2006). In areas of active armed conflict the availability of health services decrease in general as hospitals and clinics must close or limit their treatment during times of violence. Moreover, government resources that may typically be used to provide health care might be diverted to other priorities. Some argue, therefore, that the small arms problem is a public health problem and that health care considerations should be included in discussions of small arms issues (Cukier 2002; Cukier and Sidel 2006).

Loss of Educational and Training Opportunities

Similarly, other social services, such as education, also suffer in areas that are arms-affected. Like hospitals, schools of all kinds—primary, secondary and vocational training schools—often close during times of violent conflict, preventing children and adults from learning and preparing themselves for a better future (Small Arms Survey 2003b, 140–41). Schools re-open and enrollments do increase in post-conflict periods, but some students may still be scared to attend school and others may be unable to attend due to changed circumstances. Schools may also suffer from a lack of human and financial resources and the ability to provide a quality education. Moreover, schools themselves may become targets of violence with students and teachers being attacked or recruited into military service against their will (Small Arms Survey 2003b; Muggah and Bachelor 2002). Even when children can attend school in arms-affected areas, therefore, they are often fearful and cannot perform well in their school work. Examples of these kinds abound in countries like the Philippines, Cambodia, Kenya, Ethiopia, Colombia, Nicaragua, Sudan and Uganda, among others. The excess availability and misuse of weapons in these and other countries have experienced significant problems with delivering educational opportunities to their populations—and their ability to grow, develop and stabilize is ultimately affected (Small Arms Survey 2003b).

Small Arms and Human Security

Clearly, the widespread and unchecked spread and availability of small arms and light weapons—particularly in areas that are already unstable and insecure—have a significant impact on human security. Both directly, in terms of death, injury, abuse and trauma, and indirectly, in terms of social and economic development and well-being, the human security implications of the small arms issue are substantial. Sovereign states have a significant role to play regarding the human consequences of small arms and light weapons, but non-state actors are also important players. The contributions of both sate and non-state actors concerning the spread and control of small arms and light weapons must, therefore, be a focus of any study highlighting the connections between small arms and human rights.

States as the Primary Actors in the Small Arms Arena

The primary producers and suppliers of small arms and light weapons around the world are states. According to most recent arms trade data, more than 51 countries produce small arms and light weapons, approximately 117 countries import weapons, and around 46 countries export arms (Small Arms Survey 2008, 7; SIPRI 2008). The global value of the international arms trade in 2007 was more than $24 billion, of which approximately $4 billion were small arms and light weapons.[8] Complicating the matter, however, is the lack of available and accurate data on the small arms trade. Most registries and databases focus exclusively on large conventional weaponry like tanks, aircraft and artillery.[9] For various reasons related to state interests, among other things, governments rarely produce reports detailing their small arms transactions, making it difficult to understand the small arms trade. Moreover, grey and black market transfers further shroud the subject in secrecy, requiring us to study the subject as best as we can. What we do know, however, is that states are the primary producers, importers and exporters of small arms and light weapons, and have a significant role to play in solving the problems associated with small arms availability, circulation and misuse.

Accordingly, several political agreements among states at both the regional and international levels have emerged to address the small arms issue (see Table 12.1). Of all of these agreements, only one is legally binding for states—the United Nations Firearms Protocol of 2005. This agreement, however, reflects a minimum standard regarding arms transfer procedures, weapons marking, and weapons brokering. The most significant international activity on small arms has focused on the Program of Action to Prevent, Combat and Eradicate the Illicit Trade in Small Arms and Light Weapons in All its Aspects (PoA). This is a politically, not legally,

---

8 See SIPRI. 2008. SIPRI arms trade database. [Online]. Available at: http://armstrade.sipri.org/arms_trade/values.php [accessed: 25 January 2009] for the value of arms imports and exports. Also see Stohl, R. and Grillot, S. 2009. *The International Arms Trade*. London: Polity Press, forthcoming.

9 See the United Nations Register of Conventional Arms at http://disarmament.un.org/cab/register.html and the SIPRI. 2008. SIPRI arms trade database. [Online]. Available at: http://armstrade.sipri.org/arms_trade/values.php [accessed: 25 January 2009].

Table 12.1 Regional and International Small Arms Agreement among States

Date	Title of Agreement	Region/Location
1997	Inter-American Convention Against the Illicit Manufacturing of and Trafficking in Firearms, Ammunition, Explosives, and other Related Materials(OAS Convention 1997)	Organization of American States
1998	EU Code of Conduct (EU Code of Conduct)	European Union
1998	Moratorium on Importation, Exportation and Manufacture of Light Weapons in West Africa (ECOWAS 1998)	Economic Community of West African States
2000	Nairobi Declaration on the Problem of the Proliferation of Illicit Small Arms and Light Weapons in the Great Lakes Region and in the Horn of Africa (Nairobi Declaration 2001)	Great Lakes Region and Horn of Africa
2000	Bamako Declaration on an African Common Position on the Illicit Proliferation, Circulation and Trafficking of Small Arms and Light Weapons (Bamako Declaration 2000)	Organization of African Unity
2001	Protocol on the Control of Firearms, Ammunition and other Related Materials in the Southern African Development Community Region (SADC Protocol)	Southern African Development Community
2001	Program of Action to Prevent, Combat and Eradicate the Illicit Trade in Small Arms and Light Weapons in All its Aspects(United Nations 2002)	United Nations
2002	Document on Small Arms and Light Weapons (OSCE 2002)	Organization for Security Cooperation in Europe
2005	Protocol Against the Illicit Manufacturing of and Trafficking in Firearms, their Parts and Components and Ammunition, Supplementing the United Nations Convention Against Transnational Organized Crime(United Nations 2005)	United Nations
2006	Resolution to develop a comprehensive Arms Trade Treaty (United Nations 2006)	United Nations

binding document that focuses strictly on illicit trafficking of arms and reflects a "lowest common denominator" given the requirement for consensus decision-making in the United Nations (Garcia 2006, 58). At PoA biennial meetings in 2003, 2005 and 2008, and at the review conference in 2006, states reiterated their concerns about small arms and many argued for more concrete measures to combat the problem, but solid agreements that moved beyond voluntary to mandatory remained elusive.

In October 2006, in an effort to push the small arms control issue forward, the United Nations General Assembly considered a resolution authorizing the UN to develop a comprehensive Arms Trade Treaty (ATT) by 2008 (United Nations 2006). A Group of Government Experts (GGE) was tasked to begin work on an ATT and met three times in 2008 before concluding that more work is required before states can consider a treaty on this issue. The process will continue within the United Nations to determine whether there should be an ATT and what it should include, but significant difficulties concerning what an ATT should cover, how it should be structured, and whether it can be enforced remain.[10]

Given their role in producing, importing and using small arms, as well as developing instruments to control them, states are significant players. They do not, however, have a solo role in the area as non-state actors also contribute to the supply, demand and control of small arms, challenging state authority in an area where sovereign states once had a complete monopoly—on matters of military, national and human security.

Challenges for State Sovereignty

Moisés Naím argued in 2003 that arms trafficking is one of "the five wars of globalization."[11] Because trafficking in commodities of all kinds, including drugs, arms and people, transcends borders and involves sophisticated international networks, states are increasingly powerless to combat the problem. Unlike governments and their agents, illicit traffickers operate largely free from geographical and, therefore, legal constraints. This fact makes it more challenging for governments to investigate, arrest and prosecute these criminals given state agents must operate within a system characterized by state sovereignty, which binds them to territorial jurisdiction. Traffickers are not similarly constrained by jurisdictional boundaries, giving them the advantage in these new "wars of globalization" (Naim 2003, 35). Moreover, government operations to combat criminal trafficking networks are bureaucratic and centralized in nature, compared to the decentralized groups of the criminal underworld (Naim 2003). Ultimately, principles of sovereignty and differences in organizational structure and operations drastically affect the ability of governments to fight these "wars" and win.

Regarding the small arms issue, non-state actors play a significant role in both benign and nefarious ways. Arms dealers, armed insurgents, terrorists and organized criminals challenge state authority and sovereignty as they operate beyond national boundaries and often without impunity. Many of these actors are directly contesting the sovereignty and authority of state actors, and some are simply negatively affecting state effectiveness by operating on the margins of the law. More benign players in the small arms area are the various nongovernmental and transnational organizations that advocate for or against small arms control measures. These organizations seek to pressure governments to enact certain policies and prescriptions regarding small arms and light weapons transfers,

10 Author interview with a member of the GGE, August 2008.

11 The other "wars of globalization" concern the illegal trade in drugs, intellectual property, people and money. See Naím, M. 2003. The Five Wars of Globalization. *Foreign Policy* [Online], 134, 28–37. Available at: http://www.foreignpolicy.com/Ning/archive/archive/134/5wars.qxd.pdf [accessed: 26 January 2009].

acquisitions and use. Both types of non-state actors are discussed in more detail below, but ultimately, these groups make it clear that state actors are not the sole proprietors of the small arms issue as they must contend with the activities and interests of these non-state actors.

Non-state Actors and the Supply and Demand of Small Arms

In terms of the supply of small arms, brokers play an important role in arranging and profiting from weapons transfers.[12] Although not all arms dealers engage in illegal transactions, as some may be licensed by their governments to serve as intermediaries, many arms brokers operate on the margins of or outside the law as they transfer or deliver weapons between parties that may not be able to acquire arms through legal channels. Illicit arms deals facilitated by what some call "gun-runners" or "merchants of death" have caused much concern in recent years, resulting in international attempts to reduce illegal arms brokering and the excessive availability and circulation of small arms, particularly in unstable and insecure areas that are prime for violent conflict (Lumpe 2007).

Non-state actors that are often the recipients of illegally transferred weapons include insurgents, terrorists and organized criminals. Although these groups and individuals are typically on the demand side of the small arms issue, they may also engage in what is called craft production—producing rudimentary weapons in homes and shops using basic designs and spare parts of other weapons (Small Arms Survey 2003a, 26–8). The most significant sources of insurgent, terrorist and criminal weapons, however, are government or military stockpiles from which these groups steal and buy weapons, as well as the "ant trade," a small but constant stream of weapons that flow from various directions and sources (Small Arms Survey 2005c, 159).Their acquisition of weapons, therefore, flouts state law (although some governments do support insurgent and terrorist groups), as does their use of violence to achieve their goals and challenge state authority (Small Arms Survey 2005c, 159–73; Schroeder 2004).

Nongovernmental Organizations and the Battle over Small Arms Control

Other non-state, or nongovernmental, actors are involved in the small arms issue not as participants in the transfer or use of weapons, but as policy advocates regarding small arms control or availability. Shortly after the Cold War ended, activists, scholars, and policymakers began to highlight the serious problems associated with the availability, circulation, and misuse of small arms and light

---

12 For definitions of gun broker and brokering, see the United Nations. 2001. *Model Convention on the Registration of Arms Brokers and the Suppression of Unlicensed Arms Brokering* from NISAT.org [Online], 3. Available at http://www.nisat.org/Brokering/Model%20Convention%20on%20the%20Registration%20of%20Arms%20Brokers.pdf [accessed: 26 January 2009].

weapons. Throughout the early 1990s, a number of researchers published various accounts of small arms problems, ranging from arms transfers to non-state actors and the role of arms brokers to unrestrained weapons availability (Garcia 2006, 29–61; Stohl, Schroeder, and Smith 2007, 38–47). This growing "epistemic community" served to generate knowledge and heighten awareness about the dire consequences of the unchecked spread of small arms and light weapons (Haas 1992, 1–35; Garcia 2006, 35–43). In response, the United Nations took up the small arms issue with a number of resolutions, expert reports, and calls for action (United Nations 1995).

By the late 1990s, a coalition of nongovernmental organizations (NGOs) organized a transnational network to raise awareness about and lobby for strong, global gun control measures. As a result, the International Action Network on Small Arms (IANSA) was launched in 1999. As a network of more than 700 NGOs situated in over 100 countries, IANSA's purpose is to lead global efforts to enhance controls on and decrease the demand for small arms and light weapons around the world.[13]

Not to be left out of the debate, pro-gun, anti-control organizations also became involved in the global gun issue with the US National Rifle Association (NRA) registering as an NGO at the United Nations in 1996. In 1997, the NRA assisted in the establishment of the World Forum on the Future of Sport Shooting Activities (WFSA), headquartered in Brussels, Belgium. As a coalition of more than two dozen pro-gun groups and arms manufacturers, the WFSA has taken the lead at the United Nations and other international arenas for the pro-gun movement (Morton 2006; World Forum on the Future of Sport Shooting Activities).

These NGOs function to challenge, pressure and persuade state officials to develop and implement policies and procedures that conform to their specific interests regarding small arms. IANSA, the primary pro-arms-control organization, and the NRA/WFSA, the primary anti-arms-control organization, compete with each other for the attention of policy-makers, as well as work to involve ordinary citizens in the arms control debate (Grillot, Stapley and Hanna 2006; Grillot 2008).

The Impact of Human Rights Norms

One of the earliest suggestions analysts and advocates offered regarding the small arms issue was to develop new international norms and standards of behavior that outline the parameters of acceptable small arms activities (Latham 1999; Klare 1995; Renner 1998, 131–48; Renner 1997; Lumpe 1999, 151–64). Their argument

13 For details on IANSA, see the group's website at http://www.iansa.org. For specifics on the group's purpose, see IANSA. 1999–2004. *IANSA Founding Document* from IANSA.org [Online]. Available at http://www.iansa.org/about/m1.htm [accessed: 26 January 2009].

was that normative prescriptions and proscriptions must underlie all measures to address small arms problems. However, despite the numerous actions taken by states and NGOs in an effort to combat small arms problems, corresponding norms are relatively weak or non-existent. Nearly all small arms agreements are based on political promises at best, suggesting only voluntary action. Basically, there have been many national, regional, and international small arms control conferences and activities over the past decade with rather weak and voluntary normative agreements as a result (Grillot 2008).

Nevertheless, international norms—particularly human rights norms—do help us understand why states continue to discuss and attempt to tackle various aspects of the small arms issue, particularly illicit arms brokering, marking and tracing of weapons, and the collection and destruction of surplus weaponry (Garcia 2006). In fact, appealing to human rights norms is one strategy that arms control groups employ. IANSA's statement of purpose focuses on a human's right to a secure and safe environment, and the group's overall agenda and program are greatly influenced by the view that small arms inflict "violent death, injury, and psychological trauma on hundreds of thousands of people each year" (IANSA 1999–2004, 2). IANSA's focus on the conflict, violence, fear, and instability that plague civilians all around the world indicates that the organization's focus is centered on human rights. Their ability to pinpoint blame for such violence, destruction, and loss of life is complicated, however, by the secrecy shrouding weapons transactions, sales, and movements and the difficulty in determining with any certainty from where firearms have come and who specifically is responsible. Moreover, a debate exists regarding the direct links between arms transfers and conflict. Most states, in fact, suggest that small arms do not cause violence and conflict, but that they escalate and prolong violence and conflict (Craft 1999). Pro-gun groups capitalize on this questionable causality by re-iterating their well known mantra that "guns don't kill people, people kill people."

Furthermore, there remains another difficulty in that human rights norms encourage state action in one direction, while other types of norms in the international system promote behavior in another direction. There is, therefore, a collision of sorts between human rights norms and norms such as sovereignty, national defense and human liberty (Grillot 2008). Because small arms and light weapons are indeed considered "legitimate" weapons that serve a variety of purposes from policing and national defense to personal protection and sport shooting, they fall within a category of acceptable weaponry and are, therefore, difficult to control and nearly impossible to ban. Governments use these weapons to protect their homeland and serve their legitimate interests. It is the clear, therefore, that gun control norms based on human rights must be created in a very competitive normative environment where existing ideas about the role of weapons in politics and societies conflict with stricter arms controls. Norms of sovereignty, national defense and human liberty may be perceived as inconsistent with restrictions on state and non-state action, such as the ability to acquire armaments for the purpose of defense, to fight tyrannical authorities, and to protect territory. The importance of the norms of sovereignty and national defense, for example, are affirmed in the Charter of the United Nations and reaffirmed in several of the small arms instruments mentioned above, including the 2001 *Program of Action* (United Nations 1948; Program of Action 2002). Moreover, many states emphasized such norms in their small arms statements at the UN meetings in 2001 and 2006.[14] And anti-gun-control groups such as the NRA argue vehemently that individuals possess the civil liberty to own and use weapons for personal protection and sporting activities. It is not clear, therefore, which norms—human rights, sovereignty, self-defense or individual liberty—take precedence and when.[15] Despite the recognition of the small arms problem, any attempt to develop arms control based on human rights norms must begin with respect for the pre-existing norms of sovereignty, national defense and human liberty—norms that reflect the legitimacy and purpose of armaments in relations among nations and peoples. The insertion of new arms control norms must contend with this existing framework.

We do know, however, that states often act to limit the impact of weapons on human lives. The various agreements discussed above indicate state concerns about the negative consequences of weapons availability and misuse. Other evidence, such as arms embargoes, also indicate that norms of humanitarian intervention, for example, matter to state actors as they attempt to minimize and prevent the loss and destruction of human life (Sandholtz 2002, 201–25). But, arms embargos are regularly broken, intervention is often ignored, and agreements are repeatedly not honored when it comes to violent conflict in certain parts of the world (Woodrow Wilson Center for International Scholars 2008). Despite this, it does seem that international human rights norms help us understand why states would actually engage in the multitude of meetings, conferences, and agreements on small arms issues without producing significant results. This type of behavior and conflict between various norms reportedly occurs in the environmental area as well. Radoslav Dimitrov shows, for example, that states have long engaged

---

14 See, in particular, the 2001 statements of China, Egypt, Germany, Indonesia, Russia and the United States at http://disarmament.un.org/cab/smallarms/statements.htm; and the 2006 statements of Egypt, Pakistan, Vietnam, and United States at http://www.un.org/events/smallarms2006/mem-states.html.

15 The International Campaign to Ban Landmines (ICBL) and the Resulting Ottawa Treaty are outstanding examples of where and when human rights concerns actually trump other types of sovereignty and national defense priorities. For more on the ICBL and the Landmine Ban, see Price, R. 1999. Reversing the Gun Sights: Transnational Civil Society Targets Land Mines. *International Organization* [Online], 52 (3), 613–644. Available at: http://www.jstor.org.ezproxy1.lib.ou.edu/sici?sici=00208183%281998%2952%3A3%3C613%3ARTGSTCSTLM%3E2.0.CO%3B2-M&origin=serialsolutions&cookieSet=1 [accessed: 26 January 2009]; Rutherford, K., Brem, S. and Matthew, R.A. eds. 2003. *Reframing the Agenda: The Impact of NGO and Middle Power Cooperation in International Security Policy*. London: Greenwood Press; and Rutherford, K. 2006. *Landmines and Human Security: The International Movement to Ban Landmines*. Albany, NY: SUNY Press.

in much rhetoric and developed empty agreements focused on the protection of forests around the world simply because global environmental norms require states to appear as if they are doing something about a perceived environmental problem (Dimitrov 2005). Perhaps this same effect is at work regarding the impact of human rights norms on small arms issues, indicating that international norms do, in fact, have an impact on what states do, even if what they do is merely pay lip-service to the issue.

Conclusion

Despite the difficulties, there is hope that the small arms issue will continue to grow in prominence in future years as organizations such as IANSA continue to raise awareness and heighten our attention to small arms problems, particularly focusing on the human rights implications. It is precisely because of human rights norms that there has been more attention, action and commitment to the small arms problem, and it is likely to be because of human rights norms that additional norms and standards of behavior regarding the spread and misuse of small arms will emerge. But, the future is not without challenges as conflicting norms of sovereignty, self-defense, national security and human liberty will be forever present in the international system. What must occur is a shift in priorities regarding when norms of sovereignty, national defense and human liberty supersede human rights norms and the notion that human beings have a right to live without fear of death or injury from small arms and light weapons. Otherwise, millions of people around the world will continue to suffer the consequences of the supply and demand of small arms.

References

Amnesty International 2006. *Dead on Time: Arms Transportation, Brokering and the Threat to Human Rights from Amnesty International*. [Online]. Available at: http://www.amnesty.org/en/library/info/ACT30/008/2006 [accessed: 25 January 2009].

Amnesty International 2007. *Sudan: Arms Continuing to Fuel Serious Human Rights Violations in Darfur from Amnesty International*. [Online]. Available at: http://www.amnesty.org/en/library/info/AFR54/019/2007 [accessed: 25 January 2009].

Bamako Declaration on an African Common Position on the Illicit Proliferation, Circulation and Trafficking of Small Arms and Light Weapons 2005. [Online]. Available at: http://www.globalpolicy.org/security/smallarms/regional/bamako.htm [accessed: 25 January 2009].

Baron, N., Buus Jenson, S. and de Jong, J. T. V. M. 2003. Refugees and Internally Displaced People, in *Trauma Interventions in War and Peace: Prevention,*

Practice, and Policy, edited by B. L. Green, M. J. Friedman, J. T.V.M. de Jong, S. D. Soloman, T. M. Keane, J. A. Fairbank, B. Donelan, E. Frey-Wouters and Y. Danieli. New York: Springer, 243–270.

Boutwell, J. and Klare, M.T. 1999a. Introduction, in *Light Weapons and Civil Conflict*, edited by J. Boutwell and M. T. Klare. Lanham: Rowman and Littlefield, 1–8.

Cattaneo, S. 2004. Targeting the Middlemen: Controlling Brokering Activities. *Small Arms Survey 2004: Rights at Risk*. [Online]. Oxford: Oxford University Press, 141–71. Available at: http://www.smallarmssurvey.org/files/sas/publications/year_b_pdf/2004/2004SASCh5_full_fr.pdf [accessed: 20 January 2009].

Coalition to Stop the Use of Child Soldiers 2008. *Child Soldiers Global Report 2008*, Coalition to Stop the Use of Child Soldiers. [Online]. Available at: http://www.childsoldiersglobalreport.org/overview-and-benchmarks [accessed: 25 January 2009].

Control Arms Campaign 2004. *Guns or Growth: Assessing the Impact of Arms Sales on Sustainable Development from iansa.org*. [Online]. Available: at: http://www.iansa.org/un/documents/guns-or-growth-en.pdf [accessed: 27 January 2009].

Craft, C. 1999. *Weapons for Peace, Weapons for War: The Effect of Arms Transfers on War Outbreak, Involvement, and Outcomes*. New York: Routledge.

Cukier, W. 2002. Small Arms and Light Weapons: A Public Health Approach. *Brown Journal of World Affairs*. [Online]. 9(1), 261–80. Available at: http://www.ryerson.ca/SAFER-Net/issues/BroJJE03.pdf [accessed: 25 January 2009].

Cukier, W. and Sidel, V. W. 2006. *The Global Gun Epidemic: From Saturday Night Specials to AK-47s*. Westport: Praeger.

Dimitrov, R. S. 2005. Hostage to Norms: States, Institutions and Global Forest Politics. *Global Environmental Politics* 5(4), 1–24. [Online November]. Available at: http://muse.jhu.edu/journals/global_environmental_politics/v005/5.4dimitrov.pdf [accessed: 26 January 2009].

Economic Community of West Africa (ECOWAS) 1998. *Moratorium on the Importation, Exportation and Manufacture of Light Weapons in ECOWAS Member States*. [Online]. Available at: http://www.fas.org/nuke/control/pcased/text/ecowas.htm [accessed: 25 January 2009].

EU Code of Conduct on Arms Exports [Online]. Available at: http://www.fas.org/asmp/campaigns/code/eucodetext.htm [accessed: 25 January 2009].

Farah, D. and Braun, S. 2007. *Merchant of Death: Money, Guns, Planes, and the Man Who Makes War Possible*. Hoboken: John Wiley & Sons, Inc.

Fatau Musah, A. and Castle, R. 1998. *Eastern Europe's Arsenal on the Loose: Managing Light Weapons Flows in Conflict Zones*. BASIC Papers, Occasional Papers on International Security Issues [Online], No. ISSN 1353-0402. Available at: http://www.iansa.org/documents/development/eeurope_arsenal.htm [accessed: 21 January 2009].

Frey, B. A. 2004. Small Arms and Light Weapons: The Tools Used to Violate Human Rights, *Disarmament Forum*. [Online]. (3), 37–46. Available at: http://www.unidir.ch/pdf/articles/pdf-art2140.pdf [accessed: 25 January 2009].

Galeria, J., and Phebo, L. 2006. Using Public Health Information to Inform, Build Support and Implement Policies for Gun Violence Prevention: A Case Study from the Gun Ban Referendum. *African Security Review*. [Online]. 15(2), 16–37. Available at: http://www.issafrica.org/dynamic/administration/file_manager/file_links/15_2F2.PDF?link_id=3&slink_id=3331&link_type=12&slink_type=23&tmpl_id=3 [accessed: 25 January 2009].

Garcia, D. 2006. *Small Arms and Security: New Emerging International Norms*. London: Routledge.

Geneva Declaration 2008. *Global Burden of Armed Violence* [Online]. Available at: http://www.genevadeclaration.org/pdfs/Global-Burden-of-Armed-Violence.pdf [accessed: 26 January 2009].

Ginifer, J. and Ismail, O. 2005. *Armed Violence and Poverty in Nigeria*. Available at: http://www.smallarmssurvey.org/files/portal/spotlight/country/afr_pdf/africa-nigeria-2005.pdf [accessed: 26 January 2009].

Gonchar, K. and Lock, P. 1995. Small Arms and Light Weapons: Russia and the Former Soviet Union, in *Lethal Commerce: The Global Trade in Small Arms and Light Weapons*, edited by J. Boutwell, M. T. Klare, and L. W. Reed. Cambridge: American Academy of Arts and Sciences, 116–26.

Grillot, S. R. 2003a. Light Weapons, Long Reach: Bulgaria's Role in the Spread and Control of Small Arms. *Journal of Southern Europe and the Balkans* 5(3), 279–97.

Grillot, S. R. 2003b. *Small Arms Control in the Black Sea Region: A Regional Assessment of Small Arms Control Initiatives*. Eurasia Series No. 2 [Online]. Available at: http://www.smallarmssurvey.org/files/portal/spotlight/country/eu_pdf/europe-bul-mol-rom-tur-ukr-2003.pdf [accessed: 21 January 2009].

Grillot, S. R. 2003c. *Small Arms Control in Central and Eastern Europe: A Regional Assessment of Small Arms Control Initiatives*. London: International Alert [Online]. Available at: http://www.international-alert.org/pdf/CEE_June.pdf [accessed: 26 January 2009].

Grillot, S. R. 2008. *Global Gun Control: Examining the Consequences of Competing International Norms*. Unpublished manuscript.

Grillot, S. R., Stapley, C. S., and Hanna, M. E. 2006. Assessing the Small Arms Movement: The Trials and Tribulations of a Transnational Network. *Contemporary Security Policy*. [Online]. 27(1), 60–84. Available at: http://www.informaworld.com/smpp/content~content=a745976219~db=all [accessed: 26 January 2009].

Haas, P. 1992. Introduction: Epistemic Communities and International Policy Coordination. *International Organization*. [Online]. 46(1), 1–35. Available at: http://www.jstor.org/stable/2706951[accessed: 25 January 2009].

Hampson, F. O., Hay, J. B. and Daudelin, J. 2001. *Madness in the Multitude: Human Security and World Disorder*. Oxford: Oxford University Press.

IANSA 1999–2004. *IANSA Founding Document* [Online]. Available at: http://www.iansa.org/about/m1.htm [accessed: 26 January 2009].

Klare, M. T. 1995. Stemming the Lethal Trade in Small Arms and Light Weapons. *Issues in Science and Technology*. [Online]. 52–8. Available at: http://www.highbeam.com/doc/1G1-17780960.html [accessed: 26 January 2009].

Klare, M. T. 1999a. The International Trade in Light Weapons: What Have We Learned? in *Light Weapons and Civil Conflict*, editd by J. Boutwell and M. T. Klare. Lanham: Rowman & Littlefield, 13–20.

Klare, M. T. 1999b. An Overview of the Global Trade in Small Arms and Light Weapons, in *Small Arms Control: Old Weapons, New Issues*, edited by L. Lumpe and T. Gabelnick. New York: UNIDIR and Ashgate, 4–5.

Latham, A. 1999. Light Weapons and Human Security—A Conceptual Overview, in *Small Arms Control: Old Weapons, New Issues*, edited by L. Lumpe and T. Gabelnick. New York: UNIDIR and Ashgate, 11–35.

Lock, P. 1997. Armed Conflicts and Small Arms Proliferation. *Policy Sciences*. [Online]. 30(3), 117–32. Available at: http://www.springerlink.com.ezproxy1.lib.ou.edu/content/qv3p6h03n1351014/fulltext.pdf [accessed: 21 January 2009].

Lumpe, L. 1999. Curbing the Proliferation of Small Arms and Light Weapons. *Security Dialogue*. [Online]. 30(2), 151–64. Available at: http://sdi.sagepub.com.ezproxy1.lib.ou.edu/cgi/reprint/30/2/151 [accessed: 26 January 2009].

Lumpe, L. (ed.) 2007. *Running Guns: The Global Black Market in Small Arms*. London and New York: Zed Books.

Lumpe, L. and Gabelnick, T. (eds) (1999). *Small Arms Control: Old Weapons, New Issues*. New York: UNIDIR and Ashgate.

Machel, G. 2000. *The Impact of Armed Conflict on Children: A Critical Review of Progress Made and Obstacles Encountered in Increasing Protection of War-Affected Children.* Paper to the International Conference on War-Affected Children, Winnipeg, Canada, 16–17 September 2000), Available at: http://www.strategicnetwork.org/pdf/kb5736.pdf [accessed: 21 January 2009].

Morton, D. 2006. Gunning for the World. *Foreign Policy*. [Online]. 1–5. Available at: http://www.foreignpolicy.com [accessed at: 26 January 2009].

Muggah, R., and Bachelor, P. 2002. *Development Held Hostage: Assessing the Effects of Small Arms on Human Development*. Available at: http://www.smallarmssurvey.org/files/sas/publications/co_publi_pdf/2002/2002-hum_hostage.pdf [accessed: January 26, 2009].

Muggah, R. and Berman, E. 2001. Humanitarianism Under Threat: The Humanitarian Impacts of Small Arms and Light Weapons. *Small Arms Survey/Centre for Humanitarian Dialogue* 3. Available at: http://www.smallarmsnet.org/pubs/sassr1.pdf [accessed: 21 January 2009].

Muggah, R. and Buchanan, C. 2005a. No Relief: Surveying the Effects of Gun Violence on Aid Workers. *Humanitarian Exchange Magazine*. [Online]. 31. Available at: http://www.odihpn.org/report.asp?ID=2743 [accessed: 25 January 2009].

Muggah, R. and Buchanan, C. 2005b. No Relief: Surveying the Effects of Gun Violence on Humanitarian and Development Personnel, *Small Arms Survey* [Online]. Available at: http://www.reliefweb.int/library/documents/2005/hdc-norelief-20jun.pdf [accessed: 25 January 2009].

Naim, M. 2003. The Five Wars of Globalization. *Foreign Policy* 134, 28–37.

The Nairobi Declaration on the Problem of the Proliferation of Illicit Small Arms and Light Weapons in the Great Lakes Region and the Horn of Africa 2001. [Online]. Available at: http://www.smallarmsnet.org/docs/saaf04.pdf [accessed: 25 January 2009].

OAS Convention, Inter-American Convention Against the Illicit Manufacturing of and Trafficking in Firearms, Ammunition, Explosives, and Other Related Materials 1997. Department of International Law. [Online]. Available at: http://www.oas.org/juridico/English/treaties/a-63.html [accessed: 25 January 2009].

OSCE 2002. *Expert Advice on Implementation of Section V of the OSCE Document on Small Arms and Light Weapons from Organization for Security and Co-operation in EuropeForum for Security Co-operation 374th Plenary Meeting* FSC Journal No. 380, Agenda item 5. [Online]. Available at: http://www.osce.org/documents/fsc/2002/11/1166_en.pdf [accessed: 25 January 2009].

Protocol on the Control of Firearms, Ammunition, and Other Related Materials in the Southern African Development Community (SADC) Region. [Online]. Available at: http://disarmament.un.org/cab/docs/trcngexperts/sadcprotocol.pdf [accessed: 25 January 2009].

Renner, M. 1997. *Small Arms, Big Impact: The Next Challenge of Disarmament.* Worldwatch Paper, 137. Washington, D.C.: Worldwatch Institute.

Renner, M. 1998. Curbing the Proliferation of Small Arms, in *State of the World: A Worldwatch Institute Report on Progress toward a Sustainable Society*, edited by L. Brown, C. Flavin and H. French. New York. W.W. Norton & Company, 131–48.

Sandholtz, W. 2002. Humanitarian Intervention: Global Enforcement of Human Rights? in *Globalization and Human Rights*, edited by A. Brysk. Los Angeles: University of California Press, 201–25.

Schroeder, M. 2004. *Small Arms, Terrorism and the OAS Firearms Convention*, Occasional Paper No. 1. [Online]. Available at: http://www.smallarmssurvey.org/files/portal/issueareas/measures/Measur_pdf/Schroeder%20OAS%20Convention.pdf [accessed: January 26, 2009].

SIPRI 2008. SIPRI Arms Trade Database. [Online]. Available at:http://armstrade.sipri.org/arms_trade/values.php [accessed: 25 January 2009].

Small Arms Survey 2001. Fuelling the Flames: Brokers and Transport Agents in the Illicit Arms Trade. *Small Arms Survey 2001: Profiling the Problem* [Online], Oxford: Oxford University Press, 95–139. Available at: http://www.smallarmssurvey.org/files/sas/publications/year_b_pdf/2001/2001SASCh3_full_en.pdf [accessed: 20 January 2009].

Small Arms Survey 2002. The Legal-Illicit Link: Global Small Arms Transfers. *Small Arms Survey 2002: Counting the Human Cost*. Oxford: Oxford University Press, 109–53.

Small Arms Survey 2003a. Workshops and Factories: Products and Production. *Small Arms Survey 2003: Development Denied*. Oxford: Oxford University Press.

Small Arms Survey 2003b. Obstructing Development: The Effects of Small Arms on Human Development. *Small Arms Survey 2003: Development Denied*. Oxford: Oxford University Press.

Small Arms Survey 2005a. Gun Culture in Kosovo: Questioning the Origins of Conflict. *Small Arms Survey 2005: Weapons at War*. Oxford: Oxford University Press.

Small Arms Survey 2005b. Managing 'Post-conflict' Zones: DDR and Weapons Reduction. *Small Arms Survey 2005: Weapons at War*. [Online]. Oxford: Oxford University Press, 267–301. Available at: http://www.smallarmssurvey.org/files/sas/publications/year_b_pdf/2005/2005SASCh10_full_en.pdf [accessed: 21 January 2009].

Small Arms Survey 2005c. Sourcing the Tools of War: Small Arms Supplies to Conflict Zones. *Small Arms Survey 2005: Weapons at War*. Oxford: Oxford University Press.

Small Arms Survey 2005d. Behind the Numbers: Small Arms and Conflict Deaths. *Small Arms Survey 2005: Weapons at War*. [Online]. 230–56. Available at: http://www.smallarmssurvey.org/files/sas/publications/year_b_pdf/2005/2005SASCh9_full_en.pdf [accessed: 21 January 2009].

Small Arms Survey 2006. The Other Side of the Coin: Demand for Small Arms. *Small Arms Survey 2006: Unfinished Business*. [Online]. 141–163. Available at: http://www.smallarmssurvey.org/files/sas/publications/year_b_pdf/2006/French%202006/CH6%20Demand_FR.pdf [accessed: 21 January 2009].

Small Arms Survey 2008. Light Weapons: Products, Producers, and Proliferation. *Small Arms Survey 2008: Risk and Resilience*. Oxford: Oxford University Press.

Smith, C. 1999. Areas of Major Concentration in the Use and Traffic of Small Arms, in *Small Arms Control*: *Old Weapons, New Issues*, edited by L. Lumpe and T. Gabelnick, New York: UNIDIR and Ashgate, 85–90.

Stohl, R. and Grillot, S. 2009. *The International Arms Trade*. London: Polity Press, forthcoming.

Stohl, R., Schroeder, M. and Smith, D. 2007. *The Small Arms Trade*. Oxford: Oneworld Publications.

UNHCR 2007. *UNHCR, 2007 Global Trends: Refugees, Asylum-seekers, Returnees, Internally Displaced and Stateless Persons*. [Online]. Available at: http://www.unhcr.org/statistics/STATISTICS/4852366f2.pdf [accessed: 21 January 2009].

United Nations 1948. *Charter of the United Nations from UN.org*. [Online]. Available at: http://www.un.org/aboutun/charter/ [accessed: 26 January 2009].

United Nations 1995. UN General Assembly, *Supplement to an Agenda for Peace: Position Paper of the Secretary-General on the Occasion of the Fiftieth Anniversary of the United Nations,* A/50/60, S/1995/1, 3. [Online]. Available at: http://www.un.org/Docs/SG/agsupp.html [accessed: 25 January 2009].

United Nations 2002. *Program of Action to Prevent, Combat and Eradicate the Illicit Trade in Small Arms and Light Weapons in All Its Aspects (UN Document A/CONF.192/15) Program of Action from Disarmament.un.org.* [Online]. Available at: http://disarmament.un.org/cab/poa.html [accessed: 26 January 2009].

United Nations 2005. *Firearm Protocol: Curbing the Spread of Illicit Weapons.* [Online]. Available at: http://www.unodc.org/newsletter/en/200504/page005.html [accessed: 25 January 2009].

United Nations 2006. *Towards an Arms Trade Treaty: Establishing Common International Standards for the Import, Export and Transfer of Conventional Arms*, Sixty-first session First Committee Agenda Item 90 General and Complete Disarmament. [Online]. Available at: http://www.controlarms.org/en/documents%20and%20files/un-resolution-61-89-towards-an-arms-trade-treaty [accessed: 25 January 2009].

Woodrow Wilson Center for International Scholars 2008. *The Humanitarian Effect of Arms Embargos: Can Arms Embargoes End or Limit Violent Conflict?* [Online]. Available at: http://www.wilsoncenter.org/index.cfm?topic_id=1417&fuseaction=topics.event_summary&event_id=488115 [accessed: 26 January 2009].

World Forum on the Future of Sport Shooting Activities (WFSA). Available at: http://www.wfsa.net/ [accessed: 26 January 2009].

Index

For Product Safety Concerns and Information please contact our EU representative GPSR@taylorandfrancis.com
Taylor & Francis Verlag GmbH, Kaufingerstraße 24, 80331 München, Germany

www.ingramcontent.com/pod-product-compliance
Ingram Content Group UK Ltd.
Pitfield, Milton Keynes, MK11 3LW, UK
UKHW020157260926
475702UK00047B/509

* 9 7 8 0 7 5 4 6 7 7 1 9 2 *